IRISH ESSAYS

Denis Donoghue has been a key figure in Irish studies and an important public intellectual in Ireland, the UK, and US throughout his career. These essays represent the best of his writing and operate in conversation with one another. He probes the questions of Irish national and cultural identity that underlie the finest achievements of Irish writing in all genres. Together, the essays form an unusually lively and far-reaching study of three crucial Irish writers – Swift, Yeats, and Joyce – together with other voices including Mangan, Beckett, Trevor, McGahern, and Doyle. Donoghue's forceful arguments, deep engagement with the critical tradition, buoyant prose, and extensive learning are all exemplified in this collection. This book is essential reading for all those interested in Irish literature and culture and its far-reaching effects on the world.

DENIS DONOGHUE is University Professor and Henry James Chair of English and American Letters at New York University.

D1314606

IRISH ESSAYS

DENIS DONOGHUE

CAMBRIDGE
UNIVERSITY PRESS

CAMBRIDGE UNIVERSITY PRESS
Cambridge, New York, Melbourne, Madrid, Cape Town,
Singapore, São Paulo, Delhi, Tokyo, Mexico City

Cambridge University Press
The Edinburgh Building, Cambridge CB2 8RU, UK

Published in the United States of America by Cambridge University Press, New York

www.cambridge.org
Information on this title: www.cambridge.org/9780521187282

First published 2011

Printed in the United Kingdom at the University Press, Cambridge

A catalogue record for this publication is available from the British Library

Library of Congress Cataloging-in-Publication Data
Donoghue, Denis, 1928–
Irish Essays / by Denis Donoghue.
p.   cm
Includes bibliographical references and index.
ISBN 978-1-107-00690-4 (Hardback) – ISBN 978-0-521-18728-2 (Paperback)
1. English literature–Irish authors–History and criticism.   2. National characteristics,
Irish, in literature.   3. Literature and society–Ireland.   4. Ireland–In literature.   I. Title.
PR8718.D66 2011
820.9'9417–dc22

2010045701

ISBN 978-1-107-00690-4 Hardback
ISBN 978-0-521-18728-2 Paperback

For Frances, again

Contents

Contents

Introduction

My first job was as an Administrative Officer in the Irish Civil Service. I was assigned to the Department of Finance, Establishments Division. Our duty was to decide on the staffing arrangements in various government departments and their outlying services. The work was not trivial. How many air traffic controllers should be employed at Shannon Airport? That was a question for the Department of Industry and Commerce, in the first instance, and for the Department of Finance – in principle, the Minister of Finance – in the end. I found nothing wrong with the work, except that I had no particular flair for it, as my superiors Seán Ó Buachalla, Gerard McInerney, and Louis Fitzgerald had. It was a happy release, then, when Professor Jeremiah J. Hogan offered me an Assistant Lectureship in the Department of English, University College, Dublin. Hogan was the sole professor: he was in full charge of the Department, in accordance with the ordinance of Departments by the Irish Universities Act of 1908. Informally, he entrusted the teaching of Old and Middle English to T. P. Dunning, a scholar of Langland. He handed over Anglo-Irish Literature and Drama, as it was called, to Roger McHugh, a colleague he did not like: he wanted to keep him at a distance. English literature, from approximately the year 1500 to the later years of the nineteenth century – say, from Skelton to Newman and Hopkins – was Hogan's particular concern. American literature was not taught. My duty was to teach whatever courses Professor Hogan assigned to me in English literature, mainly Shakespeare and seventeenth-century poetry, prose, and drama. Being his man, not McHugh's, I did not teach Anglo-Irish literature.

I might have taught it, in other circumstances. My first published essay, I find, was on Charles Macklin. I wrote a dissertation on him for my MA. He was one of a number of Irishmen in the middle and later years of the eighteenth century who sought their fortunes in some relation to the London theatre: Arthur Murphy, Isaac Bickerstaffe, Hugh Kelly, and others even more forgotten. Macklin wrote about ten plays, three of which were published – *Love à la Mode* (1759), *The True-Born Irishman* (1763) and *The Man of the World* (1781). But he was most acclaimed for performances in the roles of Shylock (1741) and Macbeth (1772). These were the subjects of my essay, a chapter from my otherwise unpublished dissertation. Further essays I published in the first year or two of my employment were on Hopkins, Yeats, Joyce, Synge, Lionel Trilling, and William Empson – this one was my first attempt at "practical criticism," a reading of Empson's poem "Arachne." These essays and reviews brought forth no comment from Professor Hogan. Generally he did not approve of young men rushing into print, but he did not withhold his patronage from me.

Things rested so till I left UCD to take a job at Cambridge as a University Lecturer and a Fellow of King's College. It happened that the Tripos had a course called Special Author, in which the set books were supposed to be the complete works of the chosen one. The Special Author that year was Swift. I gave the formal lectures for the course and arranged a "circus" of lectures on circumambient issues. Unwilling to let my reading go to waste, I turned my lectures into a book, rather inaccurately called *Swift: A Critical Introduction* (Cambridge University Press, 1969). I had already brought out, with J. R. Mulryne, *An Honoured Guest: New Essays on W. B. Yeats* (1965), and was working on many things in English, Irish, and American literature, including a short book on Yeats for Frank Kermode's Modern Masters series, published in 1971. I returned to UCD in 1967, partly to propose a reorganization of the English Department: three equal professorships instead of one; headship of the Department to be by rotation among the three, every two years; McHugh to become Professor of Anglo-Irish Literature and Drama, Dunning to become Professor of Old and Middle English, and I to become Professor of Modern English and American Literature – "Modern" to mean, roughly, Skelton to T. S. Eliot, "American" to mean as much of American literature as my few colleagues and I could reasonably teach. In 1965 I had published *Connoisseurs of Chaos: Ideas of Order in Modern American Poetry.* Professor Hogan was now President of UCD, having been appointed to the post in October 1964.

During those years, if my memory is accurate, I taught without any ideological emphasis, except for the vague but persistent nationalism which I continued to feel from my boyhood years in Northern Ireland. I realize that that is in itself an ideological emphasis, in its adult form probably bourgeois liberal or bourgeois conservative. But I did not feel any pressure to take a stand on an issue of theory or principle. Richard Ellmann's two books on Yeats held out that agreeable possibility. I assumed that reading a poem or a novel meant interpreting it: what interpreting entailed could be best shown in practice, especially in F. R. Leavis's practice and Empson's. Leavis's *Revaluation, The Common Pursuit, The Great Tradition,* and his essays in *Scrutiny* provided instances of literary criticism I could point to, if called upon, as well as selected passages from Empson's *Seven Types of Ambiguity, Some Versions of Pastoral,* and *The Structure of Complex Words.* But my masters were mainly American – Kenneth Burke, R. P. Blackmur, John Crowe Ransom, and Cleanth Brooks. I knew that Brooks's criticism, and Ransom's were deeply conservative, but that did not trouble my sense of the usefulness of Brooks's readings of particular poems in *The Well-Wrought Urn* and Ransom's literary-philosophical meditations in *The World's Body.* It was a day of unusual splendor when I received from Mr. Ransom, as I always called him, a letter in his own hand telling me that he liked my essay on Yeats's *Words for Music Perhaps* enough to publish it in the *Kenyon Review.*

Those peaceful days ended in 1965 when Conor Cruise O'Brien published an essay called "Passion and Cunning," a revisionist survey of the work and life of W. B. Yeats: it was a chapter in a collection of essays called *In Excited Reverie,* edited by A. Norman Jeffares and K. G. W. Cross to mark the centenary of Yeats's birth. O'Brien interpreted Yeats's life and work – some of us thought invidiously, indeed maliciously – to show that the poet was always of an incipiently authoritarian and indeed cunning disposition, even before he was attracted to Mussolini and, on Irish ground, to General O'Duffy; and that even his best poems were incorrigibly marked by that disposition. Those of us who wrote about Yeats could not ignore an attack so vigorous. Nearly every critic of Yeats, from the early days of Louis MacNeice, Austin Clarke, and Stephen Spender to Ellmann, had adverted to Yeats's last years and tried to account for his authoritarian rage, but none had presented a comprehensive portrait of the artist as a deplorable man, as O'Brien had. I tried to take Empson's line, that one hoped that writers would rise above the prejudices of their time but if they didn't, there was no merit in pulling a long face about it. I'm not sure that I convinced anyone. Ideological strife could not be avoided, especially when it started taking violent form in Northern Ireland in 1968, and more generally in Europe and the USA. Killings of Loyalist and nationalist, Catholic and Protestant, in the North made it difficult to think that one could read a poem in a spirit of disinterestedness. The history of Ireland, which many of us read as "cultural nationalists," again became rough ground. Revisionist historians began to deconstruct our myths, especially the one according to which the Rising of Easter Week 1916 and the establishing of the Irish Free State amounted to good but unfinished business. The Yeats Summer School at Sligo – I was its first Director – became for several years a scene of ideological strife. Northern Ireland was now an international issue: how could Christians be killing one another? The Troubles, as we started calling them again, brought forward a new generation of poets, novelists, playwrights, and filmmakers, and gave them concentrated themes of division and betrayal. Seamus Heaney, the most famous of these, kept his poetry clear by saying not too much about the Troubles, short of saying nothing; he wrote as if anthropology or archaeology, not history, were his discipline. I made myself notorious for a day by saying, at an open meeting of students and faculty in UCD, that the aim of an education in the humanities was "to enable students to overhear a distinguished mind communing with itself about a work of art." There was an ideology of disenchantment at large, rueful, often punitive, secular (Fintan O'Toole, John Banville), Frankfurt Marxist (Seamus Deane), feminist (Nuala O' Faoláin, Eavan Boland), and Loyalist (Conor Cruise O'Brien).

In 1980 I left UCD again, this time to take up an appointment to the Henry James Chair of English and American Letters at New York University. The chair was not so called in any relation to me. I gather that it was named in honor of Leon Edel, biographer of Henry James, when Harvard tried to coax him away from New York University. I assumed, what turned out to be true, that "English" in the title of the chair would include "Irish" without any fuss. I regarded myself as a "generalist" rather than a specialist – though I learn with dismay from the *OED* that a writer in the *Economist* for December 2, 1961 referred to "the complacent belief that a well-trained 'generalist' could turn his hand to anything." I have indeed turned my hand to many things, some of which I have assembled in three books, *We Irish* (1986), *Reading America* (1987), and *England, Their England* (1988). A number of review-essays remain uncollected because I could not see how to interpret the authors I wrote about in a clear relation to their Irish settings. I think of Goldsmith, John Butler Yeats, Jack B. Yeats, Liam O'Flaherty, and Eavan Boland in this regard. I continue to teach courses in Irish Studies at New York University under its Director, J. J. Lee, along with courses in English and American literature for the Department of English. Now that the Good Friday Agreement of 1998 seems to have resolved the Troubles by yet again affirming the status of Northern Ireland within the British Empire, and giving nationalists the empty promise of some day voting for a United Ireland, it has become possible to teach Irish literature in a more-or-less equable if sad setting. There is a lull. The "culture wars" appear to be over. A year or two ago I taught a course on "Yeats and the Abbey Theatre" as if I were an art historian teaching a course on French Impressionism. I am almost nostalgic for the years in which I wrote fighting essays and books on Deconstruction. Almost: not quite.

The short pieces I have reprinted here are those which are – or seem to be – in conversation with the longer essays on Swift, Yeats, and Joyce.

PART I

Ireland

CHAPTER I

Race, nation, state

A few autobiographical sentences may not, I hope, be amiss. I was born in Tullow, one of the minor towns of County Carlow, itself a minor county of the Irish Free State, as it was then constituted. But my home – though I rarely felt at home there – was in Warrenpoint, a town only slightly larger than Tullow, in County Down, just across the Border in Northern Ireland. My father was the sergeant-in-charge of the local police force, then called the Royal Ulster Constabulary. We were a Catholic family, living in the "married quarters" of the police barracks, not a comfortable situation in domestic, social, or political terms. My impulses were entirely nationalist, and I regarded the RUC as an alien instrument of occupation: its function was to enforce the status of Northern Ireland, a political entity I deplored. Whatever misgivings my father and mother felt on this issue, they did not discuss them in my presence. Religion and politics were beyond the pale of conversation.

Warrenpoint is a seaside resort on Carlingford Lough, but it is also distinctive for having the largest public square in Ireland. For that reason, when I was growing up, it was famous for political marches, Unionist flourishes, nationalist shows of resentment. Those occasions were equal in one respect, though not ecumenical in any: each party had two days in the year to itself. We had not yet learnt to call the summer months the marching season, but the lines of ideological possession were not in dispute. Nationalists started off the year on March 17, St. Patrick's Day. Unionists took over the town on July 12, the not-quite-accurately calculated anniversary of the victory of King William III at the battle of the Boyne in 1690. There were two further occasions. Nationalists who were also Roman Catholics – as nearly all of them were – celebrated the Feast of the Assumption of the Blessed Virgin on August 15. But they marched to a softer tread on that day than on St. Patrick's Day, since they could hardly claim that the Blessed Virgin was Irish. Finally, on the last Saturday of August,

---

* The Parnell Lecture 1997–98 at Magdalen College, Cambridge, published in Warwick Gould (ed.), *Yeats and the Nineties: Yeats Annual, No. 16* (Houndmills: Palgrave, 2001), revised 2009.

Unionists celebrated Royal Black Preceptory Day, a festival I did not understand. The success of an occasion was measured by the number of bands that
joined the parade and the distances the celebrants had traveled by bus or train.
Unionists included members of the Orange Order and the Apprentice Boys:
they wore black suits and bowler hats, with orange sashes diagonally across
their chests. The bands featured banner images of King William on his white
horse casting King James to the ground. Nationalists had no event to show as
dramatic as that one, but their banners in green, white, and orange presented a
communal figure of Ireland that supposedly included the mythical Kathleen ni
Houlihan as vividly as the historical Wolfe Tone, Robert Emmet, and Daniel
O'Connell. The lettering on nationalist banners was Celtic, a notional mark of
allegiance to Irish, a language we labored to learn and on rare occasions to
speak. The music on those marching days consisted of political songs and
ballads that could be played to brass, pipe, and drum; on the Unionist side
"The Sash My Father Wore," on the nationalist side "Who Fears to Speak of
'Ninety-Eight'?" and "A Nation Once Again." It seemed a harmless custom:
there were grim faces, steadfast to some undefined purpose, but I did not feel
obliged to take them too seriously. Political passions on display in Warrenpoint were not as fierce as in other towns and villages in the North; in
Harryville, Dunloy, and Drumcree, for instance, as in recent years.

  I will put an end to these reminiscences now, because my memory has been
shown to be fallible. When I published a memoir called *Warrenpoint* some
years ago, I relied on my powers of recall to an extent I soon had cause to regret.
Errors of fact are there to embarrass me. So I will not claim that my relation to
the marches was analytic or otherwise thoughtful. I did not wonder, for
instance, as I have wondered since, when precisely Ireland had been a
nation rather than a site of quarrelsome tribes, such that in Thomas Davis's
poem of 1842 or thereabouts it must become a nation once again. It had
certainly ceased to be a nation on January 1, 1801 when the wretched Act of
Union came into force. Presumably that was what Davis had in mind:

> When boyhood's fire was in my blood
> I read of ancient freemen
> For Greece and Rome who bravely stood,
> THREE HUNDRED MEN AND THREE MEN.
> And then I prayed I yet might see
> Our fetters rent in twain,
> And Ireland, long a province, be
> A NATION ONCE AGAIN.[1]

---

[1] *The Poems of Thomas Davis* (Dublin: Duffy, 1853), p. 73.

Davis's reference to Greece and Rome recalls the three hundred who died at Thermopylae – the hot gates – and the three Romans who kept the Sublician Bridge. I didn't know the references, or stop to learn them, when I committed the song to memory or let it inhabit my mind. I should have wondered why Ireland, to become a nation rather than a province, must exhibit the bravery of Greece and Rome.

In the south of Ireland, so far as I recall, there were no parades of Orange or Green, except for an Orange march every year in Bundoran, County Donegal, for reasons I don't understand. The anthologies read in schools south of the Border featured patriotic poems but not marching songs. The most memorable poem in that context was Thomas D'Arcy McGee's "The Celts":

> Long, long ago, beyond the misty space
> Of twice a thousand years,
> In Erin old there dwelt a mighty race,
> Taller than Roman spears;
> Like oaks and towers they had a giant grace,
> Were fleet as deers,
> With wind and wave they made their 'biding place,
> These Western shepherd-seers.[2]

The Celts were thought to be mighty because epic tradition required them to be.

It is customary to say that Ireland was a nation in the twelfth century, but I don't understand how the conspiracies and struggles for power among local kings fulfilled the concept of a nation. We read of Diarmait MacMurchadha in conflict with Tighernan Ua Ruairc not only because MacMurchadha abducted Ua Ruairc's wife Dervorgilla but because the province of Meath was to be won or lost. We hear of the High King Ruairi Ua Concobhar in league with Ua Ruairc; of MacMurchadha submitting himself to King Henry II of England to gain his support in recovering his territory; of the bishops giving Henry their allegiance in the expectation that he would reform the Irish church, in the twelfth century a notoriously corrupt institution. Davis's "A Chronology of Ireland" gives the relevant dates without comment, as if they spoke their own truth, as they would if they were accurate. I'll give them so far as they have been corrected:

1156: Pope Hadrian IV's bull *Laudabiliter* granting Henry II the right to incorporate Ireland in his realms.

---

[2] Thomas D'Arcy McGee, *Poems* (Boston: Sadler, 1869), pp. 176–177.

1169, May: First Landing of the Normans
1171, October 16: Henry II arrives in Ireland
1172: Synod of Cashel assembled under the authority of Henry II. A Council, called by some a Parliament, held by Henry II at Lismore.[3]

Davis does not mention the unforgivable Diarmait and Dervorgilla "who brought the Norman in," as the Young Man on the run from the General Post Office in 1916 keeps reminding us in Yeats's *The Dreaming of the Bones*.[4] However, since 1172, according to Davis and the Young Ireland writers, Ireland has been merely a province.

In the middle of the nineteenth century, it was not universally agreed that Ireland had ever been a nation. Between December 1865 and May 1866, Matthew Arnold gave four lectures at Oxford on the study of Celtic Literature, in which he asserted that the Celts, and specifically the Irish and the Welsh, had for centuries been a race but not a nation. He spoke of "the shrunken and diminished remains of this great primitive race," but only to remark their "failure to reach any material civilisation sound and satisfying, and not out at elbows, poor, slovenly, and half-barbarous." Arnold claimed that the Celts had never achieved the degree of compos-ition that would be embodied in a polity. The epigraph he chose for the lectures was a line from Macpherson's *Poems of Ossian*: "They went forth to the war, but they always fell." Taking his bearings from Renan's *Essay on the Poetry of the Celtic Races* and Henri Martin's *France before 1789*, Arnold spoke up for the Celts, but on the clear assumption that they had never become a nation or entered into history. They were a race, recog-nizable in their spirit or genius, but they had never exceeded that condi-tion. The genius of the Celtic peoples counted for something "in the inward world of thought and science," but for nothing "in the outward and visible world of material life." As late as 1887, Arnold said that the Irish could be regarded as "a nation poetically only, not politically."[5]

I use the words "race" and "nation" with the liberty of an amateur. I will assume, in default of an erudite sense of the matter, that a race, as distinct from a nation, is what sociologists call a "social imaginary." Its status is ideal or virtual rather than palpable. It is what people living in the same country – a certain small island in the Atlantic Ocean, say – think of

[3] Thomas Davis, *Essays*, ed. D. J. O'Donoghue (New York: Lemma Publishing Co., 1974 reprint of 1914 edition), p. 250.

[4] *The Variorum Edition of the Plays of W. B. Yeats*, ed. Russell K. Alspach (London: Macmillan, 1966), p. 773.

[5] Matthew Arnold, "From Easter to August," *The Nineteenth Century*, Vol. 22 (September 1887), p. 321.

themselves as being: their feeling is primordial rather than historical, social, or economic. In that sense – Arnold's – the Irish race had left traces of itself in poems, sagas, and artifacts, but it had not otherwise entered into the history of peoples. It is what one imagines, on the evidence of archaeological and linguistic remains. But a nation is what one projects, on the strength of that imagining. A race is a people-in-waiting, exemplifying the condition of being possible, a long "perhaps." Or it marks what once was, an immemorial folk that has left evidences of itself in legends and landscapes but cannot otherwise be produced for inspection. We think of a race as a tribe or breed, descended from putative common ancestors; but we say that it has not – or not yet – taken to itself the relatively stable character of a society. Or perhaps it has been ejected from historical or territorial existence, like the Jews in Leopold Bloom's sense of them. In the "Cyclops" chapter of *Ulysses* John Wyse Nolan asks Bloom: "But do you know what a nation means?" "A nation is the same people living in the same place," Bloom answers. "What is your nation if I may ask?" the Citizen intervenes to say. "Ireland," says Bloom, "I was born here. Ireland." After a paragraph of Joyce's linguistic finery, Bloom adverts to another attribute of his inherited life. "And I belong to a race, too ... that is hated and persecuted .... At this very moment ... sold by auction in Morocco like slaves or cattle ...."[6] Bloom is not ready to expound the differences between Jews as a race and Irish men and women as a nation, but his use of the terms is acceptable so far as it goes.

Arnold derived his typology of races from scholars of ethnology, linguistics, and the historical study of the Celtic languages. He did not know the languages, so he was indebted to O'Curry, Zeuss, O'Donovan, and other scholars for his access, limited indeed, to Celtic literature. But he was charmed by the little he knew, and gratified to think of the Celtic languages as distinctive so long as he could take pleasure in their being dead. He referred to "the practical inconvenience of perpetuating the speaking of Welsh" and maintained that "the fusion of all the inhabitants of these islands into one homogeneous, English-speaking whole, the breaking down of barriers between us, the swallowing up of separate provincial nationalities, is a consummation to which the natural course of things irresistibly tends." He did not hesitate, apparently, over the metaphor of "swallowing up." He regarded the genius of the Celtic race as

---

[6] James Joyce, *Ulysses*, ed. Hans Walter Gabler with Wolfhard Steppe and Claus Melchior (3 vols., New York: Garland, 1984), Vol. II, pp. 713–717.

beautiful, but fatally defective in its inability to engage with the real conditions of life. For his main argument, he endorsed a claim of Henri Martin's: that the Celts were "always ready to react against the despotism of fact." They were imaginative, sentimental, vivid, in every respect Nature's children, but they were incapable of acting upon the real world; they lacked the power of composition and therefore the social and political capacity. It followed that the only reasonable thing for "the Celtic members of this empire" to do in 1865 was to bring their nationalist desires to a quiet end and join with English people to create a better polity in Britain, "a new type, more intelligent, more gracious, and more humane."[7] Ireland had no future of its own, but it could help to improve an English society dismally Philistine when left to its proclivities. England, in turn, should do everything to attach Ireland to itself. On Ireland's part, there must be no thought of independence.

Arnold's advice got a poor reception. Within two years, the Fenian Rising – despite its being a botched enterprise in every practical respect – at least made it clear that the Act of Union of January 1, 1801 was still in dispute. Sixteen years after lecturing on the study of Celtic literature, Arnold reported with dismay in an essay called "The Incompatibles" that England had "completely failed to attach Ireland." Worse still: "we find ourselves the object of a glowing, fierce, unexplained hatred on the part of the Irish people." But there must still be no thought of Home Rule or separation. In the spirit of Edmund Burke, Arnold urged that Ireland should be brought "to acquiesce in the English connection by good and just treatment." Specifically: Ireland would be appeased not by better Land Bills but by "the equitable treatment of Catholicism" in regard to schools and universities; and by the development of a society in England which Irish people would find worth joining.[8]

It may be said: well, Arnold is merely a particular manifestation of prejudice and vivacity; he is not representative of the relation between England and Ireland. True, but he was not alone in maintaining that the Irish were a race, not a nation. George Moore, apparently an Irish writer, expressed much the same attitude, especially in *A Drama in Muslin* and *Parnell and His Island*. Ireland was "a primitive country and barbarous people." The western Celt, as Moore described him, was "a creature quick

---

[7] Matthew Arnold, "On the Study of Celtic Literature," in *Lectures and Essays in Criticism*, ed. R. H. Super (Ann Arbor: University of Michigan Press, 1962), pp. 291, 296–298, 344–345, 385, 395.

[8] Matthew Arnold, *English Literature and Irish Politics*, ed. R. H. Super (Ann Arbor: University of Michigan Press, 1973), pp. 238–242, 269.

to dream, and powerless to execute; in external aspects and in moral history the same tale is told – great things attempted, nothing done."[9] You could find Ireland interesting so long as you were not invited to take it seriously. In *Hail and Farewell* Moore made fun of Yeats for his rejection of the social class – the middle one – to which Yeats himself belonged on both sides of his family. In the *Autobiographies* Yeats paid Moore back for this affront and many other indelicacies. Moore's face, he reported, was carved out of a turnip, his body was "insinuating, upflowing, circulative, curvicular, pop-eyed." He was so ill-mannered that "he wrote a long preface to prove that he had a mistress in Mayfair."[10] In *Hail and Farewell* Moore, who knew no Irish, laughed at Douglas Hyde for speaking it – "a torrent of dark, muddied stuff flowed from him, much like the porter which used to come up from Carnacun to be drunk by the peasants on midsummer nights when a bonfire was lighted,"[11] – and he gave a farcical account of a pilgrimage he himself made with George Russell (AE) to Slievegullion in honor of Cuchulain and Finn. Moore's sarcasm always preceded the need of it. But the main difference between Moore and Arnold on the question of the Irish as a race was that Arnold proposed to rescue them from their civic penury by attaching them to England; Moore tormented them for the fun of it. Arnold blamed successive British governments for keeping the Irish in their barbarous condition. Moore sneered at every institution in sight: Gladstone, Parnell, the Catholic Church, the Land League, Irish peasants, and the worthies of Dublin Castle. It was as if his rhetoric had only one figure of thought and he meant to keep it employed.

But Moore's insults did not inhibit the work of cultural nationalists. Nor did Joyce's gibes at Yeats and the literary movement. I have in mind "The Holy Office" (1904), "Gas from a Burner" (1912), and the account of political life after Parnell, as Joyce gives it in "Ivy Day in the Committee Room" – a story set in the Dublin of October 6, 1902. But these ironies are not definitive; they do not tell the whole story of Joyce's relation to nationalism or even to Yeats and his companions. Joyce was as deeply involved in the values of "kinship, race, and inheritance" as he was committed to those of art and the Europe of Dante, Flaubert, and Ibsen.[12] There is no reason to think that he is being sarcastic at Stephen Dedalus's

[9] George Moore, *Parnell and his Island* (London: Swan Sonnenschein, Lowrey, 1887), pp. 55, 233.
[10] W. B. Yeats, *Autobiographies* (London: Macmillan, 1966), pp. 406, 422.
[11] George Moore, *Hail and Farewell* (2 vols., New York: Appleton, 1925 reprint), Vol. I, p. 139.
[12] Cf. Emer Nolan, *James Joyce and Nationalism* (London: Routledge, 1995), p. 42.

expense when he has him exclaim: "I go to encounter for the millionth time the reality of experience and to forge in the smithy of my soul the uncreated conscience of my race."[13] It is possible to read that declaration ironically, but the irony soon becomes ashamed of itself.

In any event, none of Joyce's interventions, or Moore's, deflected Yeats from his purpose as a cultural nationalist, to summon the Irish race into historical existence as a nation. I do not claim that he accomplished this with his own hands. The work of cultural nationalism began, according to one persuasive account, when the antiquarian Edward Bunting and his assistants transcribed and published the songs played at the great harpists' festival in Belfast in 1792.[14] Bunting's achievements are clear in his *A General Collection of the Ancient Irish Music* (1796), *A General Collection of the Ancient Music of Ireland* (1809), and *The Ancient Music of Ireland* (1840). The early phase of modern Irish nationalism also includes preeminently Samuel Ferguson, Isaac Butt, Michael Davitt, John O'Leary, and Parnell; and in other respects Hyde and the Gaelic League, Michael Cusack and the Gaelic Athletic Association, Lady Gregory and the Abbey Theatre, and many men and women whose purposes did not coincide with Yeats's. Nor was Yeats the first to prepare the ground; he had many precursors, none of them his equal: Davis, Gavan Duffy, Standish O'Grady, Mangan, Ferguson, and Allingham. In 1886 Yeats published his first essay, "The Poetry of Sir Samuel Ferguson," in which he said that Ferguson's

special claim to our attention is that he went back to the Irish cycle, finding it, in truth, a fountain that, in the passage of centuries, was overgrown with weeds and grass, so that the very way to it was forgotten of the poets; but now that his feet have worn the pathway, many others will follow, and bring thence living waters for the healing of our nation, helping us to live the larger life of the Spirit, and lifting our souls away from their selfish joys and sorrows to be the companions of those who lived greatly among the woods and hills when the world was young.[15]

This became Yeats's own ambition in his early poems, plays, and essays. But he did not express Ireland at every point of its feeling and desire, as reference to Maud Gonne, the Countess Markiewicz, Pearse, Connolly, Griffith, and Collins is enough to indicate. But Parnell, Yeats, and Hyde

---

[13] James Joyce, *A Portrait of the Artist as a Young Man*, ed. Hans Walter Gabler with Walter Hettche (New York: Garland, 1993), p. 282.

[14] Katie Trumpener, *Bardic Nationalism: The Romantic Novel and the British Empire* (Princeton University Press, 1997), pp. 10 ff.

[15] W. B. Yeats, *Uncollected Prose, Vol. I: First Reviews and Articles 1886–1896*, ed. John P. Frayne (New York: Columbia University Press, 1970), p. 82.

are the major figures in the early years of modern Irish nationalism, at that time a sacred cause. Yeats's main achievement in his early work was to bring to composition and form a plethora of national desires that hardly knew themselves to be desires. He told many Irish men and women what they felt, what they wanted, and the more strenuous things they should now want. It was an achievement the more remarkable because he spoke from the experience of a social class in decline, the Protestant professional class of parsons and business men, and he thought to arouse from their sleep a people mainly Roman Catholic, a type he always disliked and in his later years feared.

The question of nationalism, its origin, and the conditions of its rise, is contentious. I assume that national sentiment is a feeling of kinship with the other people in one's vicinity rather than with people as such or in general. It is a tendency to think of one's race on the analogy of one's family. This does not entail thinking well of them, it is enough that the analogy with one's family be retained even in disappointment. The national sentiment may also provoke a habit of regarding people outside the circle of kinship as different and probably hostile. Julia Kristeva has urged people – French, to begin with – to break this habit by reflecting on "the unconscious" in Freud's description of it. By this reflection we find that we are strangers to ourselves. So we should find it possible to appreciate the strangeness of other people – the foreigners – "instead of striving to bend them to the norms of our own repression."[16] I suppose, too, that nationalism contains an aspiration to see one's kinship embodied in a nation, a territory, and ultimately a state. We are also being urged these days to think of nationalism in relation to the factors that enabled it – the printing press, modernization, Romanticism, and the rejection of Enlightenment values. Some scholars of nationalism present it as a discursive formation without any ground in one's experience. This is implausible. At least in Ireland, the nationalist conviction has not begun or ended in words, it has been provoked by issues of land, ownership, tenancy, trade, the Famine, and apparently continuous humiliation by those in power.

I am willing to be persuaded by Hans Kohn that the sentiment of nationalism reached its clearest formulation in Rousseau's *Social Contract* with his concept of the "general will." If Nationalism is, as Kohn describes it, "the state of mind in which the supreme loyalty of the individual is felt

---

[16] Julia Kristeva, *Nations without Nationalism*, trans. Leon S. Roudiez (New York: Columbia University Press, 1993), p. 29.

to be due to the nation-state," it seems reasonable to posit the general will as an essential condition of its thriving: it is not the sum of individual wills but the common will, released from every merely accidental desire and turned toward the fellowship of one's kind.[17] In that sense the United States is the first community of people who thought of themselves, at least on that occasion, as bringing a nation into existence. But it is necessary, with Irish nationalism in view, to add to Rousseau's "general will" Herder's concept of the *Volksgeist*, if only to take account of the emphasis – in Davis, Hyde, Daniel Corkery, and D. P. Moran, to name four otherwise disparate figures – on the Irish language and the valued differences between the cultures of Ireland and England. Herder devoted his work to the idea of a nation rather than the nation-state, but that, too, was a factor in some Irish nationalists. An uncle of mine, Seamus O'Néill, a rebel before 1916 and imprisoned in Ireland and England at various times thereafter, told me that the Irish people suffered far more by the loss of the Irish language than by their subjection in other respects to the British Empire.

As a cultural nationalist, Yeats set out to invigorate a sentiment closely resembling Rousseau's "general will." He hoped to do this by invoking a sense of the Irish people as they were expressed primordially in a legendary history, the sagas and lore of a people before the coming of Christianity, myths of "Oisin wandering, Cuchulain killing his son and fighting the sea, Maeve and her children, Baile and Ailinn, Angus and his fellow-immortals."[18]

I would, if I could, add to that majestic heraldry of the poets, that great and complicated inheritance of images which written literature has substituted for the greater and more complex inheritance of spoken tradition, some new heraldic images, gathered from the lips of the common people. Christianity and the old nature faith have lain down side by side in the cottages, and I would proclaim that peace as loudly as I can among the kingdoms of poetry, where there is no peace that is not joyous, no battle that does not give life instead of death; I may even try to persuade others, in more sober prose, that there can be no language more worthy of poetry, and of the meditation of the soul than that which has been made, or can be made, out of a subtlety of desire, an emotion of sacrifice, a delight in order, that are perhaps Christian, and myths and images that mirror the energies of woods and streams, and of their wild creatures.[19]

[17] Hans Kohn, *Nationalism: Its Meaning and History* (Princeton, NJ: Van Nostrand, revised edition, 1965), p. 9.
[18] Yeats, *Variorum Edition of the Plays*, p. 1283.   [19] Ibid., p. 1290.

If myth is, as Marcel D'Etienne has described it, "an autonomous discourse extracting from reality the elements over which it maintains sovereignty,"[20] it corresponds to a selected communal experience, as desire would have it, free from the despotism of fact. The three major cycles – the mythological cycle, the Red Branch cycle, and the cycle of the Fianna – gave Yeats enough motifs for any of his early purposes in poetry, fiction, and drama. He could use those sagas to appeal to unity of race as a force prior to historical divisions. They allowed him to say, and to urge others to say: I am of Ireland, not of England. England had given itself over to industrialism, the printing press, and counting house.

Several years after the little island was partitioned, Yeats maintained that "Ireland, divided in religion and politics, is as much one race as any modern country."[21] But he did not maintain a strict distinction between race and nation. The word "race" occurred to him when he scanned the far horizon of myth and legend, and when he consulted the evidences drawn from Celtic anthropology, folklore, and archaeology. In "J. M. Synge and the Ireland of his Time" he claimed that Synge "sought for the race, not through the eyes or in history, or even in the future, but where the monks found God, in the depths of the mind."[22] The word "nation" occurred to Yeats when he thought of a people being impelled toward self-expression and self-transformation. In the same essay he spoke of the nation as "a dumb struggling thought seeking a mouth to utter it or hand to show it, a teeming delight that would re-create the world."[23] The poet was its representative voice, the bard.

Yeats's first authority for these motifs was Standish O'Grady's *History of Ireland*, especially its first volume, *The Heroic Period* (1878). The second volume, *Cuculain and his Contemporaries* (1880), was more easily superseded in later years by the stories Lady Gregory assembled in her *Cuchulain of Muirthemne* and *Gods and Fighting Men*. Although Yeats protested that he wanted to see pagan Ireland and Christian Ireland reconciled in peace, it was crucial to him that he could divine the unity of the Irish race, to begin with, mainly in pagan terms. In the debate between Oisin and Patrick, Oisin should have the deeper experience and the better lines. Christianity must be made to appear a fine enough thing in its way, though Yeats did not emphasize the monastic and the missionary

---

[20] Marcel D'Etienne, *Dionysos Slain*, trans. L. and M. Muellner (Baltimore, Md.: Johns Hopkins University Press, 1979), p. 15.

[21] W. B. Yeats, *Explorations*, selected by Mrs. W. B. Yeats (London: Macmillan, 1962), p. 347n.

[22] W. B. Yeats, *Essays and Introductions* (London: Macmillan, 1961), p. 341.   [23] Ibid., p. 317.

traditions as Joyce did, especially in his lectures in Trieste in 1907. Nor
did he speculate on linguistic relations between Phoenicia, Crete, Greece,
Egypt, and Ireland, as Joyce did when his mind was on *Ulysses* and
Finnegans Wake. It was rhetorically compelling for Yeats to present early
Irish Christianity as a much reduced system of belief and practice, by
comparison with the heroic values of the legendary, pagan Ireland it
displaced.

When it came to a further choice, after the Reformation, Yeats settled
for an undemanding Protestantism as providing a more agreeable form of
life than Catholicism. He was often bitter, as O'Grady was, when he
pondered the declined social status of Protestants in nineteenth-century
Ireland. In several essays and two or three poems Yeats maintained that a
distinctively Irish form of nationalism had been promulgated by Moly-
neux, Swift, and especially by Berkeley; that it animated the otherwise
diverse lives of Burke, Goldsmith, Grattan, Wolfe Tone, Lord Edward
Fitzgerald, Robert Emmet, Davis, and Mitchel; and that it culminated in
Parnell. It was a Protestant achievement, but Yeats liked to think of it as at
one with heroic, pagan, antinomian impulses. A primitive form of it was
expressed in Gavan Duffy's and Davis's work for the Young Ireland
movement, but Yeats knew that he must refine upon the spirit of the
Nation by submitting its patriotic zeal to a much wider range of feelings
and a more intense scrutiny. That was his justification for claiming, in
"To Ireland in the Coming Times," that his rhymes, more than those of
Davis, Mangan, and Ferguson, told "Of things discovered in the deep,/
Where only body's laid asleep."[24] He respected Davis, but he thought that
the Young Ireland movement had encouraged Irish people to settle for
facile sentiments and vulgar arguments:

Young Ireland had taught a study of our history with the glory of Ireland for
event; and this, for lack ... of comparison with that of other countries, wrecked
the historical instinct. The man who doubted, let us say, our fabulous ancient
kings running up to Adam, or found but mythology in some old tale, was hated
as if he had doubted the authority of Scripture. Above all, no man was so
ignorant that he had not by rote familiar arguments and statistics to drive away
amid familiar applause all those that had found strange truth in the world or in
their minds, and all whose knowledge had passed out of memory and become an
instinct of hand or eye. There was no literature, for literature is a child of
experience always, of knowledge never.[25]

---

[24] W. B. Yeats, *Collected Poems* (New York: Macmillan, 1952), p. 50.
[25] Yeats, *Essays and Introductions*, pp. 316–317.

In "To Ireland in the Coming Times" Yeats included himself in the kinship of Protestant nationalists, and in other poems he took up in cultural terms the work that Parnell had tried to do in parliamentary terms. The sentiment he proclaimed was Parnell's, a Protestant impulse, different in kind from the Catholic drive of O'Connell, a man Yeats affected to despise as "the great comedian." O'Connell was a populist. Parnell was a tragic hero, lonely, subjective, antithetical; an ambiguous, equivocal force, maintaining his personality as a secret, his demon. He spoke in whatever voice he chose and on his own authority.

Yeats's strategy was culturally emphatic. Parnell regularly invoked "the Irish nation" and "the Irish race" which he proposed to lead, but – as F. S. L. Lyons has noted – he seems never to have asked himself what he meant by those phrases, "and the idea that Ireland might possibly contain two nations, not one, apparently never entered his head."[26] Yeats proclaimed Unity of Race, at least to begin with: divisions would be admitted later and with regret. It is often maintained that he posited for the Irish people a fixed identity, as if such a quality were independent of circumstances. I don't think he did. His reflections on race, type, and national character seem to me not at all essentialist. He allows for mobility by making every postulate yield to the transforming power of one's imagination. He submits the ostensibly fixed concepts of nature, history, character, self, and origin to subjective transformation, such that they become one's particular forms of freedom, gesture, personality, and style. Irish identity is what he wants to create, by many acts of summoning and conjuring: it is not deemed to be already there in an immutable form. Yeats's motive was Nietzschean long before he had read Nietzsche. In "The Use and Abuse of History" Nietzsche says that we seek a past from which we may spring rather than that past from which we appear to have derived.

This explains why Yeats's typical attention to a concept or a value displaces it and submits it to his own imagination. In "A General Introduction for My Work" he says that a poet "is never the bundle of accident and incoherence that sits down to breakfast; he has been reborn as an idea, something intended, complete." Evidently, the particular idea is his own, a poet's, not a novelist's:

A novelist might describe his accidence, his incoherence, he must not; he is more type than man, more passion than type. He is Lear, Romeo, Oedipus, Tiresias; he has stepped out of a play, and even the woman he loves is Rosalind,

[26] F. S. L. Lyons, *Charles Stewart Parnell* (New York: Oxford University Press, 1977), p. 623.

Cleopatra, never The Dark Lady. He is part of his own phantasmagoria and we adore him because nature has grown intelligible, and by so doing a part of our creative power.[27]

Similarly in his considerations of time and history. Yeats was not willing to see history as mere chronology, "the cracked tune that Chronos sings."[28] In his Diary of 1930 he wrote that "History is necessity until it takes fire in someone's head and becomes freedom or virtue."[29] In "The Celtic Element in Literature," as if he were ready to exchange life for art, he wrote:

> Certainly a thirst for unbounded emotion and a wild melancholy are troublesome things in the world, and do not make its life more easy or orderly, but it may be the arts are founded on the life beyond the world, and that they must cry in the ears of our penury until the world has been consumed and become a vision.[30]

The problem was not how to consume the world but how to make this apparently opaque thing appear to be transfigured, become transparent by virtue of one's imagination.

I bring these considerations forward to clarify the relation between Yeats's work as a cultural nationalist and his dealings with magic. We have only to note his emphasis on subconscious, collective experience, in the essay on Magic, to see how compatible they were:

> I believe in the practice and philosophy of what we have agreed to call magic, in what I must call the evocation of spirits, though I do not know what they are, in the power of creating magical illusions, in the visions of truth in the depths of the mind when the eyes are closed; and I believe in three doctrines, which have, as I think, been handed down from early times, and been the foundations of nearly all magical practices. These doctrines are:

(1) that the borders of our minds are ever shifting, and that many minds can flow into one another, as it were, and create or reveal a single mind, a single energy,

(2) that the borders of our memories are as shifting, and that our memories are a part of one great memory, the memory of Nature herself, and

(3) that this great mind and great memory can be evoked by symbols.[31]

So everything begins to cohere: ancestral memories, magic, the *spiritus mundi*, the summoning of a race to become a nation, the practice of an

---

[27] Yeats, *Essays and Introductions*, p. 509.　　[28] Yeats, *Collected Poems*, p. 7.
[29] Yeats, *Explorations*, p. 336.　　[30] Yeats, *Essays and Introductions*, p. 184.　　[31] Ibid., p. 28.

antinomian politics as cultural nationalism, the politics of difference, the tragic theatre, the sacred book of the arts. In the 1892 version of "To Ireland in the Coming Times," Yeats clarified the propinquity of magic and cultural nationalism by claiming for himself, by comparison with Davis, Mangan, and Ferguson, that

> My rhymes more than their rhyming tell
> Of the dim visions old and deep,
> That God gives unto man in sleep.
> For round about my table go
> The magical powers to and fro.[32]

It follows that Yeats must assert that Ireland was a nation to the extent of its cultural difference from England. If England was, as Yeats thought, rotten with positivism and industrialism, Ireland must be – and especially the West of Ireland, Synge's mythical place, too – an antinomian culture, a place of islands, villages, and townlands, mindful of ancient lore and natural magic. He must find in the West sufficient reasons, aesthetic and spiritual, for rejecting the lure of modernism. In "Literature and the Living Voice" he wrote:

Irish poetry and Irish stories were made to be spoken or sung, while English literature, alone of great literatures, because the newest of them all, has all but completely shaped itself in the printing-press. In Ireland to-day the old world that sang and listened is, it may be for the last time in Europe, face to face with the world that reads and writes, and their antagonism is always present under some name or other in Irish imagination and intellect.[33]

Those reflections justified Yeats's recourse to the theatre. "Wherever the old imaginative life lingers," he said, "it must be stirred to more life, or at the worst, kept alive, and in Ireland this is the work, it may be, of the Gaelic movement."[34] By the Gaelic movement I think he meant to include what he later called the Celtic Renaissance, with the Abbey Theatre its significant form.

But Yeats's boldest gesture was to join his work as a cultural nationalist with that of European Symbolism and the occult. By that designation I mean to include not only Mallarmé and the other poets and dramatists presented in Arthur Symons's *The Symbolist Movement in Literature* but the whole neo-Platonic tradition with Blake as its greatest adept. Symons

---

[32] W. B. Yeats, *The Variorum Edition of the Poems*, ed. Peter Allt and R. K. Alspach (London: Macmillan, 1957), p. 138.
[33] Yeats, *Explorations*, p. 206.   [34] Ibid., pp. 208–209.

wrote of Symbolism that it is "a literature in which the visible world is no longer a reality, and the unseen world no longer a dream."[35] It may seem a wild project to act upon that emphasis while conjuring a race to come forth as a nation and to take its place in history. But Yeats did not want Ireland to become a nation like any other. In "The Celtic Element in Literature" he makes the antithetical nature of his desire quite clear. Taking up the theme where he thought Renan and Arnold had left it, he did not engage with Arnold's talk of race and nation, but he construed the strange qualities of early Irish stories as cognate with the transfiguring force of Symbolism:

I will put this differently and say that literature dwindles to a mere chronicle of circumstance, or passionless fantasies, and passionless meditations, unless it is constantly flooded with the passions and beliefs of ancient times, and that of all the fountains of the passions and beliefs of ancient times in Europe, the Slavonic, the Finnish, the Scandinavian, and the Celtic, the Celtic alone has been for centuries close to the main river of European literature.[36]

I am not sure that Yeats knew those literatures well enough to pronounce upon them or to make an invidious comparison, but we may pass over that consideration.

I should note, however, Yeats's insistence on the transforming, subjective power of imagination. History becomes freedom or virtue, the force of will is changed to the creative force of imagination, character as something given is changed to personality as something chosen, nature becomes fruitful power, time is changed to what Yeats calls "the Moods," image is transformed into symbol, mind into dream – "the generative aspect of the mind," as Allen Grossman called it[37] – and at last knowledge is transfigured as wisdom. It follows that in Yeats's early work as cultural nationalist, the poet is the exemplar, the one in whom desire knows itself for what it is. He is the bard, reciting ancient lore for the benefit of the people for whom he sings. This motive animates his early work and persists, despite many inducements to disgust and rage, till the end of his life.

David Lloyd has argued in *Anomalous States* that Yeats's work as a cultural nationalist came to a crisis if not to an end in 1916. When Pearse

---

[35] Arthur Symons, *The Symbolist Movement in Literature* (London: Constable, revised edition, 1908), p. 4.
[36] Yeats, *Essays and Introductions*, p. 185.
[37] Allen R. Grossman, *Poetic Knowledge in the Early Yeats: A Study of "The Wind among the Reeds"* (Charlottesville: University Press of Virginia, 1969), p. 40.

and the other leaders of the Easter Rising took to arms, they appropriated Yeats's Ireland, seized his myths and symbols, and removed the sources of his authority. After Easter Week and the execution of the rebels, Yeats could appeal to no authority but his own: he could no longer be the national bard. In his poems of Easter 1916 he could only pay tribute to the heroic, transforming power of men who had chosen to go their own militant way – which was not his way – and to bring the people with them. The peremptory tone of Yeats's poems and plays after 1916 is partly explained by their being "speech acts" in a particular mode: performatives, imperatives.

The evidence is not decisive. It could be argued that in the years from 1907 to 1913 – that is, from the disturbances at the first performances of Synge's *The Playboy of the Western World* to the controversy over Hugh Lane's paintings and the Dublin Lock-Out of 1913 – Yeats was no longer a cultural nationalist in the original sense: he was a poet at a distance from the people he summoned to come forth; he was a critic, a satirist, a polemicist, his note was contempt rather than exhortation. But, leaving Yeats aside for the moment, it would be reasonable to argue that the work of cultural nationalism came to a crisis in 1915 when Hyde resigned from the presidency of the Gaelic League because the League had become a political rather than a cultural organization. In the same year Pearse dissociated himself, in his pamphlet *Ghosts*, from constitutional nationalists as men who had allowed themselves to be defeated by the fall and death of Parnell. It soon became clear that the conviction of identity which Yeats, Hyde, Lady Gregory, and their colleagues provoked in those who attended to them had issued in desires that those writers could not have anticipated, desires that could not be appeased by Home Rule in any of the forms in which it might be proposed.

Pearse was the crucial figure in bringing about this change and in forcing Ireland to the extremity of becoming a state after his execution, much bloodshed, and the Civil War. The word "state" appears only once in the Proclamation of the Irish Republic – the text is the work of Pearse, James Connolly, and Thomas MacDonagh, but of Pearse mainly – but that once is resolute: "we hereby proclaim the Irish Republic as a Sovereign Independent State." There are four references to the Irish "people," three to the "nation," one to "nationhood," three to the "republic," and one to "Poblacht na hEireann." It was as if the founding of a state were the culminating act in a series of acknowledgements testifying to a conviction of nationhood and identity. The sense of identity floats free of its mere history. Like Yeats, and like de Valera in the Constitution of 1937, Pearse

appeals not to Irish history as the record of events in the order in which
they have occurred but to the nation that has existed and continues to
exist "in the minds and loyalties of its people," as Liam de Paor has
expressed it, "independently, as it were, of its own history of some
centuries past."[38] Pearse implies that the true history of Ireland, as distinct
from the specious history it has officially had, is not a record of the
English presence in Ireland for more than seven hundred years but of
the six attempts in the past three hundred years to remove that presence:
he means the acts of insurrection in 1641, 1689, 1798, 1803, 1848, and 1867.
The only reference in the Proclamation to the refusal of Unionists in
certain parts of Ulster to countenance any nationalist proceeding is in this
sentence:

The Republic guarantees religious and civil liberty, equal rights and equal
opportunities to all its citizens, and declares its resolve to pursue the happiness
and prosperity of the whole nation and of all its parts, cherishing all the children
of the nation equally, and oblivious of the differences carefully fostered by an
alien government, which have divided a minority from the majority in the past.[39]

Pearse knew, as everyone should have known since 1886, that the minority
he referred to would not acquiesce in a Republic of the entire island of
Ireland, any more than it had acquiesced in Home Rule, but he hoped –
as Hyde did, and de Valera at least for some years – that Unionists would
come to acknowledge that they were Irish rather than British, and subside
into an Irish republic, if such a thing were to be brought about. The Good
Friday Agreement of 1998 has made it clear that no such yielding, on the
part of Unionists, is to be contemplated.

Meanwhile the Proclamation of 1916 summoned the Irish race not only
to believe in a transfigured history but to take part in an insurgent politics.
Pearse did not have an elaborate political philosophy, but his thinking
seems to have been compatible with a tendentious politics enunciated
fifteen years later by Carl Schmitt. The state, according to Schmitt, is "the
political status of an organized people in an enclosed territorial unit." In
its literal sense and its historical appearance, "the state is a specific entity
of a people." Jacques Derrida has phrased it differently: the State is "the
particular modality of the mode of existence of the people (*Volk*)."[40] The
main point of Schmitt's theory is that "the specific political distinction to

[38] Liam de Paor, *On the Easter Proclamation and Other Declarations* (Dublin: Four Courts Press,
    1997), p. 36.
[39] Ibid., p. 10.
[40] Jacques Derrida, *Politics of Friendship*, trans. George Collins (London: Verso, 1997), p. 119.

which political actions and motives can be reduced is that between friend and enemy."[41] It follows that the political does not exist without the figure of the enemy and the determined possibility of an actual war. The state is the teleological "end" of the political, and it is necessarily characterized by the designation of friend and enemy. In this spirit, Pearse turned Yeats's cultural nationalism of difference – between Ireland and England – into a politics of friendship and hostility. We are friends with our Unionist brothers and sisters in the North, but England – at least for the moment – is our enemy.

It is still a dispute whether the Home Rule Bill that passed in Westminster in September 1914 but was suspended for the duration of the War would have led, in the fullness of a few more years, to the complete independence of Ireland. I doubt it. I cannot regret that Pearse and his companions acted as they did and when they did, without anything resembling a mandate. Revolutions hardly ever have a mandate. What Pearse had – and justly claimed – was the authority of understanding Irish history and tradition as a long travail issuing in revolution by force of logic and desire. The fact that previous revolutions failed only made it more urgent that this latest one succeed. It is difficult to deny to Pearse the right to his own understanding, which was so much more convinced than anyone else's. Some students of Easter Week have wondered how the Rising would have turned out if it had been led by Connolly rather than by Pearse: would Ireland have turned toward European Socialism for its identity? I don't think it would. Socialism, indeed Marxism in any of its forms, needs, if it is to have a chance of thriving, an industrial society and the whole concatenation of factories and trade unions. Ireland has never had an Industrial Revolution, except for a brief period in Belfast and the Lagan Valley. Connolly understood this, and eventually committed himself – as Constance Markiewicz and other feminist leaders did – to the separatist movement under Pearse's leadership. But I feel some misgiving when I reflect that one of the main consequences of Pearse's being the leader of the Rising was the identification of nationalism and Catholicism, after more than a hundred years in which most of the leaders of nationalism were Protestants. The continuity of Pearse, Cosgrave, and de Valera meant that, in practice, Irish politics would be deduced – to the scandal of many Catholics, let me say – from Roman Catholic theology, a procedure from which the

---

[41] Carl Schmitt, *The Concept of the Political*, trans. George Schwab (New Brunswick, NJ: Rutgers University Press, 1976), pp. 19, 26.

institutions of both Church and State have inevitably suffered, as in the debacle of the Mother and Child Scheme of 1951.

Pearse could not have foreseen the consequences of the Easter Rising – the assembly of the first Dáil Eireann in January 1919, the (British) Government of Ireland Act of 1920 that established Northern Ireland and guaranteed its part in the United Kingdom, the Articles of Agreement between Britain and Ireland in 1921, the ratification of those Articles by Dáil Eireann in 1922, the Constitution of the same year, the Civil War, the defeat of de Valera's republicans, the victory of his party, Fianna Fáil, in 1932, the new Constitution of 1937, and the declaration of the Irish Republic in 1948, an entity recognized by the United Kingdom in 1949. It is sometimes maintained by disaffected nationalists that this sequence of events has merely extended British colonial rule in Ireland under the guise of independence. Such critics point out that Ireland has adopted most of its administrative institutions from the United Kingdom and has not radically changed the disposition of power and wealth among the social classes. Yeats anticipated this expression of disappointment:

> Parnell came down the road, he said to a cheering man:
> "Ireland shall get her freedom and you still break stone."[42]

Ireland has taken over from the United Kingdom most of its arrangements for the conduct of law, a two-tier system of government, a similar police-force, a system of class formations favorable to the middle- and upper-middle classes, much the same arrangements in economics, banking, and investment. I am not convinced that this decision on the part of the Free State and later governments has been either an error or a crime.

Besides, it is a fact of inescapable significance that since 1922 Ireland – most of it, twenty-six of the thirty-two counties – has been governed by Irish men and women and is otherwise subject only to the institutions the Irish people have chosen to join, notably the European Economic Community in January 1973. That makes such a difference that I am content to put up with every defect in the government of Ireland, even beyond the third generation. Perusal of Gramsci's *Prison Notebooks*, Fanon's *The Wretched of the Earth* and later work by Benedict Anderson, Edward Said, Partha Chatterjee, and Homi Bhabha has not weakened my resolve in that respect. I deplore the follies and corruptions of successive Irish governments: a misguided policy on the Irish language, a futile economic war

---

[42] Yeats, *Collected Poems*, p. 309.

between Ireland and England in the 1930s, meanness of spirit regarding the censorship of books and films, the confounding of politics and religion, the bad faith of governments on the question of Northern Ireland, the greed of Charles J. Haughey and other politicians. But I don't regret that de Valera's Ireland stayed neutral in the Second World War or that it has chosen – at least for the present –to stay out of NATO and to maintain its independent judgment, at least occasionally, in the European Union and the United Nations.

What I most deplore is the habit of Irish governments to suppress the republican tradition in practice while paying lip-service to it on the standard anniversaries. I understand that the Free State Government had its hands full: it had to set up a working system of administration, entailing arrangements in matters of law, agriculture, education, economic development, transportation, and so forth. It had to deal with the aftermath of a civil war, continued violence, assassinations. But I can't believe that the execution of republican prisoners, even for crimes of murder, was justified. What do you do with your gunmen when the revolution is over? Long-term imprisonment would have been a just response. I concede that in such circumstances the Free State Government could not have been expected to bring patient and imaginative consideration to these questions: what should we do with the separatist passions we ourselves felt and acted upon a few years ago; and how are we to comport ourselves in relation to the United Kingdom and, more particularly, to those in Northern Ireland who would take up arms rather than make common cause with us?

De Valera had less excuse than Cosgrave for doing nothing. The institutions of the State were more settled, though not entirely to his satisfaction. By 1937, after five years in power, he was in a position to bring forward a new Constitution to replace the one enacted by the Free State with effect from December 6, 1922, and to have it pass. It is clear that he tried to respect the republican tradition by making a distinction between the nation, the matter of the first three Articles of the Constitution, and the state, the matter of Articles 4 to 11. The Preamble pays tribute to the Irish people and their "unremitting struggle to regain the rightful independence of our Nation." Article 2 declares that "the national territory consists of the whole island of Ireland, its islands and the territorial seas." Article 3 begins: "Pending the re-integration of the national territory," but then goes on to accept that the jurisdiction of the Parliament and Government extends only to the twenty-six counties established as subject to the laws of the Irish Free State. These provisions have weathered many disputes in law, including a dissenting judgment in Russell v. Fanning (1988) in which Justice Hederman said that the re-unification of the national territory is "by the provisions of the Preamble to the Constitution and of Article 3 of the Constitution a constitutional imperative and not one the pursuit or non-pursuit of which is within the discretion of the government or any organ of the state."[43] This view was later endorsed by the Supreme Court in McGimpsey v. Ireland (1990). I interpret Hederman as saying that the reunification of the national territory is a constitutional imperative rather than a policy to be pursued or not according to the wishes of the government that happens to be in power. But the fact is that no government since 1937 has in any consistent degree obeyed the instruction. Gerry Adams is the only politician who has continued to speak of "the constitutional imperative of pursuing Irish unity."[44] The Good Friday Agreement has silenced him, too: he has settled, however sadly, for the permanent existence of Northern Ireland as a constituent of the United Kingdom.

De Valera accepted, after 1932, that there was nothing he could do to get rid of Partition. He continued to bring the issue up in discussions with the British government in 1932, 1936, 1938, and later years. But the Anglo-Irish Agreement, in April 1938, promised the northern Parliament, yet again, that it would never be separated from the United Kingdom. The part that Northern Ireland played – and suffered– in the Second World War was a further bond of loyalty to the United Kingdom, a fact embodied in the Ireland Act of 1949. De Valera gave up the ghost of Irish unity in 1938, though he continued to keep the aspiration notionally alive. He regarded it as the most acute tragedy of his life that he had failed to bring Partition to a peaceful end.[45]

One of the consequences of de Valera's dismal belief, as early as 1938, that he could do nothing to bring about Irish unity was the handing over of republican conviction, in effect, to the IRA especially in the years of the War, and the establishing of a new republican party, Seán MacBride's Clann na Poblachta, in time to contest the general election in January 1948. In 1957, when de Valera took up his last administration, the Northern Ireland Parliament and the single-mindedness of Unionist zeal for the union of the United Kingdom and Northern Ireland seemed to

---

[43] J. M. Kelly, *The Irish Constitution*, ed. Gerard Hogan and Gerry Whyte (London and Dublin: Butterworths, third edition, 1994), p. 6.

[44] Gerry Adams, "We Have No Exit Strategy," *Ireland on Sunday*, March 8, 1998, p. 3.

[45] Cf. John Bowman, *De Valera and the Ulster Question 1917–1973* (Oxford: Clarendon Press, 1982).

be scripted in stone. Governments in Dublin could yearn and make diminished noise on the appropriate public occasions, but they soon gave up even imagining a united Ireland. Until the Northern Ireland Civil Rights Association started protesting in the North in 1968, with violent consequences for several years, every Irish government regarded the question of Northern Ireland as beyond its reach: it was, in practice, Britain's business. As a result, no government seriously tried to imagine how republican sentiments and desires, either in the North or the South, might be acknowledged. This situation was not changed by the Sunningdale Agreement of December 1973, the Anglo-Irish Agreement of November 15, 1985, the Downing Street Declaration, the Framework Document, and the Good Friday Agreement. None of these has even committed itself to saying what "a majority of the people of Northern Ireland" means. Does it mean 51 percent? Not at all. These documents are repugnant to a few Unionists; they should also be repugnant to nationalists, because they give Unionists a veto on every proposal that might lead, in however distant a future, to a united Ireland. As a further consequence of this neglect, over a period of forty years, the leaders of Sinn Féin are in a position to claim – with some justification – that they, rather than the government in Dublin, are the authentic guardians of the republican, separatist tradition. As for my own sentiments: I remain a nationalist, but I think it most unlikely that Unionists in the North will ever be persuaded to make common cause with the South. Ian Paisley, David Trimble, Peter Robinson and their ancestors have been in the North for 370 years: they still think of themselves as British rather than as Irish. Perhaps de Valera and his associates could have done more to persuade them to sink their differences with us in a united Ireland. A few political commentators have argued that unity, according to some definition of it, is logically inescapable. I hope so. In the meantime I do not condone a single act of bloodshed, nor do I think that the social conditions in Northern Ireland, wounding to Catholics as they have been, have ever justified the taking up of arms. At the same time, the desires embodied in the republican tradition can't be merely suppressed, any more justly or effectively than loyalist desires which have a strong historical right to persist.

I have referred to bad faith on the part of Irish governments and especially of de Valera's administrations. But I do not share the common view, represented accurately enough by Neil Jordan's film *Michael Collins*, that de Valera was a sinister figure, a murderous angel. He was a devout Catholic, something of a scholar, a teacher, a leader, ardent in the cause of the Irish language and the unity of Ireland. But he was also spiritually constricted, such that he determined to express his love of Ireland even if it entailed repressing its citizens. It was hard to feel alive and at ease in the country he governed. Not surprisingly, many Irish writers deplored the narrowness of de Valera's Ireland, its joylessness. I have in mind particularly Seán O'Faoláin, Frank O'Connor, Austin Clarke, Flann O'Brien, Elizabeth Bowen, and Kate O'Brien. But a state is always disappointing, especially one that has issued from a high rhetoric of race and nation. It is bound to incur the sardonic note of disillusion. Think of the state of Israel, the grand hopes of its setting forth in the years before and after 1948, the heartbreak of its racial history, and now the degree to which Netanyahu's Israel has become a state like any other. Ireland, too: the discrepancy between the race divined through its myths, the nation it was summoned and supposed to become, and the state it became is hard to be patient with, subject to the consideration that at least it is independent in part and a feasible place, on the whole, in which to live. It does not own any nuclear or hydrogen bombs or germ weapons. That's something worth making a note of. But it could have been a better country. In "Parnell's Funeral" (1933) Yeats wrote:

> The rest I pass, one sentence I unsay.
> Had de Valera eaten Parnell's heart
> No loose-lipped demagogue had won the day ....[46]

I don't think of de Valera as a loose-lipped demagogue: he was tight-lipped to a fault. But I respond to Yeats's motif in later lines according to which one eats the heart of a dead man to acquire his qualities.[47] No Irish leader has eaten Parnell's heart or imagined what form a politics would take that honored Swift and Parnell.

But "Parnell's Funeral" was not Yeats's last word on politics, race, nation, and state. I will end with a reference to two literary episodes in 1938. In that year Samuel Beckett published his first novel, *Murphy*. The fourth chapter is set, briefly, in the General Post Office in Dublin, Pearse's chosen place for the Rising and, outside, for the Proclamation of the Republic. Neary is contemplating from behind the statue of Cuchulain, Oliver Shepherd's work:

---

[46] Yeats, *Collected Poems*, p. 276.

[47] Peter Ure traced this motif to Sordello di Goito's *planh* on the death of Lord Blatacz, a poem translated in free verse by Ezra Pound in *The Spirit of Romance*. Cf. Ure, *Yeats and Anglo-Irish Literature*, ed. C. J. Rawson (Liverpool University Press, 1974), pp. 130–132.

Neary had bared his head, as though the holy ground meant something to him. Suddenly he flung aside his hat, sprang forward, seized the dying hero by the thighs and began to dash his head against his buttocks, such as they are.

A policeman approaches, but one Wylie, a former pupil of Neary's, leads Neary off to the exit. When the policeman shouts to them, Wylie says: "John o' God's. Hundred per cent harmless ... Stillorgan ... Not Dundrum."[48] That is: a nursing home for mentally ill patients, not an asylum for the criminally insane.

Beckett wrote *Murphy* between August 1936 and June 1938. I have no evidence that Yeats read the novel then or later. We are dealing with a coincidence. In April 1938 he wrote one of his last poems, "The Statues," which is based on a conviction he arrived at by reading Adolf Furtwängler and other historians of art:

There are moments when I am certain that art must once again accept those Greek proportions which carry into plastic art the Pythagorean numbers, those faces which are divine because all there is empty and measured. Europe was not born when Greek galleys defeated the Persian hordes at Salamis, but when the Doric studios sent out those broad-backed marble statues against the multiform, vague, expressive Asiatic sea, they gave to the sexual instinct of Europe its goal, its fixed type.[49]

Yeats asks, in the last stanza of "The Statues":

> When Pearse summoned Cuchulain to his side,
> What stalked through the Post Office? What intellect,
> What calculation, number, measurement, replied?[50]

Pearse revered the name and legendary bearing of Cuchulain only less devoutly than the more ascertainable memory of Columcille, one of the three patron saints of Ireland. Summoning is what Yeats is doing, too, in this poem as in "Parnell's Funeral": it is the most typical act of his later poems. "Sect" is his word now for the earlier "race" as he bodies forth Pearse the representative Irish figure and opposes him to the filthy modern tide of democracy; and opposes Greek sculptural form – as in Phidias – to Asiatic formlessness. In several of these later poems Yeats deduces a politics from an aesthetic, more particularly from the history of sculpture: the Pythagorean theory of numbers is supposed to have made possible not only Phidias but Michelangelo and a corresponding praxis of great men. Yeats's pamphlet *On the Boiler* gives some theory in favor of

---

[48] Samuel Beckett, *Murphy* (London: Calder and Boyars, 1969, reprint of 1938 edition), p. 33.
[49] Yeats, *Explorations*, p. 451.   [50] Yeats, *Collected Poems*, p. 323.

the politics and is chiefly to be read as indicating not what the poems mean but how close Yeats was, in 1938, to the end of his tether. His talk of "rule of kindred" is noxious. In the poems it hardly matters, because there it is merely part of an elaborate mixture of allusions and invocations: it is to be valued mainly for its enabling the poet to achieve his distinctive, desperately driven tone, his personal sense of the world rather than the world as it might appear to other people. I construe the violence of the last poems as a sign of rage and desperation. He hoped against hope that the Irish people would resist the claims of democracy and climb to "our proper dark," the same darkness of subjectivity and transformation in which he found Swift and Parnell.

Yeats knew that Ireland would have nothing to do with it, and would not take pains to understand what he was saying. Modern Irish politics is a politics of the same, not a politics of difference. Many Irish people have grown tired of being told that they are interesting beyond their numbers or that the trajectory from race through nation to state has made them distinguished among their European associates. They want to be the same as everyone else, the same as England to begin with and as the United States later on. It is their right. But only with misgiving: there are other values, which we advert to when we murmur name upon name – Davis, Parnell, Yeats, Hyde, Synge – and when, as on this occasion, we honor the memory of Parnell.

PART II

On Swift

CHAPTER 2

Reading Gulliver's Travels

I

Houses of decay, mine, his and all. You told the Clongowes gentry you had an uncle a judge and an uncle a general in the army. Come out of them, Stephen. Beauty is not there. Nor in the stagnant bay of Marsh's library where you read the fading prophecies of Joachim Abbas. For whom? The hundredheaded rabble of the cathedral close. A hater of his kind ran from them to the wood of madness, his mane foaming in the moon, his eyeballs stars. Houyhnhnm, horsenostrilled. The oval equine faces, Temple, Buck Mulligan, Foxy Campbell, Lanternjaws. Abbas father, furious dean, what offence laid fire to their brains? Paff! *Descende, calve, ut ne amplius decalveris.*[1]

On October 28, 1726, the London printer Benjamin Motte issued the first volume of *Travels into Several Remote Nations of the World* by Lemuel Gulliver, "first a surgeon, and then a captain of several ships." A few readers knew that the real author was Jonathan Swift, Dean of St. Patrick's Cathedral – "the cathedral close" – in Dublin. Presumably they took the book as a squib thrown off from the Dean's official life, or a satire on those in power in London who had banished him to Dublin in 1714. The book was an immediate success: two further editions were required in 1726 and two more in 1727. John Gay wrote to Swift on November 17, 1726 to report that "from the highest to the lowest it is universally read, from the cabinet-council to the nursery."[2] Some readers enjoyed it as an attack on Whiggery in general and Sir Robert Walpole in particular. Those who brought it into the nursery read it as a yarn populated by big men and little men. Bolingbroke was evidently the first

---

* From my *The Practice of Reading* (Yale University Press, 1998).

[1] James Joyce, *Ulysses*, ed. Hans Walter Gabler with Wolfhard Steppe and Claus Melchior (3 vols., New York: Garland, 1984), Vol. I, p. 81.

[2] Jonathan Swift, *Correspondence*, ed. Harold Williams (5 vols., Oxford: Clarendon Press, 1963–1965), Vol. III, p. 182.

reader to interpret it as an offensive book, "a design of evil consequence to depreciate human nature," as Gay reported to Swift.[3] That sense of the book became common twenty-five or thirty years later: *Gulliver's Travels* is not innocent, "a pleasant humorous book," or "such a merry work,"[4] as Swift's friend Arbuthnot called it, but a libel on mankind.

It is essential to the character of *Gulliver's Travels* that it allows readers to mistake it for something else which in certain respects it resembles: a serious travel-book, a parody travel-book, a philosophical allegory like *Candide*, a vision of Utopia, like More's book. The book is a simulacrum, inserted in the space between whatever at first it may appear to be and what on second thoughts it may otherwise appear to be. It has lasted for 250 years, mainly because readers can't be certain that they know what kind of book they're reading, even if they know that a trick of impersonation is somehow being played on them. The book is as bizarre in its way as, in quite another way, *A Tale of a Tub*. Many readers have read both books and decided, like the scholars in Brobdingnag who examine Gulliver, that the object of attention is *Relplum Scalcath*, or *Lusus Naturae*, a freak of nature.

The most useful preliminary description of *Gulliver's Travels* I have seen is Northrop Frye's account of the genre it embodies. I refer to his essay, "The Four Forms of Prose Fiction," according to which the forms are novel, confession, romance, and anatomy. *Pride and Prejudice* is a novel, because while we are reading it (and maybe after that) we think of Elizabeth Bennet as if she existed: the words on the page only give her more life than she supposedly already has. *Wuthering Heights* (the part of it set in the Heights, not in Thrushcross Grange) is a romance, because it does not concentrate on the semblances of "real people" but on stylized figures which expand into psychological types. We don't ask whether or not Heathcliff is credible as a character. *A Portrait of the Artist as a Young Man* is a confession, because it is closely akin to autobiography, and offers to show what Stephen's life – parts of it, at least – was like. Most people, Frye says, would call *Gulliver's Travels* fiction but not a novel:

It must then be another form of fiction, as it certainly has a form, and we feel that we are turning from the novel to this form, whatever it is, when we turn from Rousseau's *Emile* to Voltaire's *Candide*, or from Butler's *The Way of All Flesh* to the Erewhon books, or from Huxley's *Point Counter Point* to *Brave New World*. The form thus has its own traditions, and, as the examples of Butler and Huxley show, has preserved some integrity even under the ascendancy of the novel.

---

[3] Ibid.   [4] Ibid., p. 179.

Its existence is easy enough to demonstrate, and no one will challenge the statement that the literary ancestry of *Gulliver's Travels* and *Candide* runs through Rabelais and Erasmus to Lucian.[5]

Gulliver's Travels, then, is an anatomy, as in Burton's *Anatomy of Melancholy*, where anatomy means dissection or analysis. Frye calls it Menippean satire too, a type of fiction which "deals less with people as such than with mental attitudes." In this respect it differs from the novel. In the anatomy, "pedants, bigots, cranks, parvenus, virtuosi, enthusiasts, rapacious and incompetent men of all kinds are handled in terms of the 'humor' or ruling passion, their occupational approach to life as distinct from their social behavior." It is a feature of the anatomy that characterization is stylized rather than realistic: people are presented as mouthpieces of the ideas or prejudices they hold. In an anatomy the chief character is often a pedant, a lunatic of one idea. Reading *Gulliver's Travels*, one is bemused to find Gulliver keeping on doing the same thing, getting himself into the same predicament, like Charlie Chaplin or Buster Keaton. A constant theme in the anatomy, Frye remarks, is ridicule of the *philosophus gloriosus*. Lucian ridicules the Greek philosophers, Rabelais and Erasmus the scholastics, Swift the Cartesians and the Royal Society, Voltaire the Leibnitzians, Peacock the Romantics, Samuel Butler the Darwinists, Huxley the behaviorists. The reason for this is "that, while the novelist sees evil and folly as social diseases, the Menippean satirist sees them as diseases of the intellect, as a kind of maddened pedantry which the *philosophus gloriosus* at once symbolizes and defines." The anatomy, finally, "presents us with a vision of the world in terms of a single intellectual pattern." It often achieves this pattern by imposing upon its image of life " a logical and self-consistent shift of perspective, presenting it as Lilliputian or Brobdingnagian," or by telling the story "from the point of view of an ass, a savage, or a drunk." Or else "it will take the form of a 'marvelous journey' and present a caricature of a familiar society as the logical structure of an imaginary one." Comedy arises from the disjunction between a point of view, maintained with unquestioned lucidity, and our conviction that we, not these lunatics, know what life is really like.

   Irish fiction has many anatomies: Stephens's *The Charwoman's Daughter* and *The Crock of Gold*, Eimar O'Duffy's *King Goshawk and the Birds*, Mervyn Wall's Fursey books, Flann O'Brien's *The Third Policeman*.

---

[5] Northrop Frye, "The Four Forms of Prose Fiction," *The Hudson Review*, Vol. 2, No. 4 (Winter 1950), pp. 588–589.

O'Brien's De Selby is a *philosophus gloriosus*, a pedant like the scholars in Swift's Academy of Lagado: his publications on roads, names, hallucinations, and the chemical differences between day and night are the brain-spasms of a sage and the cause of further lucubrations in his ephebe, the narrator. In such fiction we are encouraged to find it plausible that characters come to resemble the bicycles they ride. Human dilemmas are treated – Hugh Kenner made the point – as essentially epistemological, not as ethical, comedies.[6]

It follows from this bizarre logic that *Gulliver's Travels*, like *A Tale of a Tub*, exhibits instances of irony stable and unstable, to use Wayne Booth's distinction in *The Rhetoric of Irony*. In stable irony we have only to take one interpretative step and we find ourselves back on solid ground. When Gulliver offers to make cannon-guns and explosives for use by the King of Brobdingnag, we have only to make one move to see that Gulliver and the European civilization for which he speaks are being reflected on. But the irony in *Gulliver's Travels* is often unstable: if we make one interpretative move, we find ourselves still on shifting sands, as in the Voyage to the Houyhnhnms. In stable irony there is always an imaginary point from which the world is to be viewed in its entirety. In unstable irony there is no such point. Instead, there is a sequence of equivocations which we bring to an end only arbitrarily, when we have had as much equivocation as we can bear. Nor is the irony Kierkegaardian, that is, propelled by the ironist's desire to feel free, to relish the freedom of having no motive other than his own enjoyment. We have no such impression of *Gulliver's Travels*. Swift's irony in that book is local, opportunistic, and irregular. You may call it negative if, with F. R. Leavis, you construe the book as sustained by no system of values, unlike, say, Pope's *The Dunciad*. If, reading the *Tale of a Tub*, you are not happy with the serene and peaceful possession of being well-deceived, you may choose to be undeceived, with no greater boon of happiness.

It is generally held that the mischief of *Gulliver's Travels* is postponed till the fourth voyage and Gulliver's encounters with the Houyhnhnms and the Yahoos. In fact, it begins with Swift's presentation of Gulliver. Normally, when writers of fiction establish first-person narration, they give their narrators enough capacity to understand their experiences or the events they witness; not necessarily every form of intelligence, but enough to report on the events. Some writers, notably Henry James, can't bear to

---

[6] Hugh Kenner, *Samuel Beckett: A Critical Study* (Berkeley: University of California Press, new edition, 1967), p. 37.

have their tales told by an idiot, a fool, or a villain. James knew that such people exist and must be acknowledged, but he didn't think they should have the responsibility of delivering the main issues or of being themselves the chief personages of the fiction. He wondered about Fielding's procedure in *Tom Jones* and only reluctantly came to think that it was acceptable: while Tom hasn't a brain in his head, Fielding has enough brains for both of them. But in *Gulliver's Travels*, while Gulliver is not an idiot, a fool, or a villain, he is barely qualified to take the force and point of his experience. He is given some competence in navigation and the rudiments of medicine, but he can deal with experience only when it comes to him in a form he can count or measure. As Hugh Kenner has said of him, he is "aware of nothing but incremental evidence."[7] Swift has created one of the most memorable characters in fiction by giving him no character at all, no imagination, no depth of feeling, no resources of inner life beyond the attributes of a hack reporter on a local newspaper. He has no sense of anything beneath the visible surface, no powers of divination, and no inkling of the need of such powers.

We generally assume that each of us sees the world from his or her own point of view. It would be distressing if we found that our sense of the world differed in fundamental respects from everyone else's. Normally we take it for granted that our perceptions don't differ drastically from those of most other people. We assume that things, by and large, are as we see them. We make for ourselves a picture of the world, perhaps a rudimentary diagram, and we act upon it. Up to that point, we don't differ much from Gulliver. But when we say that Gulliver has no imagination, we also mean that he doesn't feel the lack of it, he is so busy reporting events as if they had only to be reckoned, weighed, and counted. He thrives – or at least gets along – on the penury of his interests. So readers must play an unusually active part in constructing the book. We can't take Gulliver's word as the true last word on any subject, though as the first word we have no choice but to rely on it. In matters of judgment, discrimination, and the relation between one thing and another, readers have to do most of the work for themselves. Gulliver has merely indicated that there is work to be done; he reports the occasions that call for judgment. Again a contrast with James's fiction is appropriate. When we read *The Ambassadors*, we find that our main task is to keep up with Lambert Strether, rising to his occasions of perception and divination. We have to think and feel with him up and down and all around the town. In the end we may

---

[7] Hugh Kenner, *Joyce's Voices* (Berkeley: University of California Press, 1978), p. 4.

decide that he's not an impeccable interpreter of the events, and that we are justified in trying to go beyond him or think aside from him. But in *Gulliver's Travels* we start with a conviction that Gulliver's sense of life differs from ours and is palpably inadequate to the reality it negotiates.

Swift sends Gulliver voyaging into several remote nations of the world, and he gives him an absurdly small supply of qualifications. He is allowed to bring with him only the attributes normally found adequate in a settled society – a simple frame of reference, modest expectations, and the disposition of a practical man. We begin to suspect that Gulliver is as he is, not because God made him so but because England made him so. If there is an English tradition in politics, education, and morality, it is inscribed in him: it discloses itself in a sense of life that settles comfortably for its constraints and regards as folly and vanity any interests that range beyond a narrow circle. We are to take things one after another, preferably in the order in which our senses encounter them. England has made Gulliver, written a program for him beyond which he does not stray. His duty coincides with his inclination: to station himself in front of events and to report them in the sequence of their impingement on him. Penuriously direct prose is the means of delivery. Someone else, the reader, must act upon the information that Gulliver supplies. The comedy of the book arises from the fact that a mind programmed to observe nothing more than ordinary events in England is found bringing its rudimentary attributes to bear upon situations inordinate and bizarre. Trained to observe certain limited constituents of experience, Gulliver's mind has never been instructed in the art of dealing with monsters.

When I say that England made Lemuel Gulliver, I mean to disagree with Terry Eagleton's claim, in *Heathcliff and the Great Hunger*, that *Gulliver's Travels* is about Ireland. Gulliver, according to Eagleton, is "an appropriate figure for an Ascendancy which was both colonized and colonialist."[8] I can't read the book that way. It seems to me a book about the susceptibility of the human mind to the experiences it happens to undergo; it denotes the conditions, mostly demeaning, under which the mind somehow manages to persist. Samuel Johnson said of *Gulliver's Travels* that when once you have thought of big men and little men, it is very easy to do all the rest. It's not at all easy. Or rather: that isn't what's going on. Swift's real achievement is to attract into the orbit of big men and little men a mind somehow capable of surviving experience without

[8] Terry Eagleton, *Heathcliff and the Great Hunger: Studies in Irish Culture* (London: Verso, 1995), p. 160.

understanding it. In the end, Swift darkens the comedy by showing the same mind succumbing to its experience and nearly dying in the event.

In the first three voyages, the comedy is fairly simple: it is the comedy of disproportion that arises from the differences between ends and means, essence and existence, absolutes and relativities, big men and little men, Big Enders and Little Enders, steady states and floating islands. It is part of the rhetoric of the voyage to Lilliput that we are to be impressed by big people and to despise little people. On every occasion on which such words as "little" and "diminutive" appear, we are to feel contempt for the people to whom they refer. Gulliver adopts the grandiloquent style of address so prevalent in Lilliput. When he prevents war between Lilliput and Blefuscu by pulling the ships out of the Blefuscu harbor, he addresses the ruler of Lilliput in a loud voice: "Long live the most puissant Emperor of Lilliput!" When he is leaving Lilliput, and the Emperor and his family come out to say goodbye, Gulliver reports that "I lay down on my face to kiss his hand." He is already brainwashed.

The rhythm of brainwashing is worked up more elaborately in the second voyage, appropriately, since Gulliver is now the diminutive one. When the King of Brobdingnag has listened for a while to Gulliver's account of life in England, he "observed, how contemptible a Thing was human Grandeur, which could be mimicked by such diminutive Insects as I." Gulliver is inclined to take offence, but on second thought not:

But, as I was not in a Condition to resent Injuries, so, upon mature Thoughts, I began to doubt whether I were injured or no. For, after having been accustomed several Months to the Sight and Converse of this People, and observed every Object upon which I cast mine Eyes, to be of proportionable Magnitude; the Horror I had first conceived from their Bulk and Aspect was so far worn off, that if I had then beheld a Company of *English* Lords and Ladies in their Finery and Birth-day Cloaths, acting their several Parts in the most courtly Manner of Strutting, and Bowing and Prating; to say the Truth, I should have been strongly tempted to laugh as much at them as this King and his Grandees did at me. Neither indeed could I forbear smiling at my self, when the Queen used to place me upon her Hand towards a Looking-Glass, by which both our Persons appeared before me in full View together; and there could nothing be more ridiculous than the Comparison: So that I really began to imagine my self dwindled many Degrees below my usual Size.[9]

Gulliver is not in a position to resent injuries, so he becomes accustomed to not resenting them. Behaviorism is at work. He starts doubting

[9] Jonathan Swift, *Gulliver's Travels*, ed. Herbert Davis (Oxford: Basil Blackwell, 1959), p. 107.

whether he has cause of resentment. He has begun – as Hermia says in *A Midsummer Night's Dream* – to "choose love by another's eyes." The Queen's eyes, for the time being. She keeps a dwarf for her amusement:

Nothing angered and mortified me so much as the Queen's Dwarf, who being of the lowest Stature that was ever in that Country, (for I verily think he was not full Thirty Foot high) became so insolent at seeing a Creature so much beneath him, that he would always affect to swagger and look big as he passed by me in the Queen's Antichamber, while I was standing on some Table talking with the Lords or Ladies of the Court; and he seldom failed of a smart Word or two upon my Littleness; against which I could only revenge my self by calling him *Brother*, challenging him to wrestle; and such Repartees as are usual in the Mouths of *Court Pages*. One Day at Dinner, this malicious little Cubb was so nettled with something I had said to him, that raising himself upon the Frame of her Majesty's Chair, he took me up by the Middle, as I was sitting down, not thinking any Harm, and let me drop into a large Silver Bowl of Cream; and then ran away as fast as he could.[10]

Here the ironies persist, but virtually every phrase sends them off in a different direction. Choosing derision by another's eyes, Gulliver affects to despise the dwarf – "of the lowest Stature that was ever in that Country." But the idiom he uses is the repartee of court pages: "affect to swagger and look big." Gulliver hardly glances at his own posture – "while I was standing on some Table talking with the Lords or Ladies of the Court" – the word "some" gaining the effect of inattention. The malice of "this malicious little Cubb" is already prepared for by the force of "dwindled," "diminished," and other such words in earlier passages. The full effect is realized by associating the affected dwarf with the English ladies in their strutting, bowing, and prating.

Forty pages later, when Gulliver has left Brobdingnag and is rescued by the ship, he tells the Captain that when he first saw the sailors, he thought them "the most little contemptible Creatures I had ever beheld":

For, indeed, while I was in that Prince's Country, I could never endure to look in a Glass after my Eyes had been accustomed to such prodigious Objects; because the Comparison gave me so despicable a Conceit of my self.[11]

In Brobdingnag, Gulliver accepts the local system of values so readily that when he goes to see the chief temple and the tower which was reckoned "the highest in the Kingdom," he comes back disappointed: it is hardly more than 3,000 feet high.

---

[10]　Ibid., pp. 107–108.　　[11]　Ibid., p. 147.

But the most thorough brainwashing takes effect in the fourth voyage. Gulliver sees the Yahoos and thinks them hideous brutes. He is still an Englishman. But after a while he comes to see himself as very like a Yahoo and different only in the clothes he wears: they run about naked. The conviction of resemblance makes him loathe the Yahoos even more, because it forces him to see his own nature in a hideous form. When he meets the whinnying horses, he finds them impressively reasonable, and they think him a Yahoo, though notably teachable for such a brute. However, the Houyhnhnms soon decide that while Gulliver's learning ability is good for a Yahoo, and while his personal habits are cleaner than one would expect of a Yahoo, in every other respect he comes out badly from the comparison. Gulliver doesn't defend himself in these adjudications: gradually, he is brainwashed enough to find them convincing. Chapter seven begins:

The Reader may be disposed to wonder how I could prevail on my self to give so free a Representation of my own Species, among a Race of Mortals who were already too apt to conceive the vilest Opinion of Human Kind, from that entire Congruity betwixt me and their *Yahoos*. But I must freely confess, that the many Virtues of those excellent *Quadrupeds* placed in opposite View to human Corruptions, had so far opened mine Eyes, and enlarged my Understanding, that I began to view the Actions and Passions of Man in a very different Light; and to think the Honour of my own Kind not worth managing; which, besides, it was impossible for me to do before a Person of so acute a Judgment as my Master, who daily convinced me of a thousand Faults in my self, whereof I had not the least Perception before, and which with us would never be numbered even among human Infirmities. I had likewise learned from his Example an utter Detestation of all Falsehood or Disguise; and *Truth* appeared so amiable to me, that I determined upon sacrificing every thing to it.[12]

"So free a Representation": free, in the sense of unceremonious, regardless of narrow conceptions of duty or loyalty, at the risk of irresponsibility. As in Swift's pamphlet against abolishing Christianity: "Great wits love to be free with the highest objects; and if they cannot be allowed a God to revile or renounce, they will speak evil of dignities." The ironies run to "I must freely confess." Must, because I have come to value truth more than anything, and this puts me under obligation, but it also leaves me free in a way you might not appreciate.

Gradually, Gulliver comes to accept the Houyhnhnm view of things, at whatever cost to his self-esteem. He agrees, for instance, that a being

---

[12] Ibid., p. 258.

whose eyes are placed directly in front, one on each side of his nose and each of them directed straight ahead, can't look far on either side without turning his head; a disability from which Yahoos are exempt. Gulliver admits the point of these comparisons. A mind brainwashed, to begin with, by the England that made him, and later by the forces he meets on the three early voyages, is ready to be brainwashed again by his new masters, the Houyhnhnms. Appropriately, the first sign of this process is that Gulliver comes to think the English language "barbarous" by comparison with the language of the Houyhnhnms. The Houyhnhnms don't accept Gulliver as a rational animal, they speak of "those appearances of reason" in him, and decide that instead of being a rational creature he has merely been taught to imitate one:

> He added, how I had endeavoured to persuade him, that in my own and other Countries the *Yahoos* acted as the governing, rational Animal, and held the *Houyhnhnms* in Servitude: That, he observed in me all the Qualities of a *Yahoo*, only a little more civilized by some Tincture of Reason; which however was in a Degree as far inferior to the *Houyhnhnm* Race, as the *Yahoos* of their Country were to me.[13]

When a further comparison arises between Gulliver and the Yahoos, the Houyhnhnms conclude that it still tells against him. After Gulliver has given his master a full account of human life in England, his master says that "when a creature pretending to reason could be capable of such enormities, he dreaded, lest the corruption of that faculty might be worse than brutality itself." He seemed therefore confident, Gulliver reports, "that instead of reason, we were only possessed of some quality fitted to increase our natural vices." When a young female Yahoo attempts a sexual assault on the naked Gulliver, he has to accept the obvious conclusion:

> For now I could no longer deny, that I was a real *Yahoo*, in every Limb and Feature, since the Females had a natural Propensity to me as one of their own Species.[14]

A few pages later Gulliver thinks to himself:

> For, supposing I should escape with Life by some strange Adventure, how could I think with Temper, of passing my Days among *Yahoos*, and relapsing into my old Corruptions, for want of Examples to lead and keep me within the Paths of Virtue.[15]

---

[13] Ibid., p. 272.   [14] Ibid., p. 267.   [15] Ibid., p. 280.

Before he has spent a year in the country of the Houyhnhnms, he has contracted, he says, "such a Love and Veneration for the Inhabitants, that I entered on a firm Resolution never to return to human Kind, but to pass the rest of my Life among these admirable *Houyhnhnms* in the Contemplation and Practice of every Virtue; where I could have no Example or Incitement to Vice." After a while, he comes to think it wonderful that these whinnying horses would condescend to distinguish him from the rest of his species, the Yahoos, and he can't bear to look at the reflection of his body in a lake. He begins to imitate the trotting of the horses and to speak in a whinnying voice. Compelled to leave the country of the Houyhnhnms, he prostrates himself to kiss his master's foot, and thinks it wonderful that his master does him the honor of raising the hoof to his mouth. When he leaves, and it looks as if he will be rescued by a passing ship, he sails off in another direction, choosing rather, as he says, to live with barbarians than with European Yahoos. Befriended by the Portuguese Captain Don Pedro de Mendez, Gulliver concludes that he should descend to treat him "like an Animal which had some little Portion of Reason." Brought to Lisbon, Gulliver can walk the streets only if his nose is "well stopped with Rue, or sometimes with Tobacco." When the Captain offers to give him his best suit of clothes, Gulliver declines the offer, "abhorring to cover myself with any thing that had been on the Back of a *Yahoo*":

I only desired he would lend me two clean Shirts, which having been washed since he wore them, I believed would not so much defile me. These I changed every second Day, and washed them myself.[16]

Restored to his home, Gulliver finds himself loathing the sight of his family:

My Wife and Family received me with great Surprize and Joy, because they concluded me certainly dead; but I must freely confess, the Sight of them filled me only with Hatred, Disgust and Contempt; and the more, by reflecting on the near Alliance I had to them. For, although since my unfortunate Exile from the *Houyhnhnm* Country, I had compelled myself to tolerate the Sight of *Yahoos*, and to converse with Don *Pedro de Mendez*, yet my Memory and Imaginations were perpetually filled with the Virtues and Ideas of those exalted *Houyhnhnms*. And when I began to consider, that by copulating with one of the *Yahoo*-Species, I had become a Parent of more, it struck me with the utmost Shame, Confusion and Horror.[17]

[16] Ibid., p. 288.   [17] Ibid., p. 289.

The irony enforces itself between "must" and "freely." As soon as Gulliver entered his home, he reports, "my Wife took me in her Arms, and kissed me; at which, having not been used to the Touch of that odious Animal for so many Years, I fell in a Swoon for almost an Hour" (289). His favorite company in England is that of two horses and their groom: "for I feel my Spirits revived by the Smell he contracts in the Stable." Gradually, the effects wear off: the next phase of brainwashing begins. At the end of the book, Gulliver is becoming an Englishman again, though he will remain for a long time incensed by the vanity and pride of his countrymen. "And although it be hard for a Man late in Life to remove old Habits, I am not altogether out of Hopes in some Time to suffer a Neighbour *Yahoo* in my Company, without the Apprehensions I am yet under of his Teeth or his Claws."

II

There are two overlapping contexts in which we may consider the force of brainwashing in *Gulliver's Travels*. So far as the violence is directed against someone's mind, the first context is epistemological, and the philosophy referred to in all but words is Locke's. I agree with those who hold that Swift had little or no interest in philosophy, and that the third voyage shows how ready he was to make fun of merely intellectual pursuits. But he was interested in religion and politics, and he liked to think he knew what he was saying in sermons and pamphlets. He needed to have some notion of knowledge. That is all I am concerned to assume. I would be surprised to find him speculating, beyond local need, on the character of a sense-datum.

In the *Essay Concerning Human Understanding* Locke argues that the mind, to begin with, is a blank page waiting to be written on. The first stage in mental activity is a sensory event: adverting to an external object or action, the mind responds with certain sensations. The only other capacity the mind certainly has is that of reflecting upon those sensations and, finally, upon its own processes, like Gulliver lying bound in Lilliput:

At length, struggling to get loose, I had the Fortune to break the Strings, and wrench out the Pegs that fastened my left Arm to the Ground; for, by lifting it up to my Face, I discovered the Methods they had taken to bind me; and, at the same time, with a violent Pull, which gave me excessive Pain, I a little loosened the Strings that tied down my Hair on the left Side; so that I was just able to turn my Head about two Inches. But the Creatures ran off a second time, before I could seize them; whereupon there was a great Shout in a very shrill Accent; and after it ceased, I heard one of them cry aloud, **Tolgo Phonac**; when in an Instant I felt above an Hundred Arrows discharged on my left Hand, which pricked me like so many Needles; and besides, they shot another Flight into the Air, as we do Bombs in **Europe**; whereof many, I suppose, fell on my Body, (though I felt them not) and some on my Face, which I immediately covered with my left Hand.[18]

Gulliver leaves nothing to be deduced. He must lift his left hand to his face before he can comprehend the methods the Lilliputians used to bind him. He can move his head two inches, an essay in precision on evidence mainly tactile. "Above an Hundred Arrows" is as accurate as he can be, the hand being out of the eye's range. "Many, I suppose, fell on my Body," supposition being necessary because he didn't feel them all. Why not? Because, five lines later, "I had on me a Buff Jerkin, which they could not pierce." "As we do Bombs in **Europe**," the neatness of the comparison being offered for what it's worth, an irony shot with force entirely disinterested. Meanwhile Gulliver's mental activity proceeds along impeccably empirical lines; first the event, followed by its sensory recognition, followed in turn by considerations punctual to the occasion, and all delivered in a style as close to the event as post-Restoration prose enabled.

My account of Locke's position in epistemology is as bare as Gulliver's in reportage. The little I have said would need to be explicated further if I were a professional philosopher, or if Swift were. My few sentences merely point to what Locke regarded as the basic materials of knowledge and why he thought that in their possession the mind has no choice. "In this part," as he says, "the understanding is merely passive; and whether or not it will have these beginnings, and as it were materials of knowledge, is not in its own power."[19] Against Descartes, Cudworth, and many other philosophers, Locke insists that there are no "innate notions," as he calls them in the first Book of the *Essay*. He maintains that if there were innate notions, an infant would be born with the idea of God and the certainty that God is to be worshipped.

Not that Locke's position on that matter was decisive. Leibniz attacked it on the grounds that it is impossible to construct knowledge from a *tabula rasa* and the exterior world. Contingent understanding, he argued, never builds from zero. Locke's "savage," the figure he posited as the zero point of knowledge, is not (in Leibnitz's view) a mere form waiting to be

---

[18] Ibid., p. 22.
[19] John Locke, *An Essay Concerning Human Understanding*, ed. Peter H. Nidditch (Oxford: Clarendon Press, 1975), p. 118.

written on, but a figure of decadence: savages are not primitives but men who have forgotten everything primitive. But the main reason for Locke's opposition to the notion of innate ideas was political or civic rather than epistemological: he saw that those who believed in innate ideas also claimed the right to say what those ideas were and to impose them upon others:

Nor is it a small power it gives one man over another to have the authority to be the dictator of principles and teacher of unquestionable truths, and to make a man swallow that for an innate principle which may serve to his purpose who teacheth them.[20]

It was for political reasons, therefore, that Locke attacked the assumption that there are innate notions or ideas. Toleration was more important to him than any other consideration. In the *Letter to a Young Clergyman* some scholars have found Swift criticizing Locke for his stand against innate notions. It seems to me clearer in the sermon "On the Testimony of Conscience" where Swift defines conscience as "that Knowledge which a Man hath within himself of his own Thoughts and Actions." God, he says, "hath placed Conscience in us to be our Director only in those Actions which Scripture and Reason plainly tell us to be good or evil."[21] Clearly if God placed Conscience in us, Conscience is innate. But nothing in Locke's account of sensation and reflection allows for conscience or a moral sense. In Swift's view the denial of Conscience as an innate power would undermine religion. Locke refused to give any credence to innate ideas, but he had no hesitation in saying that there are innate capacities: precisely, the powers of sensory perception and reflection. Only the provocative objects and events had to be supplied by experience. These powers would assure you that you could act in certain ways, but they wouldn't compel you to act in any particular way. Nor would they establish a moral propensity in the midst of their capacities. But Locke recognized an acute problem: his aim was to take the control of our thinking away from passion or any other authority and to allow us to think for ourselves and take responsibility for our actions. We are to step aside from our spontaneous interests and try to understand our processes of thinking. A man may choose a remote Good "as an end to be pursued." "Here a Man may suspend the act of his choice from being determined for or against the thing proposed, till he has examined, whether it be really of

[20] Ibid., p. 102.
[21] Swift, *Irish Tracts 1720–1723*, ed. Herbert Davis (Oxford: Basil Blackwell, 1968), p. 150.

a nature in it self and consequences to make him happy, or no."[22] The mind, according to Locke, can suspend the execution of any of its desires, consider them, and weigh them with other desires. So he included in the power of reflection what we normally call "will." In that respect one's thinking should be a declaration of independence. But in the chapter of the *Essay* on the association of ideas he meets a difficulty in distinguishing between associations that form customs – which are good – and those that form habits – which are bad. He refers at one point to "the Empire of Habit." Clearly, he thinks that associations of ideas which set up bad habits are the very definition of madness; for one thing, they veto the act of reflection by preventing the mind from feeling inclined to it. Hans Aarsleff has noted, in his *From Locke to Saussure*, that Locke didn't work out this problem; he left to Condillac's *Essay on the Origin of Human Knowledge* (1746) the development of the notion that the association of ideas was somehow innate, or might be.

One of the aims of *Gulliver's Travels*, then, is to make fun of Locke's epistemology; to show how vulnerable the mind is if it has no capacities but those of sensation and reflection; if its entire life begins with external events and objects, and depends upon them. Gulliver is a parody of Locke's empiricism, a tilt against any philosophy that considers the mind to be the slave of its contents. That is what Yeats had in view, I assume, when he wrote:

> Locke sank into a swoon;
> The Garden died;
> God took the spinning jenny
> Out of his side.[23]

The swoon is passivity: the mind, in Locke's account, depends upon the contingency of the events and objects that impinge on it. Yeats thought that Pound and Joyce, too, capitulated to this wretched assumption. Swift feared that Locke might be right, and he dealt with his fear by parodying it. Assume that Locke is right: then if you change the things a mind encounters, you change the quality of the mind. This is brainwashing, in effect. Swift is demonstrating in Gulliver what Locke's empire of habit comes to: the mind is held captive by enforced associations of ideas. Such an imperial force constrains the act of reflection, upon which Locke's philosophy relies.

---

[22] Locke, *Essay*, p. 270.
[23] W. B. Yeats, *The Poems*, ed. Daniel Albright (London: Dent, 1994), p. 260.

The second context also involves Locke, but this time the issue is moral philosophy rather than epistemology. Charles Taylor has outlined the situation so clearly in *Sources of the Self* (1989) that I can give the gist of the dispute in his terms. In Swift's time there were two relevant traditions in moral philosophy. One of them was represented by Hobbes and Locke: it expressed a naturalistic transposition of the doctrine of Original Sin. According to this tradition, God's law is doubly external to us as fallen creatures: first, because we cannot identify the good with the bent of our own natures: and second, because the law of God – if we could discover what it is – runs against the grain of our depraved wills. We cannot, therefore, deduce a morality from the natural world, so we do well to regard Nature as neutral. All we can manage is be as self-aware as possible and act responsibly under the auspices of tolerance.

The other tradition of moral philosophy is represented by the Cambridge Platonists – especially by Henry More, Ralph Cudworth, Benjamin Whichcote, and John Smith. They saw human beings as intrinsically attuned to God, hence they spoke with assurance of our "inward Nature" according to which we are in harmony with the universe. This philosophy of benevolence was clear enough in Bolingbroke and Pope, but it was most fully articulated by Shaftesbury and by Hutcheson. "I must love whatever happens," Shaftesbury says in his *Philosophic Regimen*, "and see it all as fitted to me and orderly with respect to the whole, even 'the sack of cities and the ruin of mankind.'"[24] Where Locke found the source of morality in the dignity of a disengaged subject confronting a neutral nature, Shaftesbury ascribed it to the benevolent soul participating in the divine harmony of the universe. His crucial phrase is "natural affection," by which he means the sentiment that prompts us to love the whole world and everyone in it. Taylor refers to Shaftesbury's internalization of a teleological ethic of nature, and to his transformation of the appearances of harmony, order, and equilibrium into an ethic of benevolence. Hutcheson developed this philosophy further in his *Inquiry into the Original of Our Ideas of Beauty and Virtue.* He had Locke in his sights, and attacked the assumption, common to Hobbes, Locke, and La Rochefoucauld, that the distinction between good and bad is founded upon self-love, self-interest, and nothing else. Hutcheson's first act in this dispute is to posit

---

[24] Quoted in Charles Taylor, *Sources of the Self: The Making of the Modern Identity* (Cambridge, Mass.: Harvard University Press, 1989), p. 251.

in each of us a moral sense. "Some actions have to men an immediate goodness," he says, and by "immediate" he means spontaneous, innately delivered, not the result of reflection and training. Taylor remarks that this is a risky assumption, especially as Hutcheson acknowledges that God could have given us an entirely different moral sense, or none at all. The fact that God gave us the particular moral sense we have is one of Hutcheson's proofs of His benign providence, but he doesn't see that he has opened the door wide to relativism. It is hard to claim at once that our moral sense is primordially given by God, and that God in His absolute freedom could have made a different choice.

In the *Essay on the Nature and Conduct of the Passions and Affections* Hutcheson renews his attack on Locke and the sceptical or misanthropic tradition. Some people, he says, might think the passions "too subtile for common Apprehension, and consequently not necessary for the instruction of men in morals, which are the common business of mankind."[25] But in fact certain notions are already current about the passions "to the great detriment of many a natural temper; since many have been discouraged from all attempts of cultivating kind generous affections in themselves, by a previous notion that there are no such affections in Nature, and that all Pretence to them was only Dissimulation, Affectation, or at best some unnatural Enthusiasm."

On the question of moral philosophy – but not of epistemology – Swift is of Locke's party, except that he gives far greater allowance to Revelation and Conscience than Locke did. His general sense of human life in its moral bearing puts him with Hobbes, Mandeville, and La Rochefoucauld in his belief that moral and social life is mainly propelled by self-love. The only mitigations of this dark vision that Swift is willing to concede are religion and the common decencies of friendship and commonsense. His religion was that of the Church of Ireland, unexactingly interpreted, but it was not merely a matter of morals. Faith was crucial, though Swift gave a prosaic account of it and cheerfully set aside the hard theological mysteries. "By God's great mercy," as he said with evident relief, "those difficult Points [of Divinity] are never of absolute necessity to our salvation."[26] Swift thought the Christianity of Anglicanism a good enough basis for personal and social life, but he was not theologically insistent beyond the basic articles of faith and practice. As for the decencies: his moral philosophy was mostly negative and pessimistic, but he allowed for exceptional

---

[25] Quoted in Taylor, *Sources of the Self*, pp. 262–263.   [26] Swift, *Irish Tracts 1720–1723*, p. 151.

instances of merit. Taylor says of Locke that in his philosophy we take our place in the order of nature and society through the exercise of disengaged reason. As I have suggested, Swift thought this a risky position to adopt, because the mind is appallingly susceptible to what it merely happens to encounter. But his relation to the tradition of benevolence, as in Shaftesbury and Hutcheson, was severe if not dismissive: this is clear from his presentation of the Houyhnhnms, who live as if every virtue were innate, a practice that enchants Gulliver even though it hardly adds up to life at all. As Leavis said, the Houyhnhnms have all the virtue but the Yahoos have all the life.

Brainwashing embodies the belief that "the reason of the Stronger is always the best." The *Oxford English Dictionary* defines it as "the systematic and often forcible elimination from a person's mind of all established ideas, especially political ideas, so that another set may take their place." The earliest recorded use of the word dates from 1950, during the "Cold War," a time we associate with the trial of Cardinal Stepinac and the publication of Richard Condon's novel of brainwashing, *The Manchurian Candidate* (1959). Later we had the case of Patty Hearst, which featured brainwashing at least in its early stages. The *OED* also says that brainwashing is "a kind of coercive conversion practised by certain totalitarian states on political dissidents." But the degree of coercion depends upon the degree of resistance offered by the victim. The U2 pilot Gary Powers didn't offer as much as Cardinal Stepinac. Gulliver offers little or no resistance. Nothing about him is more revealing than his willingness to have his brain washed by new masters. The book appeals to our comic sense of discrepancy and disproportion, but it touches us also in our sense of imprisonment; not imprisonment in a concentration camp, but in any system of ideas and values that is imposed upon us. In those conditions the enforced system becomes our second nature and determines our fate. In his book on Proust, Beckett says that habit has this effect; it becomes our second nature and prevents us from seeing our first.

Any system can become a prison: a tradition we have inherited, a style we have adopted, an official terminology that tells us what to think. These days, we often refer to it as ideology, a system of assumptions on which people are persuaded to live; it is all the more powerful, the more it seems to be self-evidently valid. *Gulliver's Travels* is only superficially about big men and little men: it is really about entrapment; and the most disturbing episode in the book deals with the Struldbrugs, those people in Luggnagg who are immortal in the appalling sense that they get older but can't die. They can't leave the system. In Greek mythology

Tithonus is the figure whose fate speaks to us most touchingly in this regard. He was loved by Eos, goddess of the dawn. She asked Zeus to grant him immortality, but she neglected to ask that he also be granted eternal youth. Immortal, he withered away and at last became a grasshopper. Tennyson's "Tithonus" begins:

> The woods decay, the woods decay and fall,
> The vapours weep their burthen to the ground,
> Man comes and tills the field and lies beneath,
> And after many a summer dies the swan.
> Me only cruel immortality
> Consumes: I wither slowly in thine arms, ...

The pathos of the poem is that Tithonus speaks to Eos, not to Zeus, and asks her to take back the gift: he invokes "the homes/Of happy men that have the power to die":

> Yet hold me not for ever in thine East:
> How can my nature longer mix with thine? . . .
> Release me, and restore me to the ground;[27]

The Struldbrugs are Swift's imagining of the same fate. They are the most terrible emblems of such a thing. But they are only an extreme manifestation of Gulliver's fate, to be imprisoned in one system of forces after another.

   As long as Gulliver is inside a system, he doesn't bring any irony to bear upon it. Irony is the counterforce to brainwashing: it brings to bear upon a given system other values antithetical to those in place; it holds out against the official blandishments. Gulliver doesn't. That is shown with particular clarity in a passage in the fourth voyage where he describes the certitude of reasoning among the Houyhnhnms:

As these noble *Houyhnhnms* are endowed by Nature with a general Disposition to all Virtues, and have no Conceptions or Ideas of what is evil in a rational Creature; so their grand Maxim is, to cultivate *Reason*, and to be wholly governed by it. Neither is *Reason* among them a Point problematical as with us, where Men can argue with Plausibility on both Sides of a Question; but strikes you with immediate Conviction; as it must needs do where it is not mingled, obscured, or discoloured by Passion and Interest. I remember it was with extreme Difficulty that I could bring my Master to understand the Meaning of the word *Opinion*, or how a Point could be disputable; because *Reason* taught us to affirm or deny only

---

[27] *Tennyson: A Selected Edition*, ed. Christopher Ricks (Berkeley: University of California Press, 1989), pp. 584–590.

where we are certain; and beyond our Knowledge we cannot do either. So that Controversies, Wranglings, Disputes, and Positiveness in false or dubious Propositions, are Evils unknown among the *Houyhnhnms*.[28]

The irony here is turned upon the Houyhnhnms, who have such a boring life of certitude that there is nothing to be discussed or questioned. But the sentence about Controversies, Wranglings, Disputes, and Positiveness doesn't offer a value to be set against the blankness of intellectual and moral life among the Houyhnhnms. It refers to a pedagogical tradition, practiced by the Sophists, in which children were trained to argue, interchangeably, on one side of a proposition or the other. The long-term result was the faction-fighting that Swift professed to loathe. Gulliver can't stand aside from his local experience to the extent of imagining what the proper form of reasoning might be. Swift appears to be saying: if you send the human mind into the world without the benefit of Revelation, religious belief, and an innate conscience, it will succumb to every force it meets.

IV

There is a passage in Andrei Sinyavsky's *A Voice from the Chorus* in which the Russian writer, imprisoned in Lefortovo in 1966, recalls certain books he had read as a child, among them *Gulliver's Travels*. Sinyavsky makes the point that Gulliver is well fitted to represent mankind in general, precisely because he has no personality, no permanent qualities: everything depends upon the circumstances in which he is placed. As Sinyavsky has it: "he is short or tall, clean or unclean only by comparison; he is a man by comparison and a non-man by comparison; he is a giant among Lilliputians, a Lilliputian among giants, an animal among the Houyhnhnms, a horse among men."[29] Sinyavsky thinks that Swift is saying that man is a fiction, a sham. But there is another way of phrasing the conclusion. Man is a function of his environment, trapped in a structure that determines him so long as it holds him there. The only escape is into another structure, where the brainwashing begins all over again, according to another set of ideas and principles, equally arbitrary. The comedy of *Gulliver's Travels* arises from the discrepancy between our vaguely acquired sense of what it means to be human and our

---

[28] Swift, *Gulliver's Travels*, p. 267.
[29] Abram Tertz (Andrei Sinyavsky), *A Voice from the Chorus*, trans. Kyril Fitzlyon and Max Hayward (New York: Farrar, Straus and Giroux, 1976), p. 22.

more pressing fear that "being human" depends – more than we care to realize – upon favorable local circumstances. When circumstances change, being human is the last thing we can be assured of being. *Gulliver's Travels* has become a dauntingly "modern" book again in the past thirty or forty years because it presents as fiction what many people are worried about as fact.

These worries are provoked by ideas of mind and society. Marx said that social existence determines consciousness, but he allowed for a dynamic relation between mind and environment. One of the major axioms of Structuralism went far beyond Marx to say that we are determined by the codes we have been given. We don't hear much of Structuralism these days, but none of its successors has claimed that the human mind is autonomous. It is now regularly assumed that reality and knowledge are socially constructed and that sociologists of knowledge are fully equipped to understand the processes of this construction. In *The Social Construction of Reality* (1966) Peter L. Berger and Thomas Luckmann define "reality" as "a quality appertaining to phenomena that we recognize as having a being independent of our own volition (we cannot 'wish them away')"; and they define "knowledge" as "the certainty that phenomena are real and that they possess specific characteristics."[30] This is old-style Positivism translated into sociology: it allows no place for metaphysical, religious, or visionary values. More to the point, it hands over to "society," by which Berger and Luckmann appear to mean the accredited social institutions that happen to be in place at this moment, the right to decide what constitutes knowledge in any particular. I don't see how this sociology of knowledge differs from the brainwashing I've been describing in *Gulliver's Travels*.

Gulliver's Travels touches upon another issue, close to the one I've just described but perhaps distinguishable from it, because it adverts to the possibility that man may not be the son of God but identical with something he resembles – an artifact, a machine, a gadget made like any other to perform a few rudimentary operations. Kenner has examined this motif in *The Counterfeiters*, which he subtitles *An Historical Comedy* presumably because one source of comedy, according to Bergson, is a sense of discrepancy between axioms of life as organism and appearances of life as gadgetry. The normal optimistic answer to this sense of discrepancy is the assertion that if man is a machine, he is a machine with a

---

[30] Peter L. Berger and Thomas Luckmann, *The Social Construction of Reality: A Treatise in the Sociology of Knowledge* (New York: Doubleday, 1966), p. 1.

difference, and that this difference makes all the difference. We say, for instance, that man is an animal with the further distinguishing power of reason or symbolic action: he can reflect upon his experience and represent it in symbolic terms. If we think the difference exhilarating, we conclude that man's perfection in his kind enables him to transcend his kind: he is not a mere animal at all. This optimism depends upon our emphasizing in man's favor a spiritual dimension, a particular quality or aura that makes men and women what they are.

Gulliver's Travels incites us to think or to fear that this optimism is false, that the "x" factor is a delusion, merely yet another manifestation of pride. Hazlitt said that Swift took a new view of human nature, "such as a being of a higher sphere might take of it." Precisely: because it is a matter of perspective. Swift presents in Gulliver a man bereft of spiritual radiance; he is merely the sum of his attributes, and these are few. He is someone to whom certain things happen. This is Swift's main satiric device: to present every ostensibly spiritual quality in a material form, reducing qualities to quantities and counters. And if an optimistic reader declares that man is more than the sum of a few attributes, Swift accepts the challenge. We can almost hear him say: "Prove it."

In the end, Gulliver is restored to himself. But what is the self to which he is restored? Is it that of the true-born Englishman, the ideologically propelled figure projected after the Restoration and the Glorious Revolution by an England desperately anxious to avoid another Civil War and the execution of another king? Something like that. Gulliver is an empiricist without memory or the need of it; a man restored to sanity who does not know that he has been mad. He is as close as possible to being "a man without qualities."

CHAPTER 3

Swift and the association of ideas

But now I would battle in the interests of orthodoxy, even of the commonplace; and yet could find nothing better to say than: "It is not necessary to judge every one by the law, for we have also Christ's commandment of love."

He turned and said, looking at me with shining eyes:

"Jonathan Swift made a soul for the gentlemen of this city by hating his neighbour as himself."[1]

In March 1934 F. R. Leavis published "The Irony of Swift," the essay which, more than any other, has persuaded many readers that Swift's mind is characterized by a peculiarly intense animus not accounted for by its objects. It is widely agreed that there is a quality of exorbitance in Swift's work, a force which issues, as if unprovoked, from the mind itself. Only one of Leavis's arguments in that essay has failed to gain much credence. The comparison of Swift and Blake, to Blake's advantage in point of intelligence, has not been taken up as a matter that can be profitably discussed. But the main burden of the essay, that the general character of Swift's irony is a case of extraordinary energy turned upon negation, has been received, it appears, with pleasure and relief; it is thought to be the crucial issue. We have in Swift's writings, Leavis says, "probably the most remarkable expression of negative feelings and attitudes that literature can offer – the spectacle of creative powers (the paradoxical description seems right) exhibited consistently in negation and rejection."[2]

The sentence is more regularly quoted than analyzed: in particular, what remains unexamined is Leavis's distinction between positive and negative feelings and attitudes, a distinction he seems to regard as self-evident.

* *The Yearbook of English Studies, Vol. 18 (1988): Pope, Swift, and their Circle.*
[1] W. B. Yeats, "The Tables of the Law," in *Mythologies*, ed. Warwick Gould and Deirdre Toomey (New York: Palgrave Macmillan, 2005), pp. 196–197.
[2] F. R. Leavis, *The Common Pursuit* (London: Chatto and Windus, 1952), pp. 73–88.

An ideological imperative is at work. The distinction, if I understand it, thrives in its bearing on satire but not on irony. It is one of the marks of irony that it makes the reader doubt that the situation in hand can be adequately judged by appeal to a distinction between negative and positive impulses. One's satisfaction in such discriminations and lucidities is what irony was devised to undermine. In the end, Leavis clarifies his position: it is by comparison with Gibbon and the fifteenth chapter of *The Decline and Fall of the Roman Empire* that he feels justified in saying that Swift's irony is negative. "The decorously insistent pattern of Gibbonian prose," he says, "insinuates a solidarity with the reader (the implied solidarity in Swift is itself ironical – a means to betrayal), establishes an understanding and habituates to certain assumptions." The positive standards that Gibbon calls upon "represent something impressively realized in eighteenth-century civilization." Gibbon invokes certain positive continuities of attitude and conviction which he is deemed to share with his readers and with the culture they together constitute:

Gibbon's irony, then, habituates and reassures, ministering to a kind of judicial certitude or complacency. Swift's is essentially a matter of surprise and negation: its function is to defeat habit, to intimidate and to demoralize.[3]

Leavis's terms of reference are strange. It would normally be taken as a mark of a writer's moral incapacity if the tendency of his work were to habituate and reassure, or to minister to the reader's complacency. It would be a sign of an artist's creative power if his work were directed to defeat habit or at least to make it doubt its security. The issue is between custom and habit: habit is custom congealed. Leavis's account of Donne's poems, in *Revaluation*, acts on that difference. But in writing of Swift his moral sense is perturbed to find evidence (in the writing, line by line) of intensities not already sanctioned by the society Swift addresses.

I'll look at the passage on which Leavis's diagnosis mainly relies, the section of the "Digression on Madness" in *A Tale of a Tub*, about the state of being a fool among knaves. Leavis's analysis offers to show that Swift's reader is being lulled into the security of thinking that the object of attack is "curiosity" (a pretentious or vain insistence on prying beneath the surface of things) and that the positive values being called upon are those of a contented residence among the "common forms" and external appearances:

Yesterday I ordered the Carcass of a Beau to be stript in my Presence; when we were all amazed to find so many unsuspected Faults under one Suit of

---

³ Ibid., p. 75.

Cloaths: Then I laid open his *Brain*, his *Heart*, and his *Spleen*; But, I plainly perceived at every Operation, that the farther we proceeded, we found the Defects encrease upon us in Number and Bulk: from all which, I justly formed this Conclusion to my self; That whatever Philosopher or Projector can find out an Art to sodder and patch up the Flaws and Imperfections of Nature, will deserve much better of Mankind, and teach us a more useful Science, than that so much in present Esteem, of widening and exposing them (like him who held *Anatomy* to be the ultimate End of *Physick*.) And he, whose Fortunes and Dispositions have placed him in a convenient Station to enjoy the Fruits of this noble Art; He that can with *Epicurus* content his Ideas with the Films and Images that fly off upon his Senses from the *Superficies* of Things; Such a Man truly wise, creams off Nature, leaving the Sower and the Dregs, for Philosophy and Reason to lap up.[4]

The reader's assumption that the object of attack is curiosity, Leavis says, "has become habit, and has been so nourished that few readers note anything equivocal to trouble them in that last sentence: the concrete force of 'cream off,' 'sour,' 'dregs' and 'lap up' seems unmistakably to identify Swift with an intense animus against 'philosophy and reason' (understood implicitly to stand for 'curiosity' the anatomist)."[5]

But there is nothing equivocal in Swift's sentence. The motif of the outside and the inside, with which the passage began, has implied that the inside of things is best taken for granted. If we don't trouble it, it won't trouble us. The figure is certainly dismissive, because it says that there is much in life that we should throw away so as to retain the better part. It is true, as Leavis says, that the reader's place is with Swift; at least "when we were all amazed" pretends to take this fellowship for granted. But only a remarkably sacramental sense of life would find itself affronted by the claim that some things in life are waste matter. "The trap," Leavis says, "is sprung in the last sentence of the paragraph. ...This is the sublime and refined Point of Felicity, called, *the Possession of being well deceived*; The Serene Peaceful State of being a Fool among Knaves. ...What is left?" Leavis exclaims. The positives disappear. Swift "never found anything better to contend for than a skin, a surface, an outward show."[6]

We can agree that when Swift begins a sentence with the words "sublime" and "refined" an ironic tone is intended. But it would still be possible to read it as saying that if it comes to a choice between being a fool or a knave, an honest man will choose to be a fool, and will make the

---

[4] Jonathan Swift, *The Prose Writings of Jonathan Swift*, ed. Herbert Davis et al. (16 vols., Oxford: Basil Blackwell, 1939–1974), Vol. I, pp. 109–110.
[5] Leavis, *The Common Pursuit*, p. 83.   [6] Ibid., p. 84.

best of his situation, the best being in all probability more than it is worth. Dustin Griffin has pointed out that Swift took the phrase from Rochester: his "Artemisia to Chloe" has "the perfect joy of being well deceived."[7] We need not quarrel about the degree to which Rochester's manner infects Swift's: the high-pitched pleasure that Rochester expresses when libertinage and cuckoldry are invoked is not one of Swift's notes. Cuckoldry provides the general context in which fools are distinguished from knaves, but Swift is not much charmed by the theme. He is more interested in taking command of a space of sentiment by ordaining the terms on which the discourse may be allowed to proceed. It is a regular mark of his irony that it insists upon a desperate choice between two values or two predicaments, as if the situation admitted of no other. We are to choose between those claimants: if we decline the choice and demand some third value, or a different set of alternatives, we put ourselves out of the discourse. In the present case there are two possibilities. One is that the choice is no choice, since the conditions of fool and knave are equally repugnant to an honest reader. In *The Structure of Complex Words* William Empson maintained that Swift's sentence is the earliest use of a distinctively modern feeling. "The modern use of fool I think gets its power from a suggestion of nausea, which is a new stock reaction to the presence of a lunatic (not even an eighteenth century reaction)." Empson thought it likely that Swift for personal reasons felt "all our present-day revulsion from lunacy."[8] Leavis's interpretation is much the same as Empson's, though he is far more outraged by the evidence than Empson is.

The second possibility arises when Empson quotes a passage from Enid Welsford's *The Fool: His Social and Literary History*, where she says that "the first thing to be remembered is that the words 'fool' and 'knave' were constantly coupled together, but not always in quite the same way; for sometimes they were treated as synonyms, sometimes emphasis was laid on the distinction between them." She has been discussing Sebastian Brant's *Narrenschiff* and Barclay's loose English version of it:

To religious moralists such as Brant and Barclay, a knave was simply a fool regarded *sub specie aeternitatis*, for he was neglecting his true, ultimate self-interest, and what could be more ridiculous than that? In view of Hell and Heaven, the worldly man is penny wise and pound foolish.[9]

---

[7] Dustin H. Griffin, *Satires against Man: The Poems of Rochester* (Berkeley: University of California Press, 1973), p. 280.

[8] William Empson, *The Structure of Complex Words* (London: Chatto and Windus, 1951), p. 110.

[9] Enid Welsford, *The Fool: His Social and Literary History* (New York: Farrar and Rinehart, 1935), p. 237.

It seems odd that two terms that generally make up a standard antithesis could be synonyms or mere opposites, but Empson is probably right in holding that when this occurs, "at least one of them will try to cover the whole field."[10] Presumably if you took an earthy view of these alternatives you would hold them apart by saying that at least the knave lives up to his dramatic possibilities while the fool misses them. Welsford makes it clear that if you think of fool and knave as different you can see each of them as invading the other's space, even if in practice you let one of them be the first of two stout contenders. Knave here, as Empson remarks, is the biblical fool who says in his heart "There is no God." If you think of them as the same you still have to decide whether to express their common character in genial or sinister terms. Erasmus took the genial way. In the *Encomium Moriae* Stultitia gives a lively account of herself and shows that you can live a decent life under her auspices. Ultimately what Erasmus is defending is the Christ-like way of being a child. In the long run, being one of Christ's fools will prove to have been the right way, and even in the meantime there are pleasures to be found. Worldlings only seem to have a good time, and besides their end is nigh.

It is commonly assumed that Swift's meaning cannot have coincided with Erasmus's or drawn upon a similar set of feelings. Empson thought Erasmus's sentiments no longer available, probably since Freud told us that children are not as innocent as they look. The argument is a poor one, if only because Christianity could not exist without the Christ-child sentiment and the Sermon on the Mount. Stultitia is ingenious in showing how much of the best in life is compatible with being, in her special sense, a fool; she allows us to feel, too, how much of the worst goes with the worldly sense of fool. Erasmus's contribution to the conceit is his smiling amusement at those sophisticates who are dismayed by the evidence.

There is no reason to think that Erasmus and Swift must be regarded as living in different worlds. Leavis despised Swift's religious beliefs, thought them mere show, and I agree that a culture that was willing to settle for Occasional Conformity was well on the way to letting politics take the place of religion. After the Restoration it was widely felt that the only security against another civil war was to have a consensus broad and strong enough to sink theological differences or evade them. The idea of the true-born Englishman was a safer bet than an enthusiast, an apostle, or a fanatic. Peace on earth and goodwill to men should begin with peace among Englishmen.

[10] Empson, *The Structure of Complex Words*, p. 107.

Swift might have settled for the amenities the philosophers offered. An artist could sidestep the issues, just as Bolingbroke did. In *Praisers of Folly* Walter Kaiser says of the passage about fools and knaves, that Swift "would without hesitation strike through the mask of deception."[11] The striking phrase comes from *Moby-Dick* and seems incongruous. There is no reason to think that Swift must have forced every issue of theology and philosophy further than David Hume did. He had more immediate problems on his mind. Hume accepted that knowledge depends upon "those impressions, which arise from the senses," and that "their ultimate cause is, in my opinion, perfectly inexplicable by human reason, and 'twill always be impossible to decide with certainty, whether they arise immediately from the object, or are produc'd by the creative power of the mind, or are deriv'd from the author of our being." If so, Hume advises, "where Reason is lively, and mixes itself with some propensity, it ought to be assented to."[12] Nothing in the *Treatise* encourages anyone to strike through a mask.

What Swift seems to be saying in the contested sentence is that if we force the issue, we are all inevitably deceived by appearances, so it is a question of behaving ourselves decently or not. A fool is indeed thoroughly deceived, if the strictest epistemological criteria are insisted on, but he will be justified in the end, and in the meantime he is wise to persist in his folly. A cuckold is unfortunate, but he has the chance of acting decently despite his predicament. A knave will never be justified. The irony is that this advice, too, is arrived at only upon otherwise bewildered reflection: it is not given by nature.

Leavis assumes, and I have left the assumption unquestioned, that someone is saying these things in the "Digression on Madness" and that the someone is Jonathan Swift. He does not advert to any of the questions raised by reference to implied authors or personae. I hold that most of the difficulties of the *Tale* arise from the fact that some of the sentiments it puts on show are silly, vain, pretentious, or (as we might say) modernist; but many of them are not, and the difference is rarely signaled. I think that Swift was capitalizing on the discrepancy between words that come from an implied speaker and words that issue anonymously and as if spontaneously from a printing press. If you wanted stability you could ascribe it to personal identity and a conversible style audible in its vicinity.

---

[11] Walter Kaiser, *Praisers of Folly: Erasmus, Rabelais, Shakespeare* (Cambridge, Mass.: Harvard University Press, 1963), p. 75.

[12] David Hume, *A Treatise of Human Nature*, ed. T. H. Green and T. H. Grose (London: Aalen, 1964 reprint), Vol. I, p. 385.

That would be the standard axiom. It must have seemed a bizarre thing to be able to set words loose from the voice of a speaker responsible for them and instead to have a printing press deliver semblances of speech with apparent impartiality. In *The Counterfeiters* Hugh Kenner considers the consequences, for eighteenth-century literature, of a language that theory has separated from its speakers. It does not seem implausible to me that a writer might choose to effect such a separation, in an intermittent and apparently capricious way, as in digressions where an impression of unmoored and arbitrary authority could be enforced, to the dismay of his readers. The anonymity of the printing press was of course politically expedient in times of censorship and prosecution.

I can think of two theoretical vocabularies which would give this argument some support. One is Derrida's distinction (he made it in his lecture "Structure, Sign, and Play in the Discourse of the Human Sciences") between two kinds of interpretation:

There are two interpretations of interpretation, of structure, of sign, of freeplay. The one seeks to decipher, dreams of deciphering, a truth or an origin which is free from freeplay and from the order of the sign, and lives like an exile the necessity of interpretation. The other, which is no longer turned toward the origin, affirms freeplay and tries to pass beyond man and humanism, the name man being the name of that being who, throughout the history of metaphysics or of ontotheology ... has dreamed of full presence, the reassuring foundation, the origin and the end of the game.[13]

Now suppose a book were to be written in which the narrative parts, allegorical indeed, were stable, coherent, and turned towards a meaning in the history of Christian sects since the Reformation; and in which the digressions practiced Derridean play in a void between persons and things, between voices and the mechanisms of a printing press. I can imagine such a book, and that it might coincide with *A Tale of a Tub*.

The second vocabulary might be deduced from Leavis's essay, but he does not make the deduction. He remarks that in Swift's irony "we more often, probably, feel the effect of the words as an intensity in the castigator than as an effect upon a victim: the dissociation of animus from the usual signs defines for our contemplation a peculiarly intense contempt or disgust."[14] This is true, but it is not clear why Leavis thinks it scandalous: it is a variant of T. S. Eliot's assertion, in his essay on Marvell, that Dryden is "the great master of contempt," Pope "the great master of

[13] Jacques Derrida, *Writing and Difference*, trans. Alan Bass (University of Chicago Press, 1978), pp. 278–279.
[14] Leavis, *The Common Pursuit*, pp. 76–77.

hatred," and Swift "the great master of disgust."[15] In that formulation, contempt, hatred, and disgust brought with them no rebuke: they involve neutral descriptions. Leavis's view seems to depend upon an abstract notion of equipoise, a balance supposedly fair between a mind's attention and the object in view. But unless we are to ban every prejudice, or the pretence of prejudice, from the domain of irony, we must put up with the discrepancy. Henry James said, in a letter to Thomas Sergeant Perry, that a prejudice is "a judgement formed on a subject upon data furnished, not by the subject itself, but by the mind which regards it."[16] It would be idle to plead that a writer, more especially an ironist by gift and practice, should not resort to such a discrepancy.

A few pages later in the essay Leavis says that "the only thing in the nature of a positive" that most readers of Swift will find convincingly present "is self-assertion – *superbia*."[17] But Leavis does not pursue the matter beyond a point that I suppose he took as conclusive. His clear implication is that Swift's form of irony is corrupt because of the self-assertion that animates it: it is damaging because it testifies to nothing beyond the energy it develops. No value or conviction at large in the world is invoked.

Many attempts have been made to refute Leavis's argument by finding in Swift's work values which might count as positives: usually they amount to the commonplaces of an unexactingly proclaimed Christianity. But there is at least one theory of irony according to which irony cannot be other than a produced *superbia*. It may appear that Kierkegaard's theory does not recognize unstable irony, because he says that in irony "the phenomenon is not the essence but the opposite of the essence": the word is not the meaning, but the opposite of the meaning. That would bear on stable irony, since a reader would soon learn to construe a meaning by taking it as its opposite. But Kierkegaard goes on to allow for unstable irony (he does not call it that) by saying that in irony "the subject is negatively free": if what I say is neither my meaning nor the opposite of my meaning "then I am free both in relation to others and in relation to myself."[18] This marks the exclusiveness of irony, since even if it is understood at last it is not directly or immediately understood. The

---

[15] T. S. Eliot, *Selected Essays: New Edition* (New York: Harcourt, Brace, and World, 1964), p. 252.
[16] Henry James, *Letters, Vol. 1: 1843–1875*, ed. Leon Edel (Cambridge, Mass.: Belknap Press of Harvard University Press, 1975), p. 45.
[17] Leavis, *The Common Pursuit*, p. 80.
[18] Søren Kierkegaard, *The Concept of Irony*, trans. Lee M. Capel (Bloomington, Ind.: Indiana University Press, 1971), pp. 264–265.

delay between the utterance and its being understood corresponds to a certain subjective freedom. The ironist, since he does not coincide with his meaning, has within his power the possibility of a beginning which is not "generated from previous conditions." The ironist masters every moment by traveling *incognito*. The purpose of irony is to enable the ironist to feel free to move in any direction he chooses: he is not intimidated by an object in view or by any commitment he is supposed to accept. The sign of that freedom is superior detachment not from this or that value but from the whole actuality of his time and situation. Irony therefore "has an apriority in itself, and it is not by successively destroying one segment of actuality after another that it arrives at its total view, but by virtue of this, that it destroys in the particular." It is not this or that phenomenon but the totality of existence "which it considers *sub specie ironiae*."[19]

What follows from this is Kierkegaard's distinction between satire, comedy, and irony. Satire hopes to destroy the phenomena it hates. Comedy (and he means, let us say, Shakespearian rather than Jonsonian comedy) hopes to reconcile the conflicting forces in the end. But irony "reinforces vanity in its vanity and renders madness madder."[20] The ironist requires an object as universal as the "being-for-itself of Subjectivity" which is Kierkegaard's characterization of irony: requires it, so that his superiority to it may be correspondingly complete. If the vain phenomenon is merely local, it must be immensely enlarged to make it appear to be worth the ironist's attention. But Kierkegaard emphasizes that the object never acquires any reality for the ironist, either in its own corrupt right or in its malign transformation. The ironist enforces his freedom by talking every object out of its reality: the object merely provides yet another occasion on which he may detach himself from a situation too specious to engage his interest. Finally, Kierkegaard says that irony is healthy "insofar as it rescues the soul from the snares of relativity." But it is a sickness "insofar as it is unable to tolerate the absolute except in the form of nothingness."[21]

Kierkegaard's idea of irony is derived from the example of Socrates: we may admit that Socratic poise is the last quality one would associate with Swift. But Swift's irony answers to Kierkegaard's description in several respects. The animus to which Leavis refers is indeed the sign of Swift's appalling insistence on being free and superior to whatever his mind encounters. If there is sickness, it is there, in his Kierkegaardian inability

---

[19] Ibid., p. 271.   [20] Ibid., p. 274.   [21] Ibid., p. 275.

to tolerate the absolute except in the form of nothingness. But Swift protected himself against a doomed absolutism by resorting, day by day, to an easygoing Protestantism and a conventional epistemology. I do not suppose that he resorted to these with conviction, or that they are adequate as values in their own right and to be contended for. His relation to the commonplaces of religion and philosophy was chiefly strategic: better those (or at least safer) than news from nowhere or from the abyss. I do not claim that his recourse to these commonplaces gave him, at every moment, the stability he wanted.

The point can be made by comparing Swift and Locke on a subject of concern to both of them, the force of Enthusiasm in religion. Locke deals with it in the fourth Book of the *Essay Concerning Human Understanding* and Swift in *A Tale of a Tub* and "The Mechanical Operation of the Spirit." Each of them regarded Enthusiasm as vanity of a peculiarly vulgar and disgusting kind, and dangerous, too. Locke's way of dealing with it was to adjudicate between Reason, Revelation, and Enthusiasm. Reason is natural revelation, the means by which God discloses to men such truth as comes within the reach of their natural faculties. Revelation is natural reason enlarged by direct communications from God: it is the work of reason to determine that these communications indeed come from God. So it is necessary to maintain one's reasoning power even in the presence of such deliveries. As for Enthusiasm:

This I take to be properly Enthusiasm, which though founded neither on Reason nor Divine Revelation, but arising from the Conceits of a warmed or over-weening Brain, works yet, where it once gets footing, more powerfully on the Perswasions and Actions of Man, than either of those two, or both together: Men being most forwardly obedient to the impulses they receive from themselves; And the whole Man is sure to act more vigorously, where the whole Man is carried by a natural Motion. For strong conceit like a new Principle carries all easily with it, when got above common Sense, and freed from all restraint of Reason, and check of Reflection, it is heightened into a Divine Authority, in concurrence with our own Temper and Inclination.[22]

The notion of Enthusiasm as a noxious vapor rising from the conceit of a warmed or overweening brain and taking possession of the whole man as if it were a revelation from God is common to Locke and Swift. But Locke's account of it is subdued to the decorum of exposition and discrimination. If Enthusiasm is vanity, he must take it seriously as a

---

[22] John Locke, *An Essay Concerning Human Understanding*, ed. Peter H. Nidditch (Oxford: Clarendon Press, 1975), p. 699.

motive for action. Swift is not obliged to take it seriously or even to rebuke it; he plays fast and loose with it so that his imagination may take supreme freedom to itself:

Upon these, and the like Reasons, certain Objectors pretend to put it beyond all Doubt, that there must be a sort of preternatural Spirit, possessing the Heads of the Modern Saints; And some will have it to be the Heat of Zeal, working upon the Dregs of Ignorance, as other Spirits are produced from Lees, by the Force of Fire. Some again think, that when our earthly Tabernacles are disordered and desolate, shaken and out of Repair; the Spirit delights to dwell within them, as Houses are said to be haunted, when they are forsaken and gone to Decay.[23]

"Our earthly Tabernacles" is blasphemous to a Christian who believes that by the Incarnation the human body was accorded supreme privilege. The point of Swift's rhetoric is to reduce the body to its decrepit form, and tabernacles to houses, so that he can effect a corresponding reduction of spirits to mere ghosts. As haunters of houses they are bug-bears, sustained only by superstition. The sentence advances with the resolve of a rhyming couplet. In *Some Versions of Pastoral* Empson raised the possibility that Swift's ironies released in him a force of doubt of which he may have been unconscious: as if to say, "could it be the case, truly, as etymology suggests, that everything spiritual is merely a sublimation of something physical or mechanical?" "What Swift was trying to say is a minor matter; he was rightly accused of blasphemy for what he said; his own strength made his instrument too strong for him."[24] Swift's style often ran away with him. If he divined a verbal possibility, it became at once a necessity; he could not set it aside merely out of consideration for propriety or justice. He said more than he intended, and in some sense had to believe (and often to fear) what he had said. The words compelled the disgust they preceded.

Swift indeed resorted to the common forms of attitude and belief, but as a matter of strategy rather than of conviction. His aim coincided with his greatest need, to hold himself free. The ideas he negotiated were commonplaces, and his sense of them was mostly opportunistic, but there were a few ideas which troubled him and could not easily be disposed of within common forms. One of these, I think, provided some of the impulse towards *Gulliver's Travels*. Let us assume that Swift's irony is well enough indicated by Kierkegaard's assertion that the ironist, since he

---

[23] Swift, "A Discourse concerning the Mechanical Operation of the Spirit," in *Prose Writings*, Vol. I, pp. 185–186.
[24] William Empson, *Some Versions of Pastoral* (London: Chatto and Windus, 1962), p. 62.

does not coincide with his meaning, has the power of beginning again at any moment, independently of previous conditions.

Now suppose a helpful colleague (it might be Gay, hardly Pope) were to argue that the sentiment of being free from previous conditions is a delusion, since those conditions have already secreted themselves in Swift's mind as its contents. If that were the case, his mind would not be an independent power but a rigmarole of figures, mere stuff, the result of chance and circumstance. What then would the sentiment of freedom amount to? Suppose further that Swift already feared that the argument might be true, since it was in keeping with the reductive bias of his mind, the grim pleasure he knew he took in saying that high A was nothing but low B. Then he might express his fears, and do something to control them, by projecting a man, Gulliver, of whom these wretched things could truly be said. I have tried to describe, in an earlier essay, the imaginative possibility that such a thought would entail. I've called it brainwashing.

Locke is again close to these motifs. The chapter "Of the Association of Ideas" which he added in 1700 to the *Essay Concerning Human Understanding* was an inevitable consequence of his rejection of innate ideas: he chose instead a theory of experience largely based on Boyle's corpuscular physics and Newton's optics. But he was much disturbed by the tendency of certain ideas to run together for no good reason:

Some of our *Ideas* have a natural Correspondence and Connexion one with another: It is the Office and Excellency of our Reason to trace these, and hold them together in that Union and Correspondence which is founded in their peculiar Beings. Besides this there is another Connexion of *Ideas* wholly owing to Chance or Custom; *Ideas* that in themselves are not at all of kin, come to be so united in some Mens Minds, that 'tis very hard to separate them, they always keep in company, and the one no sooner at any time comes into the Understanding but its Associate appears with it; and if they are more than two which are thus united, the whole gang always inseparable shew themselves together.[25]

Locke thought the association of ideas a real phenomenon, and a dreadful one, a form of madness, because it prevented the mind from reasoning. The reference to "gang" makes his dismay clear. He held the association of ideas responsible for virtually all the mischief and folly in the world, including sectarian violence. In the *Essay* he urged parents and teachers to prevent such associations from forming in their children, so that a clear

---

[25] Locke, *Essay*, p. 395.

space might be available to the mind for dealing with impressions according to rational processes. How parents were qualified to do this, he does not say.

The association of ideas remained a problem. If you argue, as Hartley does in *Observations on Man* (1749), that knowledge is the result of repeated juxtapositions of corpuscular vibrations, you expose the possibility that these could be enforced. Hume, in the *Inquiry Concerning Human Understanding* (1748), gives a copious account of the principles upon which ideas rush into association. There are three: resemblance, contiguity in time or place, and cause or effect. He thought we could not survive without the association of ideas, because it prompts us to believe, and to act upon our beliefs. But the association makes nonsense of the axiom that man is a reasoning animal. What we regard as knowledge is irrational, because there is no good reason to link the impressions which habit and custom insist on linking. In the chapter "Of the Reason of Animals" in the *Inquiry*, Hume reduces the supposed difference between animals and men by arguing that animals, like men, learn by experience; that men and animals believe and act upon the deliveries of custom rather than upon ratiocination; that some parts of knowledge, in animals as in men, are derived "from the original hand of nature," and finally:

The experimental reasoning itself, which we possess in common with beasts, and on which the whole conduct of life depends, is nothing but a species of instinct or a mechanical power that acts in us unknown to ourselves, and in its chief operations is not directed by any such relations or comparison of ideas as are the proper objects of our intellectual faculties.[26]

It was for this reason that in the 1748 edition of the *Philosophical Essays* Hume sketched a non-Aristotelian theory of epic poetry, history, and tragedy, predicated on the affections and the association of ideas rather than upon an Aristotelian theory of *mimesis*. He was afraid that the claims of cognitive independence, vested in the mimetic act, were specious.

Hume does not consider the possibility that one of the principles of the association of ideas (that is, contiguity) might be ordained (or, as we say, programmed) rather than circumstantial. The figure of metonymy could be deployed by repeated insistence upon it. Worry on this score has

---

[26] David Hume, *Inquiry Concerning Human Understanding*, ed. Charles W. Hendel (Indianapolis: Bobbs-Merrill, 1955), p. 116.

become explicit from time to time. In the *Enquiry Concerning Political
Justice* Godwin regarded it as a scandal that every idea, however complex,
offers itself to the mind under the conception of unity. The blending of
many impressions into one perception was, he conceded, a law of nature,
but the mind's prejudice in favor of unity made thinking virtually
impossible. Standard education, which he thought had a deplorably
vested interest in maintaining unity was, as I would say, a form of
brainwashing.

The only way to elude the dismal implications of the association of
ideas (or, more accurately, the association of images or figures) is by
showing that cognition is indeed an independent power, however frus-
trated it may be by unconscious gangs of images. In 1805 the notion of the
association of ideas was so rife that Hazlitt had to attack Hartley's version
of it directly in the hope of claiming autonomy for mind, imagination,
and volition. In the *Essay on the Principles of Human Action* he insisted,
with little evidence, that volition could not be explained "from mere
association."[27] All would be well if associations of ideas could be
attributed not to chance or custom but to the first gestures of cognition.
C. S. Peirce tried to remove the irrational harm from these associations by
arguing, in "Some Consequences of Four Incapacities" (1868), that what is
called "the association of ideas" is in reality an association of judgments
amounting to inference:

The association of ideas is said to proceed according to three principles – those
of resemblance, of contiguity, and of causality. But it would be equally true to
say that signs denote what they do on the three principles of resemblance,
contiguity, and causality. There can be no question that anything is a sign of
whatever is associated with it by resemblance, by contiguity, or by causality:
nor can there be any doubt that any sign recalls the thing signified. So, then,
the association of ideas consists in this, that a judgement occasions another
judgement, of which it is the sign. Now this is nothing less nor more than
inference.[28]

This ingenious attempt to turn a psychological embarrassment into an
entirely respectable form of judgment to be understood by a theory of
semiotics did not end the matter. Many thinkers continued to be
dismayed, even when they were not philosophers. Yeats worried about
what he called "a new naturalism that leaves man helpless before the
contents of his own mind," and he thought that Pound's *Cantos* (so far as

[27] William Hazlitt, *Works*, ed. P. P. Howe (21 vols., London: Dent, 1930–1934), Vol. I, p. 73.
[28] C. S. Peirce, *Selected Writings*, ed. Philip P. Wiener (Stanford University Press, 1958), p. 67.

he had read and understood them) and Joyce's "Anna Livia Plurabelle" (assuming he read it) were "works of an heroic sincerity, the man, his active faculties in suspense, one finger beating time to a bell sounding and echoing in the depths of his own mind."[29] Remy de Gourmont thought that the only way to deal with associations of ideas was to explode them, else the supposedly rational faculty could not proceed: his essay on the dissociation of ideas was a program of demolition. If the mind is not a capacity in some sense independent of its contents, the next questions arise: how did its contents come to be those and not other, and who put them there?

It is not necessary to maintain that Swift was a behaviorist, but only that he feared that something like what we call behaviorism might be true, or at least more probable than the axiom that there is an inviolable human essence and that it consists in the distinctive power of reasoning. I accept, as most readers do, R. S. Crane's account of the rhetorical and ironic structure of Book 4 of *Gulliver's Travels*, that it exhibits a simple reversal of the conventional distinction, common to textbooks of logic from Porphyry to Burgersdicius, between man as the reasoning animal and the horse as the whinnying animal.[30] But Crane does not quite say (perhaps he thinks it follows from his argument) that what Swift is mocking is essentialism as such. If you turn Porphyry's tree upside down you still get an essentialism, though a humiliating one. But Swift goes further, as if to say "and in any case if you take your essentialism seriously, and preen yourself upon your typology as the reasonable animal, I'll show you what your vanity entails." It is hard to say how seriously he took the distinction, which he conveyed in a letter to Pope and Bolingbroke, between man as reasoning animal and man as merely an animal capable of reasoning.[31] He seems to have felt that the author of the *Essay on Man* was not taking him seriously enough, and that the production of a wide-ranging thought might make Pope pay attention. Bolingbroke told Swift that the distinction would not stand scrutiny, and I suppose it does not, but Swift was serious in rejecting essentialist notions. He was not much interested in philosophy, but I think he felt that essentialist definitions, and especially the enhancing ones, did a lot of damage and made people more pretentious than they would otherwise be. My reading of Swift

[29] W. B. Yeats, *Essays and Introductions* (London: Macmillan, 1961), p. 405.
[30] R. S. Crane, *The Idea of the Humanities* (University of Chicago Press, 1967), pp. 261–282.
[31] Jonathan Swift, *Correspondence*, ed. Harold Williams (5 vols., Oxford: Clarendon Press, 1963–1965), Vol. III, p. 121.

suggests that he was exasperated by high-minded claims for man and his
cognitive powers, but that he was dismayed, too, by the readiest alterna-
tive notion, that the mind is merely the sum of its arbitrary and haphazard
contents.

Gulliver's Travels mocks the euphemistic typology (as in the *Essay
on Man*) which elides the differences between one man and another
by providing a category, Man as such, in which the differences are
transcended. Swift's serious thinking is far closer to Locke's remark that
while "the difference is exceeding great between some Men, and some
Animals," if we "compare the Understanding and Abilities of some
Men, and some Brutes, we shall find so little difference, that 'twill
be hard to say, that that of the Man is either clearer or larger."[32]
The descents, and the ascents, in the scale of being are very gradual.
Rochester seems to have felt much the same: the famous line in the
"Epilogue" of the "Satyre against Mankind" ("Man differs more from
man, than man from beast") seems to say that the moral difference
between the best people and the worst is greater than that between the
best people and the general run of animals.

But a lot depends upon the particular animal you have in view. If you
merely want to make a thundering attack on man, you don't need to
specify the animal you prefer: I'd be a dog, a monkey, or a bear, Rochester
says in the "Satyre," or indeed anything rather than that vain animal, man,
who is so proud of being rational. Nearly any animal would do, if you
wanted to attack man's self-conceit. But if you wanted to make a more
pointed case, the particular animal might make a difference. Empson
argues that in the seventeenth and eighteenth centuries it was common to
feel that animals "blow the gaff" on human nature, and the thought is
either dreadful or not, depending on the animal. He thinks that it was
tolerable if you had dogs in mind, rather than monkeys, even though it
was agreed that among the lower animals the elephant, the ape, the dog,
and the horse are intelligent in that descending order. In any case it was
sound strategy to think of yourself as the most triumphant of animals
rather than as the most fallen angel. If you thought of the dog you could
start building yourself into a man, and not hate yourself:

The important point about the noble animal is that he is a deeply reassuring
object to contemplate. The fact that he can be patronized as no more than
fundamental makes you think better of the race of man.[33]

---

[32] Locke, *Essay*, p. 666.   [33] Empson, *The Structure of Complex Words*, p. 170.

Empson makes the point that Swift refused this genial sentiment:

The fact that monkeys were so like men was "sadly humbling" to Boswell; Monboddo only dared to say what many had suspected, and Johnson agreed he was not a fool. Swift might fall back on the Houyhnhnm in accepting this about the Yahoo, but that was a refusal of humanity; the only real animal to use was the dog.[34]

But Swift could not have used the dog, man's faithful friend, without making the fourth book a cozy fireside thing. He had to pick an animal sure to keep his distance even in a domestic setting. It was an advantage that in Greek mythology and in Plato's *Republic* horses were given wings splendid enough to make them fly as poetic inspiration or as the noble soul. It has always been possible to say, as D. H. Lawrence did in many poems, that virtually any organism (bird, beast, or flower) is more completely itself than man is. The most recent version of this I have seen is Stanley Cavell's assertion that what is splendid in the horse is his willingness to be known:

The horse, as it stands, is a rebuke to our unreadiness to be understood, our will to remain obscure. And the more beautiful the horse's stance, the more painful the rebuke. Theirs is our best picture of a readiness to understand. Our stand, our stance, is of denial. We feel our refusals are unrevealed because we keep, we think, our fences invisible. But the horse takes cognizance of them, who does not care about invisibility.[35]

Gulliver's Travels does not require us to think that horses are finer than we are – or than some of us are. The Houyhnhnms do not, in fact, exhibit ideal powers of reasoning: if they did they would distinguish at once and without fuss between their leader's hospitality to Gulliver and Gulliver's relation to the other Yahoos. It is enough for the irony of the book that the Houyhnhnms are more intelligent than Englishmen who quarrel about matters entirely indifferent and run wild into factions and sects. There is no need to drive the matter to superlatives; comparatives are enough. Reason has a better chance, a clearer run, among the Houyhnhnms because it meets fewer obstacles: they are more content than we are, because they propose to themselves fewer wants. But they, like Gulliver, are what they are not by some essentialist or categorical imperative but as a consequence of the experiences which have made them.

---

[34] Ibid.

[35] Stanley Cavell, letter to Vicki Hearne, quoted in her "Tracking Dogs, Sensitive Horses, and the Traces of Speech," *Raritan*, Vol. 6, No. 4 (Spring 1986), p. 34.

I do not claim that this was Swift's settled position: clearly, it could be tipped in either of the available directions. He was far more determined to hold himself free and to convince himself – or at worst to hope – that he had escaped the humiliation of the association of ideas. The practice of irony was his way of retaining that consolation, despite every consideration that told against it.

PART III

On Yeats

CHAPTER 4

Three Presences: Yeats, Eliot, Pound

I

On April 2, 1916 one of Yeats's plays for dancers, *At the Hawk's Well*, received its first performance in Lady Emerald Cunard's drawing-room in Cavendish Square, London before an invited audience. Michio Ito danced the Guardian of the Well. The guests included Ezra Pound and T. S. Eliot. For all I know, this may have been the only afternoon on which Yeats, Eliot, and Pound were together in the same room. Many years later, Samuel Beckett wrote a play, like *At the Hawk's Well*, about waiting; waiting for someone who is supposed to arrive but doesn't, a variant of waiting for a transforming flow of water which is never received because the guardian of the well distracts those who are longing for it. In *Happy Days* Winnie utters the first line of *At the Hawk's Well*, "I call to the eye of the mind," one of many literary allusions that she recalls – or rather, that Beckett recalls on her behalf. I draw a loose connection between these occasions to suggest a literary context for the relations I propose to describe: Yeats and Eliot, Yeats and Pound.

We know when Eliot converted to the Anglican Communion – he made his formal profession on June 9, 1927 – but we don't know precisely when he converted to Yeats: that took much longer. The first time he wrote formally about Yeats was in the *Athenaeum*, the issue for July 4, 1919, a memorably severe review of the reprinted *The Cutting of an Agate*. Eliot apparently found Yeats's entire sensibility weird. As much in his prose as in his verse, he said, Yeats "is not 'of this world' – *this* world, of course, being our visible planet with whatever our theology or myth may conceive as below or above it." Eliot assumes that he is central, by comparison with whom Yeats is exotically peripheral. The difference between Yeats's world and ours, Eliot continued to say in consternation,

* *The Hudson Review* (Winter 2010).

"is so complete as to seem almost a physiological variety, different nerves and senses." It was not – or not merely – a matter of Yeats's interest in ghosts, mediums, leprechauns, and sprites. "When an Englishman explores the mysteries of the Cabala," Eliot said, "one knows one's opinion of him, but Mr. Yeats on any subject is a cause of bewilderment and distress":

The sprites are not unacceptable; but Mr. Yeats's daily world, the world which admits these monsters without astonishment, which views them more familiarly than Commercial Road views a Lascar – this is the unknown and unknowable. Mr. Yeats's mind is a mind in some way independent of experience; and anything that occurs in that mind is of equal importance. It is a mind in which perception of fact, and feeling and thinking are all a little different from ours.

Eliot did not define whom he had in view by "ours," or justify bringing forth their values as a decisive criterion. He did not explain how "experience" could be appealed to as a system supposedly held in common. He claimed that Yeats's sensibility could not be assessed by any available standard:

In Mr. Yeats's verse, in particular, the qualities can by no means be defined as mere attenuations and faintnesses. When it is compared with the work of any English bard of apparently equivalent thinness, the result is that the English work in question *is* thin; you can point to something that it ought to be and is not; but of Yeats you cannot say finally that he lacks feeling. He does not pretend to more feeling than he has, perhaps he has a great deal; it is not feeling that standards can measure as passionate or insipid.

Eliot's problem with Yeats was that he could not see either his thought or his feeling as having issued from any common source:

He seems, in his disembodied way, to happen on thoughts, thoughts of "wisdom," and if we are not convinced, it is because we do not see by what right he comes by them.

Perhaps, Eliot allows, Yeats got these wise thoughts from his dreaming, but even if this is so, "Mr. Yeats's dream is identical with Mr. Yeats's reality," a qualification or continuation of himself.[1]

Eliot quoted, in evidence, four short passages from *The Cutting of an Agate*, including one – inaccurately quoted, indeed – in which Yeats says that the poet must "be content to find his pleasure in all that is for ever passing away that it may come again, in the beauty of woman, in the

---

[1] T. S. Eliot, "A Foreign Mind," *The Athenaeum*, No. 4653, July 4, 1919, pp. 552–553.

fragile flowers of spring, in momentary heroic passion, in whatever is most fleeting, most impassioned, as it were, for its own perfection, most eager to return in its glory."[2] "It is a style of Pater," Eliot justly said, but then he indulged himself in a little racial prejudice, saying "it is a style of Pater, with a trick of the eye and a hanging of the nether lip that come from across the Irish Channel, all the more seductive." "Mr. Yeats," he says, "sometimes appears, as a philosopher of aesthetics, incoherent":

But all of his observations are quite consistent with his personality, with his remoteness. His remoteness is not an escape from the world, for he is innocent of any world to escape from; his procedure is blameless, but he does not start where we do.

At this point in his review, Eliot moves toward thinking that to make sense of Yeats you have first to remember that he is an Irishman. Eliot evidently thought that to be an Irishman was to be deprived of certain attributes of sensibility, notably of wit, a quality he defined in his essay on Andrew Marvell as featuring "a tough reasonableness beneath the slight lyric grace":

You cannot find it in Shelley or Keats or Wordsworth; you cannot find more than an echo of it in Landor; still less in Tennyson or Browning; and among contemporaries Mr. Yeats is an Irishman and Mr. Hardy is a modern Englishman – that is to say, Mr. Hardy is without it and Mr. Yeats is outside of the tradition altogether.[3]

What "the tradition" was, Eliot on this occasion did not say: presumably he meant a structure of values which Irish men and women lacked, even though Irish culture could point to various forms of intelligence exemplified by Swift, Yeats, Wilde, Joyce, and Shaw. Yeats's mind, Eliot said further,

is, in fact, extreme in egoism, and, as often with egoism, remains a little crude; crude, indeed, as from its remoteness one would expect. There is something of this crudity, and much of this egoism, about what is called Irish Literature: the egoism which obstructs from facing, and the crudity which remains through not having had to face direct contacts. We know also of an evasion, or rather an evacuation of reality by the very civilized; but people civilized to that extent are seldom artists, and Mr. Yeats is always an artist. His crudity and egoism are present in other writers who are Irish; justified by exploitation to the point of greatness, in the later work of Mr. James Joyce.

---

[2] W. B. Yeats, *The Cutting of an Agate* (New York: Macmillan, 1912), p. 97. Eliot gives the last phrase as "most eager to return to its own glory."
[3] T. S. Eliot, *Selected Essays: New Edition* (New York: Harcourt, Brace and World, 1964), p. 252.

Eliot seems to have received directly from Arnold his notion of what is entailed by being Irish. Joyce, too, is understandable only if you remember that he was an Irishman, with the attributes and defects which go with that fate:

Mr. Joyce's mind is subtle, erudite, even massive; but it is not like Stendhal's, an instrument continually tempering and purifying emotion; it operates within the medium, the superb current of his feeling. The basis is pure feeling, and if the feeling of Mr. Yeats were equally powerful, it would also justify his thought. Very powerful feeling *is* crude; the fault of Mr. Yeats's is that it is crude without being powerful. The weakness of his prose is similar to that of his verse. The trouble is not that it is inconsistent, illogical or incoherent, but that the objects upon which it is directed are not fixed; as in his portraits of Synge and several other Irishmen, we do not seem to get the men themselves before us, but feelings of Mr. Yeats projected. It must always be granted that in verse at least Mr. Yeats's feeling is not simply crudeness and egoism, but that it has a positive, individual and permanent quality.[4]

It may have been this quality, common to Yeats and Joyce, which enabled Eliot to think that Yeats had anticipated Joyce in the most far-reaching invention in modern literature. Reviewing *Ulysses* in 1923, Eliot wrote:

It is here that Mr. Joyce's parallel use of the *Odyssey* has a great importance. It has the importance of a scientific discovery. . . . In using the myth, in manipulating a continuous parallel between contemporaneity and antiquity, Mr. Joyce is pursuing a method which others must pursue after him. . . . It is simply a way of controlling, of ordering, of giving a shape and a significance to the immense panorama of futility and anarchy which is contemporary history. It is a method already adumbrated by Mr. Yeats, and of the need for which I believe Mr. Yeats to have been the first contemporary to be conscious . . . . Instead of narrative method, we may now use the mythical method. It is, I seriously believe, a step toward making the modern world possible for art.[5]

Eliot doesn't say where Yeats adumbrated the mythical method. I assume it entailed redeeming a mere fact from its penury by presenting it in the light of a higher or a larger perspective. If so, I think Yeats did this notably in such poems as "A Woman Homer Sung" and "No Second Troy."

It is surprising, then, in view of this achievement, that Eliot continued for several years to comment derisively on Yeats's dealings with occult images and motifs; though these were also the years in which

---

[4] Eliot, "A Foreign Mind," p. 553.
[5] T. S. Eliot, "*Ulysses*, Order, and Myth," *The Dial*, November 1923, reprinted in *Selected Prose of T. S. Eliot*, ed. Frank Kermode (London: Faber and Faber, 1975), pp. 177–178.

he recognized the power of Yeats's later poems. In *The Use of Poetry and the Use of Criticism* he wrote:

No one can read Mr. Yeats's *Autobiographies* and his earlier poetry without feeling that the author was trying to get as a poet something like the exaltation to be obtained, I believe, from hashisch or nitrous oxide. He was very much fascinated by self-induced trance states, calculated symbolism, mediums, theosophy, crystal-gazing, folklore and hobgoblins. Golden apples, archers, black pigs and such paraphernalia abounded. Often the verse has an hypnotic charm: but you cannot take heaven by magic, especially if you are, like Mr. Yeats, a very sane person. Then, by a great triumph of development, Mr. Yeats began to write and is still writing some of the most beautiful poetry in the language, some of the clearest, simplest, most direct.[6]

In *After Strange Gods* – the Page-Barbour lectures that Eliot delivered at the University of Virginia in 1933 – he referred to Pound as "probably the most important living poet in our language" and to Yeats as "the other important poet of our time," while subjecting both poets to some rebuke.[7] His complaint against Yeats, which he adopted largely from I. A. Richards's *Science and Poetry* only to make the criticism even more pointed than Richards made it, was that Yeats's "supernatural world" was "the wrong supernatural world":

It was not a world of spiritual significance, not a world of real Good and Evil, of holiness or sin, but a highly sophisticated lower mythology summoned, like a physician, to supply the fading pulse of poetry with some transient stimulant so that the dying patient may utter his last words. In its extreme self-consciousness it approaches the mythology of D. H. Lawrence on its more decadent side. We admire Mr. Yeats for having outgrown it; for having packed away his bibelots and resigned himself to live in an apartment furnished in the barest simplicity. A few faded beauties remain: Babylon, Nineveh, Helen of Troy, and such souvenirs of youth: but the austerity of Mr. Yeats's later verse on the whole, should compel the admiration of the least sympathetic.

Not that Eliot had entirely done with rebuke:

Though the tone is often of regret, sometimes of resignation:

> Things said or done long years ago,
> Or things I did not do or say
> But thought that I might say or do,

---

[6] T. S. Eliot, *The Use of Poetry and the Use of Criticism: Studies in the Relation of Criticism to Poetry in England* (London: Faber and Faber, 1950 reprint), p. 140.

[7] T. S. Eliot, *After Strange Gods: A Primer of Modern Heresy* (New York: Harcourt, Brace and Company, 1934), pp. 45, 47.

> Weigh me down, and not a day
> But something is recalled,
> My conscience or my vanity appalled.

and though Mr. Yeats is still perhaps a little too much the weather-worn Triton among the streams, he has arrived at greatness against the greatest odds; if he has not arrived at a central and universal philosophy he has at least discarded, for the most part, the trifling and eccentric, the provincial in time and place.[8]

Eliot seems to have in mind, without saying so much, that Yeats is inferior to Dante in the matter of a central and universal philosophy.

It appears that Eliot's conversion to Yeats – to the later Yeats – was made sometime between late 1933 and 1935. By 1935 he had come to appreciate Yeats's significance; first in relation to the Abbey Theatre, which "kept poetry in the theatre" and "maintained literary standards which had long since disappeared from the English stage"; and then for the poetry itself, of which Eliot said that "Mr. Yeats has been and is the greatest poet of his time." "I can think of no poet, not even among the very greatest, who has shown a longer period of development than Yeats." Development "to this extent is not merely genius, it is character; and it sets a standard which his juniors should seek to emulate, without hoping to equal."[9] I think Eliot had Shakespeare in view when he appealed to a long period of development as evidence of genius and character. Presumably he meant that in a long period of development one suffers disappointments, false starts and vain experiments only to overcome them at last and come to know the nature of one's individual talent.

When Yeats died in 1939 and Eliot accepted the invitation to deliver the first annual Yeats lecture to the Friends of the Irish Academy, at the Abbey Theatre in 1940, he retained the theme of a poet's development and remarked how Yeats "had to wait for a later maturity to find expression of early experience." Reading the poems again in the light of a complete development, Eliot found the turning point in the 1914 volume *Responsibilities* with its "violent and terrible epistle" and the great lines

> Pardon that for a barren passion's sake,
> Although I have come close on forty-nine,
> I have no child, I have nothing but a book,
> Nothing but that to prove your blood and mine.

---

[8] Ibid., pp. 50–51.
[9] T. S. Eliot, "A Commentary," *The Criterion*, Vol. 14, No. 56 (July 1935), pp. 610–613.

So he regarded Yeats, poet and dramatist, as "pre-eminently the poet of middle age," by which he appears to have meant that in the play *Purgatory* and in such poems as "In Memory of Eva Gore-Booth and Con Markiewicz" and "Coole Park 1929," "one feels that the most lively and desirable emotions of youth have been preserved to receive their full and due expression in retrospect. . . . For the interesting feelings of age are not just different feelings; they are feelings into which the feelings of youth are integrated."[10]

I have quoted enough to show that Eliot changed his critical assessment of Yeats, probably in 1934, and that his sense, up to that point, of Yeats's achievement was ungenerous and erratic. The impersonal animosity of the review of *The Cutting of an Agate* – for it amounts to that – can be explained, but only in part, by Eliot's need to put a considerable distance between himself and Yeats, each of whom could be regarded as a Symbolist, however differently they responded to French Symbolism as Arthur Symons expounded it in *The Symbolist Movement in Literature*. He did not wish to be associated with Yeats's party. It is my understanding that Symons led Yeats through the early chapters of the book on the Symbolist movement with Mallarmé as the main figure, and that Eliot made his own way quickly through the several chapters until he reached Laforgue, the poet he found most useful in his attempt to discover his own voice. Still, Eliot's animosity is hard to explain. The poems in *Responsibilities* and the play *At the Hawk's Well* were available to him for several years before he committed the asperities in his review of *The Cutting of an Agate*. In *The Use of Poetry and the Use of Criticism* he scolded Richards for not quite appreciating Yeats's later work, though he himself was slow to appreciate it. Richards could only plead that he had written *Science and Poetry* before *The Tower* came out in 1928.[11] The presence of Yeats, Swift, and Mallarmé in the "familiar compound ghost" of "Little Gidding" is Eliot's final tribute to three great predecessors; if we add Dante and Shakespeare, we make up nearly the whole account.

It is worth noting that Eliot apparently paid no attention to Yeats's later politics: he does not refer to Yeats's engagement – if it was an engagement – with the Fascism of Mussolini and Gentile. Presumably he thought that this sentiment or whatever it was did not come into the

[10] T. S. Eliot, *On Poetry and Poets* (New York: Farrar, Straus and Cudahy, 1957), pp. 299, 301, 303.
[11] Cf. Eliot, *The Use of Poetry and the Use of Criticism*, p. 140n and I. A. Richards, *Coleridge on Imagination* (London: Kegan Paul, Trench, Trubner, 1934), p. 207n.

poetry or the plays and therefore it might well be ignored. Or that even if it came into them, it did not undermine their irrefutable quality.

II

Yeats and Eliot were not familiars; they met occasionally and agreeably from as early as 1915 – at least once at a meeting of the Omega Club, and again when they lunched together at the Savile. Eliot published Yeats in *The Criterion*. Yeats and Eliot were active together in their support of Rupert Doone's Group Theatre. Eliot's *Sweeney Agonistes*, published on December 1, 1932, was performed by the Group in their rooms in London on November 11, 1934, the text as we have it being eked out with music by William Alwyn, masks by Robert Medley, and presumably a good deal of stage-business drawn from various sources. That was its first English performance: it had already been done by Hallie Flanagan's Vassar College Experimental Theatre during Eliot's months in the United States in 1933. Yeats attended another performance of it by the Group Theatre in London on December 16, 1934. Eliot and Yeats also tried to found a Poets' Theatre in London in 1935, with no success.[12] So they were associates from time to time, but not companions. Yeats and Pound make a different relation: they were friends and remained friends especially after the three winters they spent in Stone Cottage, Coleman's Hatch, Sussex. The friendship continued over the years and found fulfillment in a shared Rapallo. One of the many differences between Eliot and Pound, in their relations to Yeats, was that Pound did not change his opinion. From the first years in London, he sought out the writers he regarded as important, but he did not haggle over their attributes. When he had decided on their quality, he rarely changed his mind. On December 10, 1912, three years after meeting Yeats, he wrote a letter to *Poetry*, Harriet Monroe's new magazine:

The state of things here in London is, as I see it, as follows: I find Mr. Yeats the only poet worthy of serious study. Mr. Yeats' work is already a recognized classic and is part of the required reading in the Sorbonne. There is no need of proclaiming him to the American public. ... I would rather talk about poetry with Ford Madox Hueffer [not yet Ford Madox Ford] than with any man in London. Mr. Hueffer's beliefs about the art may be best explained by saying that they are in diametric opposition to those of Mr. Yeats.

---

[12] Cf. Michael J. Sidnell, *Dances of Death: The Group Theatre of London in the Thirties* (London: Faber and Faber, 1984), pp. 266–269.

Mr. Yeats has been subjective; believes in the glamour and associations which hang near words. "Works of art beget works of art." He has much in common with the French symbolists. Mr. Hueffer believes in an exact rendering of things. He would strip words of all "association" for the sake of getting a precise meaning. He professes to prefer prose to verse. You would find his origins in Gautier or in Flaubert. He is objective. This school tends to lapse into description. The other tends to lapse into sentiment.

Mr. Yeats' method is, to my way of thinking, very dangerous, for although he is the greatest of living poets who use English, and though he has sung some of the moods of life immortally, his art has not broadened much in scope during the past decade. His gifts to English art are mostly negative; i.e., he has stripped English poetry of many of its faults. His "followers" have come to nothing. Neither Synge, Lady Gregory nor Colum can be called his followers, though he had much to do with bringing them forth, yet nearly every man who writes English verse seriously is in some way indebted to him.[13]

It is clear that Pound was on Hueffer's side. Poetry should be at least as well-written as prose, especially the prose of Stendhal and Flaubert. The unit of perception is the visual image. Beware of glamour and associations. If mind is "the regenerative part of nature," you should not rely on impressions that merely happen to reach your retina.[14] If you do, you will find one impression displacing another: your work will not develop.

In his memoir of Gaudier-Brzeska, Pound stated the same preference without naming names:

There are two opposed ways of thinking of a man: firstly, you may think of him as that toward which perception moves, as the toy of circumstance, as the plastic substance *receiving* impressions; secondly, you may think of him as directing a certain fluid force against circumstance, as *conceiving* instead of merely reflecting and observing. One does not claim that one way is better than the other, one notes a diversity of the temperament. The two camps always exist.[15]

But Pound evidently thought that one way – the way of conceiving instead of merely reflecting – was better than the first: it was the basis of his aesthetic. "Imagisme is not Symbolism."[16]

Over a few years, Pound came to think that whatever Yeats did in the way of Symbolism, Eliot did it better; and whatever Hueffer did in the way of realism, Joyce did it better, at least in *Dubliners, A Portrait of*

---

[13] Ezra Pound, "Status Rerum," *Poetry*, Vol. 1, No. 4 (January 1913), pp. 123, 125.
[14] Hugh Kenner, *The Pound Era* (Berkeley and Los Angeles: University of California Press, 1971), p. 164.
[15] Ezra Pound, *Gaudier-Brzeska: A Memoir* (New York: New Directions, fourth printing, 1970), pp. 89–90.
[16] Ibid., p. 84.

the Artist as a Young Man, and the realistic chapters of *Ulysses*. Pound's review of *Responsibilities* in May 1914 may be thought to point to a change of style on Yeats's part, but it doesn't, not quite. There is a new note, as Pound remarks, in such poems as "No Second Troy" and "The Magi," but Yeats is still a Symbolist; although his work has become "gaunter, seeking greater hardness of detail." It is "no longer romantically Celtic."[17] Pound seems to say that Yeats, still incorrigibly Symbolist, has recognized the force of contingent detail: the change, the new note, is evident in some of the poems in *The Green Helmet and Other Poems* (1910) and *Responsibilities* (1914). But Yeats has not changed his fundamental allegiance to Symbolism. He has not joined Pound, Gaudier-Brzeska, Wyndham Lewis, H. D., Hueffer, and Joyce in the service of what we now call Objectivism. Even in later years, when Pound wrote of his early days with Yeats, he recalled him as a convinced Symbolist.

Sometime in 1911, Yeats and Pound happened to be in Paris together, but perhaps not on the day on which Pound emerged from the Metro at La Concorde and saw beautiful faces all around him. He wrote a poem of thirty lines, but he destroyed it because he judged it work of second intensity. Six months later he wrote a poem of half that length, and destroyed that, too. A year later, with the Japanese *hokku* in mind, he wrote a poem of three lines including the title, IN A STATION OF THE METRO:

> The apparition of these faces in the crowd;
> Petals on a wet, black bough.

Later he said of it:

I dare say it is meaningless unless one has drifted into a certain vein of thought. In a poem of this sort one is trying to record the precise instant when a thing outward and objective transforms itself, or darts into a thing inward and subjective.[18]

The poem, as Hugh Kenner said of it, "is energy, is effort. It does not appease itself by reproducing what is seen, but by setting some other seen thing into relation."[19] It is an instance of "juxtaposition without copula," to use a phrase we associate with Marshall McLuhan. That is why it points toward Objectivism, an option taken up by Pound and several poets of similar disposition, including William Carlos Williams, Marianne

---

[17] Ezra Pound, "The Later Yeats," *Poetry*, Vol. 4, No. 11 (May, 1914), pp. 64–68.
[18] Pound, *Gaudier–Brzeska*, p. 89.   [19] Kenner, *The Pound Era*, p. 186.

Moore, Louis Zukofsky, Basil Bunting, and George Oppen. Objectivism steps aside in favor of the thing seen, to begin with, even though the sense of that thing must eventually become, as Pound says, "inward and subjective." On the same visit to Paris, as Pound recalled it in Canto 83, he saw Yeats as

> Uncle William dawdling around Notre Dame
> in search of whatever
>   paused to admire the symbol
> with Notre Dame standing inside it
> Whereas in St Etienne
>   Or why not Dei Miracoli:
> mermaids, that carving ....[20]

Most of the work in that passage is done by "Whereas." Yeats is merely receiving impressions. Notre Dame is not seen by an act of conceiving, a flow of energy directed upon its stone. Yeats's mind is "in search of whatever," of nothing in particular. Whereas Pietro Lombardo's carved mermaids on Santa Maria dei Miracoli in Venice are there only to be seen: the mind of the one who looks at them is concentrated on their detail, it does not wait for a symbolic halo to surround them. It is the difference between modeling and carving, in Adrian Stokes's terms. The passage I've quoted from Canto 83 gave credence to a common view of Yeats – Donald Davie expressed it, all too well, in his first book on Pound – as a poet who never looked hard at anything; that he divined the emblem more ardently than the swan that produced it: "Another emblem there!" In Symbolism, you could nearly keep your eyes closed and attend only to the echo of word and word, so little are objects in space allowed to enforce their claim on you. Paul Valéry said of the poets who succeeded the French Symbolists that "they opened again, upon the accidents of being, eyes we had closed in order to make ourselves more akin to its substance."[21] When Pound noted that Yeats was susceptible to the associations that hang near words, he pointed to the Symbolists' interest in effects purely linguistic, not derived from the world or verifiable by appeal to that value: they are linguistic through and through. In his earliest years as a poet, Pound was himself susceptible to those effects, but he worked free of them and turned for guidance to the poet Gautier

---

[20] Ezra Pound, *The Cantos* (New York: New Directions, 1975), p. 548.

[21] Paul Valéry: "Ils ont réouvert aussi sur les accidents de l'être les yeux que nous avions fermés pour nous faire plus semblables à sa substance": "Avant-Propos à la connaissance de la déesse" in *Oeuvres*, ed. Jean Hytier (Paris: Gallimard, 1957), Vol. I, p. 1276.

and his insistence on the detail of apprehension. Pound became a Luminist even before he called his allegiances Imagism or Vorticism.

Pound's references to Yeats are genial nonetheless. He never forgot the friendship that developed between them in their winters at Stone Cottage where Yeats had him read scholarly works about witches and demonology as well as Doughty's *The Dawn in Britain*. Late in Canto 98 Pound scolds Yeats, Eliot, and Wyndham Lewis for having "no ground beneath 'em," by contrast with Orage who apparently had plenty of such ground. Orage, like Pound, knew that the quality of a society depends upon the system of economics that governs it – a system clarified to Pound's satisfaction by C. H. Douglas. Sometimes, as in Canto 80, Pound made a little fun of Senator Yeats, but in the same Canto he agreed with "old William" that "the crumbling of a fine house/profits no one/(Celtic or otherwise)" and in Canto 77 he recalled with no sign of dissent "uncle William" murmuring "Sligo in Heaven" when "the mist finally settled down on Tigullio," a tribute repeated in Canto 114.

III

Yeats's most sustained comments on Eliot's poetry are in his Introduction to *The Oxford Book of Modern Verse* (1936) and a BBC talk on "Modern Poetry" which he gave in the same year. On both occasions he referred to Eliot as a satirist, indeed as a mere satirist. In the *Oxford Book* he represented him through the four "Preludes," "The Hippopotamus," "Whispers of Immortality," and "Sweeney among the Nightingales." Eliot, he said,

> has produced his great effect upon his generation because he has described men and women that get out of bed or into it from mere habit; in describing this life that has lost heart his own art seems grey, cold, dry. He is an Alexander Pope, working without apparent imagination, producing his effects by a rejection of all rhythms and metaphors used by the more popular romantics rather than by the discovery of his own, this rejection giving his work an unexaggerated plainness that has the effect of novelty.

Maintaining the reference to Pope, Yeats said that Eliot "has the rhythmical flatness of the *Essay on Man* – despite Miss Sitwell's advocacy I see Pope as Blake and Keats saw him – later, in *The Waste Land*, amid much that is moving in symbol and imagery there is much monotony of accent" – to illustrate which, Yeats quoted these lines:

> When lovely woman stoops to folly and
> Paces about her room again, alone,

> She smooths her hair with automatic hand,
> And puts a record on the gramophone.

"I was affected, as I am by these lines," Yeats recalled, "when I saw for the first time a painting by Manet." "I longed," he said, "for the vivid colour and light of Rousseau and Courbet, I could not endure the grey middle-tint – and even to-day Manet gives me an incomplete pleasure; he had left the procession." And as if the word "procession" reminded Yeats of another one, he continued: "Nor can I put the Eliot of these poems among those that descend from Shakespeare and the translators of the Bible":

I think of him as satirist rather than poet. Once only does that early work speak in the great manner:

> The host with someone indistinct
> Converses at the door apart,
> The nightingales are singing near
> The Convent of the Sacred Heart,
> And sang within the bloody wood
> When Agamemnon cried aloud,
> And let their liquid siftings fall
> To stain the stiff dishonoured shroud.

There, Yeats seems to say, Eliot rose to the grand occasion of Agamemnon, as Yeats himself did in "Leda and the Swan." Yeats praised those lines because he himself, I infer, might have written them.

But Yeats comes close to being insolent when he refers to Eliot's religion as lacking "all strong emotion" by comparison with the religion of John Gray, Francis Thompson, and Lionel Johnson: "a New England Protestant by descent, there is little self-surrender in his personal relation to God and the soul." *Murder in the Cathedral*, Yeats says, is "a powerful stage play because the actor, the monkish habit, certain repeated words, symbolize what we know, not what the author knows." But Yeats has one complaint about the play:

Nowhere has the author explained how Becket and the King differ in aim; Becket's people have been robbed and persecuted in his absence; like the King he demands strong government. Speaking through Becket's mouth Eliot confronts a world growing always more terrible with a religion like that of some great statesman, a pity not less poignant because it tempers the prayer book with the results of mathematical philosophy.[22]

---

[22] W. B. Yeats, "Introduction," in *Oxford Book of Modern Verse 1892–1935* (New York: Oxford University Press, 1937), p. iii.

To enforce the point, Yeats quotes Becket's speech beginning: "Peace. And let them be, in their exaltation."

In the BBC talk on modern poetry, after describing Eliot as "the most revolutionary man in poetry during my lifetime, though his revolution was stylistic alone," Yeats associated him with writers to whom "what we call the solid earth was manufactured by the human mind from unknown raw material":

> They do not think this because of Kant and Berkeley, who are an old story, but because of something that has got into the air since a famous French mathematician wrote "Space is a creation of our ancestors." Eliot's historical and scholarly mind seems to have added this further thought, probably from Nicholas of Cusa: reality is expressed in a series of contradictions, or is this unknowable something that supports the centre of the see-saw.

To illustrate this, Yeats quoted from "Burnt Norton" the passage that begins: "At the still point of the turning world."[23]

IV

Yeats was much more warmly disposed toward Pound than toward Eliot. Especially in their conversations at Rapallo, Pound and Yeats argued fundamental philosophic questions. Pound seemed to Yeats a thorough-going skeptic: he insisted that causation couldn't be proved and that apparent sequences were the most one could trust. If you press the electric light switch, the light will probably go on: "all our knowledge is like that." But Yeats chose what Richard Ellmann called "the more solid fare of affirmation." In a journal entry of January 1929, after such a conversation, Yeats wrote of Pound's "search for complete undisturbed self-possession":

> In Eliot, and perhaps in [Wyndham] Lewis, bred in the same skepticism, there is a tendency to exchange search for submission ... I agree with Ezra in his dislike of the word belief. Belief implies an unknown object, a covenant attested with a name or signed with blood, and being more emotional than intellectual may pride itself on lack of proof. But if I affirm that such and such is true, the more complete the affirmation, the more complete the proof, and even when incomplete, it remains valid within some limit. I must kill skepticism in myself, except in so far as it is mere acknowledgement of a limit.[24]

---

[23] W. B. Yeats, "Modern Poetry," in *Essays and Introductions* (New York: Macmillan, 1961), pp. 499, 503.

[24] Quoted in Richard Ellmann, *The Identity of Yeats* (New York: Oxford University Press, second edition, 1964), p. 239.

Pound thought he could escape skepticism "by assuming a self of past years"; by re-writing his early poems, he could touch "a stronger passion, a greater confidence than I possess, or ever did possess":

Ezra when he re-creates Propertius or some Chinese poet escapes his skepticism. The one reason for putting our actual situation into our art is that the struggle for complete affirmation may be, often must be, that art's chief poignancy. I must, though [the] world shriek at me, admit no act beyond my power, nor thing beyond my knowledge, yet because my divinity is far off I blanch and tremble.[25]

It follows that Yeats liked Pound's poetry more than Eliot's, but the more he thought of Pound's poems, the more he talked himself into vehemence and exasperation. He represented Pound in the *Oxford Book* by "The River-Merchant's Wife: A Letter," a passage from "Homage to Sextus Propertius," and Canto 17. But he begged off saying anything about the Cantos as a whole. As in the revised *Vision*, with twenty-seven Cantos available to him, he could make nothing of them: it was as if he wanted to see causation and saw only arbitrary sequences:

I have often found there brightly printed kings, queens, knaves, but have never discovered why all the suits could not be dealt out in some quite different order.[26]

In the Introduction to the *Oxford Book* he said of the Cantos that "like other readers I discover at present merely exquisite or grotesque fragments," but he was content to suspend judgment till the poem was complete – a fulfillment he did not live to see. Meanwhile he was irritated by Pound's "unbridged transitions, unexplained ejaculations, that make his meaning unintelligible."[27] "Ezra Pound," Yeats said, "has made flux his theme; plot, characterization, logical discourse, seem to him abstractions unsuitable to a man of his generation." "He hopes," Yeats continued, "to give the impression that all is living, that there are no edges, no convexities, nothing to check the flow; but can such a poem have a mathematical structure?" Pound told Yeats that the Cantos would eventually number one hundred, but not that the structure of the poem would be mathematical. Yeats saw flux everywhere in them, but he did not see – what Kenner saw – that "Pound's work, say from *Lustra* to the last Cantos, is the longest working-out in any art of premises like those of

---

[25] Ibid., pp. 239–240.
[26] W. B. Yeats, *A Vision* (London: Macmillan, second edition 1937, corrected 1962), p. 4.
[27] Yeats, "Introduction," in *Oxford Book of Modern Verse 1892–1935*, pp. xxiv, xxv.

Cubism."[28] Indeed, one wonders how much of Pound's poetry Yeats kept up with and liked. It appears that whenever he thought of the poetry, he let one poem stand for the rest, and quoted it – "The Return" – without comment both in the Introduction to the *Oxford Book* and the revised *Vision*. The poem gratified Yeats, I infer, because of its theme, the return of the pagan gods. Pater wrote two stories – "Apollo in Picardy" and "Denys L'Auxerrois" – in which a god of the old dispensation survives and comes into the modern world still as a force of nature, to destroy or be destroyed. Pound's poem, which Yeats evidently liked even though he never understood *vers libre*, conducts the reader's mind through syntactic changes, variations of rhythm and phrase, and changes of grammatical tense which represent the gods as they were and as they, waveringly, are:

> See, they return; ah, see the tentative
>   Movements, and the slow feet,
>   The trouble in the pace and the uncertain
>   Wavering!
> See, they return, one, and by one,
> With fear, as half-awakened;
> As if the snow should hesitate
> And murmur in the wind,
>   and half turn back;
> These were the "Wing'd-with-Awe,"
>   Inviolable.
> Gods of the winged shoe!
> With them the silver hounds,
>   Sniffing the trace of air!
> Haie! Haie!
>   These were the swift to harry;
>   These the keen-scented;
>   These were the souls of blood.
> Slow on the leash,
>   pallid the leash-men![29]

v

One of the most admirable qualities of the men of 1922 – to call them that for short – was their readiness to accept strong criticism from their friends, and see it in print, without letting it damage the friendship.

---

[28] Kenner, *The Pound Era*, p. 142.
[29] Ezra Pound, "The Return," in *Poems and Translations* (New York: Library of America, 2003), pp. 244–245.

Eliot acknowledged, in effect, that he had no interest in Pound's poetry for what it said but every interest in the ways it discovered of saying it. Pound had nothing good to say about Eliot's later poetry. In *Time and Western Man* Wyndham Lewis attacked a quality of modern style, with Joyce as a chief exemplar. Pound tried to show Yeats the error of his diction, but his failure made no difference to their friendship. He admired Joyce's realism but regarded *Finnegans Wake* as an elaborate mistake. Yeats referred to Pound as a man "whose art is the opposite of mine, whose criticism commends what I most condemn, a man with whom I should quarrel more than with anyone else if we were not united by affection. ..."[30] He had intended to put Pound into the first version of *A Vision* as an exemplar of Phase 23 of his lunar cycle, but thought better of it. The only reference to Pound that remained in the first version was in a remarkable paragraph of apocalyptic criticism:

I discover already the first phase – Phase 23 – of the last quarter in certain friends of mine, and in writers, poets and sculptors admired by these friends, who have a form of strong love and hate hitherto unknown in the arts.

Yeats is thinking of Wyndham Lewis and Brancusi and of other artists who are "masters of a geometrical pattern or rhythm which seems to impose itself wholly from beyond the mind," the artist "standing outside himself":

I find at this 23rd Phase which is it is said the first where there is hatred of the abstract, where the intellect turns upon itself, Mr Ezra Pound, Mr Eliot, Mr Joyce, Signor Pirandello, who either eliminate from metaphor the poet's phantasy and substitute a strangeness discovered by historical research or who break up the logical processes of thought by flooding them with associated ideas or words that seem to drift into the mind by chance; or who set side by side as in [Pirandello's] *Henry IV*, "The Waste Land," *Ulysses*, the *physical primary* – a lunatic among his keepers, a man fishing behind a gas works, the vulgarity of a single Dublin day prolonged through 700 pages – and the *spiritual primary*, delirium, the Fisher King, Ulysses' wandering. It is as though myth and fact, united until the exhaustion of the Renaissance, have now fallen so far apart that man understands for the first time the rigidity of fact, and calls up, by that very recognition, myth – the *Mask* – which now but gropes its way out of the mind's dark but will shortly pursue and terrify.[31]

---

[30] Ibid., p. 3.
[31] George Mills Harper and Walter Kelly Hood (eds.), *A Critical Edition of Yeats's "A Vision" (1925)* (New York: Palgrave Macmillan, 1978), pp. 211–212.

Pound is not characterized there by his works. Ellmann has elucidated the
pursuit and terror by saying: "Yeats implies that in these writers myth,
instead of merging with fact in a symbolic whole, has collided with it to
produce a frenzied miscellany." "This is a prelude," Ellmann says, "to the
manifestation of myth in some fearful, dehumanized form."[32] It is as if
these writers forgot the lesson of Eliot's review of *Ulysses* and of Yeats's
adumbration of a particular production of meaning and value. Myth has
become ideology, a rough beast we cannot hope to understand or control.

                                   VI

I have called these three writers "presences," mainly in deference to Yeats's
use of that word as the title of one poem and a crucial invocation in
another. The poem "Presences" impels one to say that a presence is
someone who doesn't need to be named; a figure, an archetype, in this
poem harlot, child, or queen. In "Among School Children" Yeats invokes,
as if this poem were an ode – which it partly is –

> O Presences
> That passion, piety or affection knows,
> And that all heavenly glory symbolize –

The word "Presences" is capitalized, as if to honor the entities addressed,
before exercising harsher justice upon them at the end of the stanza as
"self-born mockers of man's enterprise." I interpret the Presences as
perfections projected by human desire – passion, piety or affection –
and therefore fit to symbolize heavenly glory: what else could do so? They
are bound to be "self-born mockers of man's enterprise," since that
enterprise is necessarily imperfect by comparison with those perfections.
So I follow Helen Vendler at a distance when she says that "the presences
are not Divinities to be addressed in vertical aspiration; they are self-born
and deceiving solaces, created by our longing for perfection in the things
we love."[33] They are not, I think, solaces. "Created by our longing for
perfection in the things we love," they mock our imperfections, subject
only to the consideration that the imperfections are categorical, they are in
the nature of the human case. Stevens writes that "the imperfect is our
paradise," which is to say that it is as much of paradise as we shall know,

[32] Richard Ellmann, *Eminent Domain: Yeats among Wilde, Joyce, Pound, Eliot, and Auden* (New York: Oxford University Press, 1967), p. 51.
[33] Helen Vendler, *Our Secret Discipline: Yeats and Lyric Form* (Cambridge, Mass.: Belknap Press of Harvard University Press, 2007), p. 282.

unless we believe in a greater paradise and find it fulfilled at length in another mode of being. The *OED* allows us to think of a presence also as an absence, "a divine, spiritual, or incorporeal being or influence felt or conceived as present": it points us toward the "sovran Presence" in *Paradise Lost* and, in Wordsworth's "Tintern Abbey," "I have felt/A presence that disturbs me with the joy/Of elevated thoughts." So it is not fanciful to think of our three poets as presences, not divinities indeed but objects of our devotion, so far as we love the literature they embody, imperfect as that, too, is. If we have to think of them as self-born mockers of man's enterprise, we do so only in the fateful end and after we have spent most of our lives addressing them in vertical aspiration. If these poets mock man's enterprise, they practice such mockery by misunderstanding one another; they are not deaf, but they find it hard to hear rhythms other than their own.

CHAPTER 5

The occult Yeats

One afternoon in May 1911 Yeats, visiting his friend and former lover Olivia Shakespear in London, was introduced to an English girl named Bertha Georgiana Hyde-Lees. He was nearly forty-six years old, "George," as her friends called her, was a few months over eighteen. A friendship soon developed, enthusiastic on her part, warier on his. They had much in common, including an interest in esoteric philosophy, astrology, the Tarot, and magic. They started attending séances together. In 1914 George was admitted, with Yeats as sponsor, to the Stella Matutina Section of the Golden Dawn, a secret society in London devoted to occult science and magic. By November 1915 the question of marriage had arisen, but there were difficulties. Yeats was still enchanted with Maud Gonne, although she had desecrated their love in 1903 by marrying Major John MacBride:

> My dear is angry that of late
> I cry all base blood down
> As if she had not taught me hate
> By kisses to a clown.[1]

Maud's marriage ended in 1905, and a legal separation was effected the following year, but her Catholicism made it impossible for her to think of marrying again. Besides, she didn't want to marry Yeats. They had first met on January 30, 1889, and he had fallen in love with her. But Maud was politically and soon to be sexually involved with Lucien Millevoye, a Boulangist campaigner. Millevoye and Maud had a child, Georges, who died in infancy; their second child, Iseult, was born on August 6, 1894 and survived. Maud broke with Millevoye in the summer of 1900. MacBride then entered her life, first as a companion in her fight for the

* The New York Review of Books, April 21, 1994, revised 2010.
[1] Quoted in The Gonne-Yeats Letters 1893–1938: Always Your Friend, ed. Anna MacBride White and A. Norman Jeffares (London: Hutchinson, 1992), p. 31.

independence of Ireland, then as her suitor. When the marriage came to an end, Maud sought Yeats's help in getting advice on legal and political questions. In December 1908 Yeats and Maud became lovers, but she soon gave up the sexual part of their intimacy and reverted to its spiritual or ideal mode. To complicate matters, from the spring of 1908 Yeats had been having an affair with Mabel Dickinson: it ended with a row on June 6, 1913 and Yeats felt free thereafter to call her a harlot. Meanwhile he had started to swoon over Maud's daughter Iseult, a beautiful, vivid girl who charmed him by reciting French poems.

By the end of 1915 it was clear to Yeats and his friends that he must do something, he was in an emotional mess. Better to marry than to burn; more to the point, better to marry than to run the risk of making a lover pregnant. There had been a scare of that kind with Mabel Dickinson, followed by telegrams and anger. In 1916, while Yeats was worrying about his life, John MacBride was transformed from drunken clown to martyr: the British Government executed him for his part in the Easter Rising. Maud was now free. On July 1, 1916 Yeats proposed to her again, but she gave him her usual answers, that she preferred his friendship and that posterity would appreciate her wisdom in letting a great poet concentrate on his poems. A week later, Yeats surprised her by asking whether or not she would object if he were to propose to Iseult. Maud gave him permission, but said she did not think her daughter would take his proposal seriously. In the event, Iseult took it seriously enough to keep Yeats dangling for several months. At the end of September 1917 she said no, and he at once thought of George Hyde-Lees. He proposed to her, was accepted, and they were married on October 20, 1917.

The auspices were not good. In the first days of the honeymoon Yeats was miserable, distraught that by marrying he had betrayed three women, Maud, Iseult, and George. Four days after the wedding, according to his account of the episode, he started thinking, "I have lived all through this before." On October 29 he wrote to Lady Gregory:

Then George spoke of the sensation of having lived through something before (she knew nothing of my thought). Then she said she felt that something was to be written through her. She got a piece of paper, and talking to me all the while so that her thoughts would not affect what she wrote, wrote these words (which she did not understand), "with the bird" (Iseult) "all is well at heart. Your action was right for both but in London you mistook its meaning."[2]

[2] W. B. Yeats, *The Letters of W. B. Yeats*, ed. Allan Wade (London: Rupert Hart-Davis, 1954), p. 633.

George was evidently trying to divert him and to bring assurance from the spirits that in marrying her he had done the right thing.

Having attempted automatic writing, George found she could do it, and produced it in formidable quantities. These writings gave Yeats much of the material he arranged in *A Vision* (1925). In the introduction to the revised version of the book (1937) he has this report:

What came in disjointed sentences, in almost illegible writing, was so exciting, sometimes so profound, that I persuaded her to give an hour or two day after day to the unknown writer, and after some half-dozen such hours offered to spend what remained of life explaining and piecing together those scattered sentences. "No," was the answer, "we have come to give you metaphors for poetry."[3]

In *The Making of Yeats's "A Vision": A Study of the Automatic Script* (1987) George Mills Harper revises the date of the revelation, makes it October 27, and explains how Yeats and his wife, seer and medium, engaged in the automatic writing. There were no séances, no darkened rooms, no observers. George did not go into a trance. Over a period of about two-and-a-half years, they had four-hundred-and-fifty sittings in Ireland, England, and – when George accompanied Yeats on a money-raising lecture tour – California. (When this became known, W. H. Auden mocked "the Southern Californian element" in Yeats.) The procedure was that Yeats raised a theme, asked a question – "Is then the knowledge of god easier to the artist than the saint?" – and George transmitted the answer – "Much."[4] Question: "Is butterfly symbolic of cleared subconscious?" Answer: "No Butterfly symbol of innocence of emotion Eagle complexity & unbalanced emotion anger overcoming wisdom – Butterfly wisdom overcoming anger – the clearing of subconscious destroys anger."[5] The Communicators – as Yeats called them – answered his questions to the extent eventually of 3,600 pages. George found it hard on her wrist, and on her patience. She often got bored. From March 28, 1920 they adopted an easier method by which "George speaks while asleep."[6] On September 18, 1922 they decided to give up these activities so that Yeats could set about bringing the mass of automatic writing into the order of a philosophic system, "this task [which] has been laid upon me by those

---

[3] Yeats, *A Vision* (London: Macmillan, second edition 1937, corrected 1962), p. 8.
[4] Steve L. Adams, Barbara J. Frieling, and Sandra L. Sprayberry (eds.), *Yeats's "Vision" Papers, Vol. I: The Automatic Script 5 November 1917–18 June 1918* (London: Macmillan, 1992), p. 407.
[5] Ibid., p. 104.
[6] George Mills Harper, *The Making of Yeats's "A Vision": A Study of the Automatic Script* (2 vols., London: Macmillan, 1987), Vol. II, p. 395.

who cannot speak being dead & who if I fail may never find another interpreter."[7] Yeats acted upon Blake's principle, that he "must Create a System or be enslav'd by another Man's."[8] *A Vision*, dated 1925, was privately printed on January 15, 1926. George's words to Yeats during her "sleeps" are now published as the third volume of *Yeats's Vision Papers*; the automatic scripts are given in the first two volumes.

This may be the place to report that Phillip L. Marcus, in his *Yeats and Artistic Power*, maintains that the automatic writing was a fabrication on George's part. The theme of his book is Yeats's sense of artistic power, and he wonders why there is virtually no reference to this power in *A Vision* or the automatic writing:

> That it occupies no such place in *A Vision* seems best explained by the fact that the automatic writing and the "sleeps" that eventually replaced it were from first to last a conscious or unconscious fabrication of George's, and although she carried over into the "spirit" communications most of Yeats's abiding literary and occult preoccupations she did not give that of artistic power any significant place, perhaps because she did not recognise its importance but possibly rather because the act of collaboration between her and her husband was in fact an expression of her own creativity and thus in a sense a covert act of artistic power that competed with his own.[9]

A bold claim. It is true that some of the communications are wifely. In one, Yeats is told to take more exercise and see his doctor for a check-up. In another, on June 27, 1919, he is warned against having anything to do with the increasing political agitation in Ireland: "That method is most wicked in this country – wholesale slaughter because a few are cruel – The leader should never incite."[10] That sounds like George rather than the Communicator "Ameritus." But the sitting goes straight from this admonition into technical questions about "initiatory moments" that are clearly Yeats's. I don't suppose that automatic writing is like sitting down to play the piano: there is probably a blurred period before Ameritus calls the meeting to order. Marcus wrote his book before *Yeats's Vision Papers* became available, so he had to rely on Harper's account of them in *The Making of Yeats's "A Vision"*, where the notable moments are necessarily detached a little from their contexts. In the *Vision Papers*

---

[7] Robert Anthony Martinich and Margaret Mills Harper (eds.), *Yeats's "Vision" Papers, Vol. III: Sleep and Dream Notebooks, Vision Notebooks 1 and 2, Card File* (London: Macmillan, 1992), p. 7.

[8] Quoted in *Yeats's "Vision" Papers*, Vol. III, p. 2.

[9] Phillip L. Marcus, *Yeats and Artistic Power* (New York University Press, 1992), p. 129.

[10] Steve L. Adams, Barbara J. Frieling, and Sandra L. Sprayberry (eds.), *Yeats's "Vision" Papers, Vol. II: The Automatic Script: 25 June 1918–29 March 1920* (London: Macmillan, 1992), p. 320.

I don't find any sign of fabrication or deception on George's part. The difference between wifely stuff and the rest is always clear. George had a mind of her own, she was not just taking dictation from the Communi-cators, but this didn't prevent her from feeling she was a genuine medium.

Not that the writing was always as automatic as it was supposed to be. Yeats wanted to ask about his relations with Maud, Iseult, and George, and to make occasional inquiries about Olivia and Mabel. "Will MG attain a wisdom older than the serpent?" he asked on January 9, 1918, and the Communicator, evidently a student of Blake's *The Marriage of Heaven and Hell* – "If the fool would persist in his folly he would become wise" – answered: "She will attain to the wisdom of folly."[11] After a while, George wanted to steer Yeats away from these delicate subjects to matter of philosophic import. But the going was often slow. On August 28, 1918 at Ballinamantane House the Communicator was out of sorts:

> Today the bucket will draw no water
> You have not prepared
> I indicate what I wish to do – you choose another topic
> Yes but I did not choose definitions
> I dont like the atmosphere of this house – better put it
>   right before more writing.[12]

At Oughterard on August 1, 1919 the sitting started badly: an imprecise question got a dusty answer in italics: "*Please attend & dont fidget.*"[13] At Oxford on February 1, 1918 the Communicator made it clear that he was not a mere professor:

> Do you know Boehmes symbolism?
> No I do not know any symbolism from book and I cannot get
>   it from your minds because I am here only to create.[14]

When one of the several Communicators was especially sluggish, Yeats concluded that the sitting was thwarted by Frustrators. But most of the sessions read like rather disheveled seminars on passion, emotion, love, sex, genius, memory, the transference of images from one mind to another, reincarnation, and the desirability of having children (memo: no more than two for the Yeatses). In retrospect, Yeats thought that the Communicators were "the personalities of a dream shared by my wife, by myself, occasionally by others – they have, as I must some day prove,

---

[11] *Yeats's "Vision" Papers*, Vol. I, p. 233.   [12] *Yeats's "Vision" Papers*, Vol. II, p. 29.
[13] Ibid., p. 351.   [14] *Yeats's "Vision" Papers*, Vol. I, p. 325.

spoken through others without change of knowledge or loss of power – a dream that can take objective form in sounds, in hallucinations, in scents, in flashes of light, in movements of external objects."[15]

The Communicators may not have read Boehme but they were well versed in Yeats's writings. Their main service was to enable him to extend and put in systematic form the divinations he had expressed (with Edwin John Ellis) in his edition of *The Works of William Blake* in 1893, his essays "Magic" (1901), "Swedenborg, Mediums, and the Desolate Places" (1914), and the first sketch of his visionary system, *Per Amica Silentia Lunae* (1917). In "Magic," Yeats said he believed "in what I must call the evocation of spirits, though I do not know what they are, in the power of creating magical illusions, in the visions of truth in the depths of the mind when the eyes are closed." He held to three doctrines:

(1) That the borders of our mind are ever shifting, and that many minds can flow into one another, as it were, and create or reveal a single mind, a single energy.

(2) That the borders of our memories are as shifting, and that our memories are a part of one great memory, the memory of Nature herself.

(3) That this great mind and great memory can be evoked by symbols.[16]

Sixteen years later, in *Per Amica Silentia Lunae*, he placed this mind and this memory in what the neo-Platonist Henry More called the *Anima Mundi*, a garden of ancestral images, apparitions, and memories that recur again and again, "for passion," as Yeats said, " desires its own recurrence more than any event."[17] "The dead," he continued, "as the passionate necessity wears out, come into a measure of freedom and may turn the impulse of events, started while living, in some new direction, but they cannot originate except through the living."[18] Hence the merit of séances, evocation of spirits, and automatic writing. Not surprisingly, one of the first questions Yeats asked the Communicator on November 20, 1917 was: "What is the relation of Anima Mundi to individual or to his subconsciousness?" Answer: "The relation is from human to the anima mundi – not from the subconscious but from the *acts* which the

---

[15] Yeats, *A Vision* (1937, corrected 1962), pp. 22–23.
[16] W. B. Yeats, *Essays and Introductions* (London: Macmillan, 1961), p. 28.
[17] W. B. Yeats, *Mythologies* (London: Macmillan, 1959), p. 354.   [18] Ibid., pp. 355–356.

subconscious stores up."[19] The answer didn't close the question; the nature of the Anima Mundi is one of the pervasive themes of the automatic writings.

Yeats's dealings with magic started when he was a boy in Dublin and Sligo. His uncle, George Pollexfen, was an astrologer. His friend the artist and poet George Russell (AE) was a seer. Aunt Isabella Pollexfen gave Yeats a copy of A. P. Sinnett's *Esoteric Buddhism* (1884). On June 16, 1885 Yeats, Charles Johnson, and some friends founded the Dublin Hermetic Society. After a few months it developed into the Dublin Theosophical Lodge. When the Brahman Mohini Chatterji visited Dublin in the same year, Yeats learned much from him about oriental religion and reincarnation and wrote a few poems under his gentle sway. In London at Christmas 1887, greatly impressed by Madame Blavatsky, Yeats joined the Esoteric Section of her Theosophical Society. On March 7, 1890, at MacGregor Mathers's invitation, he was initiated into the Hermetic Order of the Golden Dawn. In July 1892, when the old Fenian John O'Leary rebuked him for these interests, he defended himself:

If I had not made magic my constant study I could not have written a single word of my Blake book, nor would *The Countess Kathleen* have ever come to exist. The mystical life is the centre of all that I do and all that I think and all that I write. It holds to my work the same relation that the philosophy of Godwin held to the work of Shelley and I have always considered myself a voice of what I believe to be a greater renaissance – the revolt of the soul against the intellect – now beginning in the world.[20]

In *Reveries over Childhood and Youth*, more urbanely, Yeats gave a further reason for his recourse to the occult:

It was only when I began to study psychical research and mystical philosophy that I broke away from my father's influence. He had been a follower of John Stuart Mill and so had never shared Rossetti's conviction that it mattered to nobody whether the sun went round the earth or the earth round the sun. But through this new research, this reaction from popular science, I had begun to feel that I had allies for my secret thought.[21]

Instead of reading George Eliot, he read Baron Reichenbach on Odic Force. He wanted to turn aside from the official culture of England, mid-Victorian science, his father's rationalism, and positivism. In Dublin and London he gathered his friends into Bohemian fellowship, predicated on

[19] *Yeats's "Vision" Papers*, Vol. I, p. 86.   [20] Yeats, *Letters*, p. 211.
[21] W. B. Yeats, *Autobiographies* (London: Macmillan, 1961), p. 89.

the privileging of consciousness and vision. It wasn't hard to find allies for his secret thought. During those years at the end of the century, irregular knowledge and unorthodox spiritual experiences were deemed exciting, and not only by members of the Society for Psychical Research. Varieties of religious experience – often religious in a loose sense – were interesting enough to gain William James's attention.

The practice of magic was also, as Yeats said to George's mother about astrology, "a very flirtatious business."[22] The most erotic moments in Maud Gonne's letters to Yeats are those in which the theme is a shared vision, a dream of spiritual union. Maud was keen on such intimacies with Yeats, it was only physical conjunction with him she avoided. Besides, she was always busy with good causes: there were speeches to be made, prisoners for whom amnesty might be arranged, tenants in the west of Ireland who must be sustained after their eviction. There was an Order of Celtic Mysteries to be devised, however implausibly, by Maud, Yeats, and Mathers. Someone always arose to be denounced, or a race to be vilified, the English, the Jews. But Maud kept up her dreams and reported them to Yeats: he entered the details in his notebook and often quoted them to her, comparing her spiritual experiences to his. Sometimes he quoted them in evidence against her.

Early in 1903, making a last-minute attempt to prevent Maud from marrying MacBride, Yeats wrote her three letters, in one of which he transcribed from his diary for December 12, 1898 a dream he had of her coming to him lovingly at Lady Gregory's Coole Park. He also quoted against her the dream she had on the same night, in which the god Lug (the Celtic sun god who possessed a spear of light) took her hand and put it into Yeats's and pronounced them married. "Now I claim that this gives me right to speak," Yeats wrote with some effrontery, demanding that Maud draw back from infidelity and "become again as one of the Gods."[23] She not only went through with the marriage but made a political plan for her honeymoon in Spain; the newly-weds would assassinate King Edward VII on his visit to Gibraltar. MacBride got drunk and forgot about the plan.

The *Vision Papers* is more likely to be consulted than read. The automatic writings and the notebooks are difficult, often arbitrary and harsh, minding the deads' business, but they are essential to anyone who wants to take possession of *A Vision* in either of its versions. "I wished,"

---

[22] Quoted in A. Norman Jeffares, *Yeats: A New Biography* (London: Continuum, 2001), p. 217.
[23] *The Gonne-Yeats Letters*, p. 165.

Yeats said in the first version, "for a system of thought that would leave my imagination free to create as it chose and yet make all that it created, or could create, part of the one history, and that the soul's."[24] He had hardly published the book before he became ashamed of it: "I had misinterpreted the geometry, and in my ignorance of philosophy failed to understand distinctions upon which the coherence of the whole depended."[25] He decided he must read a lot of philosophy and try again. The revised version needed great labour and was not published till October 7, 1937, two years before he died. After his death, George Yeats and Thomas Mark, Yeats's editor at Macmillan, corrected several errors in the revised version and issued the book again in 1956 and with further corrections in 1962. The 1962 text is the one most readers of Yeats consult.

In the introduction to the 1937 version Yeats noted how close the automatic communications were to the original visionary intuitions in his *Per Amica Silentia Lunae*:

The unknown writer took his theme at first from my just published *Per Amica Silentia Lunae*. I had made a distinction between the perfection that is from a man's combat with himself and that which is from a combat with circumstance, and upon this simple distinction he built up an elaborate classification of men according to their more or less complete expression of one type or the other. He supported his classification by a series of geometrical symbols and put these symbols in an order that answered the question in my essay as to whether some prophet could not prick upon the calendar the birth of a Napoleon or a Christ.[26]

In a discarded sentence Yeats said that in *Per Amica* he had described "the whole of human life as man's attempt to become the opposite of himself or to create the opposite of his fate."[27] The situation Yeats had in mind is the one that Stevens describes in "Notes toward a Supreme Fiction":

> From this the poem springs: that we live in a place
> That is not our own and, much more, not ourselves
> And hard it is in spite of blazoned days.[28]

Poetry is the art by which the world is made to appear to be our own and ourselves. Imagination is the means of effecting this miracle. In *A Vision*

---

[24] W. B. Yeats, *A Critical Edition of "A Vision"*, ed. George Mills Harper and Walter Kelly Hood (New York: Palgrave Macmillan, 1978), p. xi.

[25] Yeats, *A Vision* (1937, corrected 1962), p. 19.   [26] Ibid., pp. 8–9.

[27] Quoted in Connie K. Hood, "The Remaking of *A Vision*," in *Yeats: An Annual of Critical and Textual Studies*, ed. Richard J. Finneran (publishers vary, 1983–1999), Vol. 1, 1983, p. 49.

[28] Wallace Stevens, *Collected Poems* (New York: Vintage Books, 1990), p. 383.

and other works Yeats uses the word "primary" to refer to the energy of one's combat with external circumstances: one's primary energy accepts that the world is not oneself, and by daily reasoning makes the best of that bad job. He describes as "antithetical," and associates with the unconscious, the energy of one's combat with oneself. The purpose of this latter combat is to choose other fates for oneself and thereby seem to transfigure the world. Both forms of energy are supposedly necessary and equal, but Yeats favored the antithetical, as a romantic poet in fellowship with Blake and Shelley would. Most of his leading questions in the occult sittings were designed to establish this preference and to find evidence for it. "The antithetical self is the source of creative power."[29]

In both versions, *A Vision* consists of an aesthetic, a poetics, a defense of poetry, a theory of imagination, a treatise of human nature predicated on the freedom of one's imagination within the obduracies of time, space, and history. To the degree to which it recognizes necessity, it is also a horoscope of persons and historical periods, taking for granted the inevitability of conflict and making a virtue of it:

> My instructors identify consciousness with conflict, not with knowledge, substitute for subject and object and their attendant logic a struggle towards harmony, towards Unity of Being.[30]

History is presented as a dynamic exchange of forces, coming into definition as phases and cycles, correlated to the twenty-eight phases of the moon. "A man of, say, Phase 13 is a man whose *Will* is at that phase."[31] So *A Vision* includes a description of psychological types and it describes exemplars of each type, mostly artists and writers: this is the most accessible part of the book, and the most winning. Finally, the book is an interpretation of tradition, rejecting the ideology of progress and Enlightenment by invoking the Anima Mundi as a treasury of images, perennial, invulnerable to rationalist irony. Like many poets, Yeats was inspired by unofficial lore, he gathered motifs wherever he felt their force and he was indifferent to their being archaic, Ptolemaic or otherwise frowned upon in the schools. These values are still to be found, though they are scarcer than they were some years ago. During the "Age of Aquarius," as we called it, Gary Snyder listed among "what you should know to be a poet – at least one kind of traditional magic:

[29] Yeats, quoted in Harper, *The Making of Yeats's "A Vision,"* Vol. I, p. 18.
[30] Yeats, *A Vision* (1937, corrected 1962), p. 214.   [31] Ibid., p. 79.

divination, astrology, the *Book of Changes*, the tarot; dreams, the illusory demons and illusory shining gods."[32]

The claim Yeats made for the revised *A Vision* is sensible:

> Some will ask whether I believe in the actual existence of my circuits of sun and moon. Those that include, now all recorded time in one circuit, now what Blake called "the pulsation of an artery," are plainly symbolical, but what of those that fixed, like a butterfly upon a pin, to our central date, the first day of our Era, divide actual history into periods of equal length? To such a question I can but answer that if sometimes, overwhelmed by miracle as all men must be when in the midst of it, I have taken such periods literally, my reason has soon recovered; and now that the system stands out clearly in my imagination I regard them as stylistic arrangements of experience comparable to the cubes in the drawing of Wyndham Lewis and to the ovoids in the sculpture of Brancusi. They have helped me to hold in a single thought reality and justice.[33]

Responses to the book have often been dismissive. Frank Pearce Sturm, a learned occultist, told Yeats that "all these gyres & cones & wheels are parts of a machine that was thrown on the scrap heap when Ptolemy died."[34] In *Science and Poetry* (1926) I. A. Richards had already maintained that Yeats's esoteric lore was as regressive as D. H. Lawrence's dealings in solar myths. T. E. Hulme had decided that Yeats was trying to restore to his poems an intuition of infinity, without having to believe in any of the accredited religious doctrines. In *After Strange Gods* (1934) T. S. Eliot said that Yeats's visions were of no moral significance. Yeats made himself a great poet by discarding this nonsense.[35] It is not true. Yeats retained it to the end, as his last poems and plays show. Hostility to *A Vision* in either of its forms culminated in Auden's contempt for it: ". . . mediums, spells, the Mysterious Orient – *how* embarrassing."[36]

It is my impression that this phase of the reception of the book is over. No one I know of finds it a scandal. Some readers hold that if Yeats needed occult communications to help him write *The Tower*, *The Winding Stair*, and his later plays, well and good. They assume that he found the elaboration of a philosophic system useful as homework, scales and arpeggios, or – as R. P. Blackmur said – "for purposes of scaffolding,

---

[32] Quoted in Eliot Weinberger (ed.), *American Poetry since 1950* (New York: Marsilio Publishers, 1993), p. 271.

[33] Yeats, *A Vision* (1937, corrected 1962), pp. 24–25.

[34] Quoted in Hood, "The Remaking of *A Vision*," p. 43.

[35] T. S. Eliot, *After Strange Gods: A Primer of Modern Heresy* (New York: Harcourt, Brace and Company, 1934), p. 50.

[36] Cf. James Hall and Martin Steinmann (eds.), *The Permanence of Yeats* (New York: Macmillan, 1950), p. 309.

for hints on how to ad lib, and how to run the frame of the dramatization of an idea."[37] Or they conclude that only a few poems, and those not the best, notably "Ego Dominus Tuus" and "The Phases of the Moon," rely on esoteric lore. These readers note, with evident pleasure, that in Yeats's finest poems, such as "Among School Children," "Nineteen Hundred and Nineteen," "Sailing to Byzantium," "The Second Coming," and "Leda and the Swan," the *Vision* is either unnecessary or the parts of it that count may easily be deduced. To read "The Second Coming," according to this assumption, all you need is to guess that the displacement of one age by another may take a violent form, as the Christian age may be displaced by some rough beast slouching towards Bethlehem to be born.

These attitudes are not, I think, quite sufficient. It is true that the *Vision Papers* clarifies a few difficult poems. "Veronica's Napkin" becomes clearer, though not pellucid, when the automatic script for November 4, 1919 has Yeats's communicator directing his attention to a passage in Frazer's *The Golden Bow* and a reference to Berenice. She was Ptolemy III's wife and she dedicated to the gods a lock of her hair as an offering for his safe return from war. Ptolemy named a constellation "Berenice's Curls" in her honor. Admittedly, this is not bohemian knowledge. The Heavenly Circuit is the title of an essay by Plotinus. According to Plotinus, God is the centre of a perfect circle; heavenly bodies and human souls rotate around Him in concentric circles. Veronica's napkin is well known to Christians, a holy relic, the handkerchief that Veronica gave the suffering Christ on his way to crucifixion on Mount Calvary. He wiped his face with it, and by miracle the imprint of his face is impressed on the handkerchief. On one level, as Harper says in *The Making of Yeats's "A Vision"*, "the poem contrasts God and Christ, suggesting ironically 'the ideal man changing into the real man.'" On another, these two figures "are symbolic of the two concentric circles representing the world and the individual." *A Vision* is Yeats's attempt, Harper says, "to explain the relationship of these two symbolic spheres."[38] Berenice's hair is invoked because the Communicator put the story into Yeats's mind when the theme was the transfer of images from one mind to another. The first lines of the poem have only the syntax of putting one phrase after another: there are no verbs or other connectives. No syntax is required, because no further authority than the Communicator's is needed. Yeats leaves it to readers to make sense of the phrases in sequence.

[37] R. P. Blackmur, *Anni Mirabiles 1921–1925* (Washington: Library of Congress, 1956), p. 38.
[38] Harper, *The Making of Yeats's "A Vision,"* Vol. II, p. 346.

The scripts and the book they led to are valuable not merely as annotations to a few poems. If we add the essays "Magic" and "Swedenborg, Mediums, and the Desolate Places" to *Per Amica Silentia Lunae*, the *Vision Papers*, and *A Vision* in its two versions, we have an apocalypse, a book of prophecy. It is an "irregular metaphysics," a phrase I take from Blackmur. In *Anni Mirabiles* he says that "where the great novelists of our times have dealt with the troubles caused by the new knowledges (and the erosion of some of the old ones) in a kind of broad and irregular psychology, so the poets have been led to deal with them (or to repel them, or rival them) in a kind of irregular and spasmodic but vitalized metaphysics." One reason for this desperate recourse is "the relative disappearance of generally accepted (if only for argument) systematic metaphysics that bears on daily life." As a consequence, we find in modern poetry the proliferation of syntaxes, each of them good only for the occasion and issuing from arbitrary force beneath or apart from reason. Blackmur speaks of poets who "quivered with horror at all statements not drawn from dreams."[39] So, too, Yeats. *A Vision* is not doctrine or dogma but, in default of those, a testament: it is authoritative only in its origin, and is content thereafter to be merely what it is. It does not ask to be acted upon or even to be believed. It is a work of literature, in that respect like *The Golden Bough*, Jung's *Psychology and Alchemy*, Freud's *The Interpretation of Dreams*, and Spengler's *The Decline of the West*.

It is not surprising that Phillip Marcus has largely put *A Vision* aside, since he deems it mainly George's work. She must count as a Frustrator in his sense of Yeats's poetry. He is concerned with the bardic tradition as it reached Yeats through Standish O'Grady, Samuel Ferguson, George Russell (AE), Arthur O'Shaughnessy, and other writers. In *Yeats and the Beginning of the Irish Renaissance* (1970, revised edition 1987) he made a strong start on this theme, Yeats's aesthetic of artistic power, and in *Yeats and Artistic Power* he develops it much further. Some of his most telling chapters are commentaries on several poems and plays including "Blood and the Moon," "Coole Park and Ballylee, 1931," "Parnell's Funeral," and *The Death of Cuchulain*. In each case his question is: to what extent does Yeats assume in this work, and act upon the assumption, that a poem or a play may have consequences in the world? His method is to place the poems and plays in their historical and literary settings. "The Tower," for instance, he relates to Yeats's Senate speech on divorce, his negotiations with the Free State Government on the release of the republican hunger-striker Mary MacSwiney, his opposition to "compulsory Irish" in the

---

[39] Blackmur, *Anni Mirabiles 1921–1925*, p. 39.

schools, and his fear that the new middle-class Catholic Ireland would set aside the heroic values he associated with the Protestant Ascendancy of the eighteenth century.

Near the end of the book, Marcus refers to Auden's claim in the (in my opinion not-very-good) poem "In Memory of W. B. Yeats," that "poetry makes nothing happen" except its own survival "in the valley of its making." That is not good enough for Marcus, who wants to see the power of poetry extending through the world. He prefers to quote, as a motto for that power, Yeats's favorite lines from O'Shaughnessy's "Ode":

> We, in the ages lying
> In the buried past of the earth,
> Built Nineveh with our sighing,
> And Babel itself in our mirth.[40]

Beside these, Marcus puts the sentence from "A General Introduction for My Work" in which Yeats says that we adore poets because in them "nature has grown intelligible, and by so doing a part of our creative power."[41] But although this comes from a late essay, Marcus has to report that Yeats lost confidence in the social and cultural effectiveness of art as he got older and Ireland became more exasperating. Marcus's book is formidable in the evidence it offers, but I think he expresses the wrong hope for poetry, that in some local and immediate respect it will change things. I would like to avoid the disappointment of finding that it doesn't. I try to read poems as if I were looking at sculptures by Brancusi, objects in which an artist has discovered aesthetic possibilities, objects added to the world for pleasure. As Stevens said: "*Esthétique* is the measure of a civilization: not the sole measure, but a measure."[42]

In *Running to Paradise* M. L. Rosenthal refers to *A Vision* only in passing, when he notes that the moon-imagery in a speech by Cuchulain's Ghost in *The Only Jealousy of Emer* is "derived from the system of fatality that Yeats and his wife were working out (published in 1925 as *A Vision*)."[43] Well, it is a system of fatality, but it is also a philosophy of will. Yeats wrote in his diary for 1930: "History is necessity until it takes fire in someone's head and becomes freedom or virtue."[44] And in a late poem,

[40] Marcus, *Yeats and Artistic Power*, pp. 9, 34. [41] Yeats, *Essays and Introductions*, p. 509.
[42] Wallace Stevens, *Opus Posthumous*, ed. Milton J. Bates (New York: Knopf, 1989), p. 197.
[43] M. L. Rosenthal, *Running to Paradise: Yeats's Poetic Art* (New York: Oxford University Press, 1993), p. 161.
[44] W. B. Yeats, *Explorations*, selected by Mrs. W. B. Yeats (London: Macmillan, 1962), p. 336.

"The lot of love is chosen." Rosenthal says of Yeats that "the body of folk-magical, Rosicrucian, cabalistic, spiritualist, and even theological lore he absorbed lies deep within subjective tradition," and he seems happy to let it lie there. I suppose it does, much of the time, and comes up to the surface only on local provocation. My own view is that Yeats valued irregular knowledge to the degree to which it provided him with a relatively clear space for his imagination to practice its magic; and that he valued it all the more when he felt that most of his experience was forced on him by immediate contingencies, externalities of the local culture which compelled his attention and which he would never have chosen.

CHAPTER 6

Yeats's Shakespeare

I

Whereas Shakespeare showed, through a style full of joy, a melancholy
vision sought from afar; a style at play, a mind that served . . . .[1]

The word "Shakespeare" does not appear in any of Yeats's poems or plays,
but "Shakespearean" does, in "Three Movements," a poem included in
Words for Music Perhaps and Other Poems (1932) and *The Winding Stair
and Other Poems* (1933). It consists of three lines:

> Shakespearean fish swam the sea, far away from land;
> Romantic fish swam in nets coming to the hand;
> What are all those fish that lie gasping on the strand?[2]

Most readers probably find the poem obscure; they wonder what
"Shakespearean" means, and what "Romantic" means and what "those
fish" denote in the allegory, if the poem is an allegory. They want to
have these obscurities clarified, if only for the satisfaction of moving on
to the next poem in the *Collected Poems*. Presumably there are readers
who don't find the obscurity a nuisance; they appreciate it as an extreme
form of discretion on Yeats's part. They may happen to know that
Elizabethan rhetoricians had four words for this figure, they called it
aenigma, noema, syllogismus, or *intimatio.* In *Elizabethan and Metaphysical Imagery* Rosemond Tuve explains that there were several ways of
"beautifying the subject," one of which was precisely by withholding
ornamentation from it. By happy choice she quotes "Three Movements"
to illustrate Yeats's use of enigma, though few readers would now
recognize that this is what he is doing:

---

* Forthcoming in *Yeats Annual.*
[1] Yeats, *A Vision* (London: Macmillan, second edition 1937, corrected 1962), p. 166.
[2] *The Variorum Edition of the Poems of W. B. Yeats,* ed. Peter Allt and Russell K. Alspach (New York:
Macmillan, 1987), p. 485.

113

A great many figures other than those I have examined were thought beautiful for their lack of elaboration. Such figures were neither more nor less "ornaments" of a poem than were the obvious or the detailed figures, and all found their chief beauty in their suitableness. I quote three lines from Yeats, chiefly to underline this difference in critical vocabulary, with which we must reckon; it would seem to us a misuse of language to comment on Yeats's "beautifying of his subject, through the figure *aenigma*," yet this is a normal Elizabethan commendation of just such uses of just such figures.

Tuve then quotes "Three Movements" and says:

This tripartite image would have been called *aenigma* by the slower-minded and *allegoria* by the quick. If anyone doubts that it "beautifies the subject," let him try to state Yeats's idea without it.[3]

The idea is not at all clear, but there is satisfaction in trying to work it out. If you like the poem by admiring its decorum, you take pleasure in the demands it makes on your quickness: you have to be quick to see what the three lines are doing together. The poem is authoritative, but not perspicuous. The theme is evidently some form of cultural crisis in the twentieth century, but to make sense of it you have to discover or intuit not only what "Shakespearean" and "Romantic" mean, but what the unspecified referent is in the third line, probably the suppressed word "Modern." The more genial aspect of the crisis is expressed in "The Nineteenth Century and After," a poem of four lines, close to "Three Movements" in *Words for Music Perhaps* and *The Winding Stair*, that makes the best of the conditions at large:

> Though the great song return no more
> There's keen delight in what we have:
> The rattle of pebbles on the shore
> Under the receding wave.[4]

That, too, is *allegoria*, but in a different mood: the sensation of hearing pebbles rattling on the shore is to be enjoyed, assuming we know what it is we are enjoying and the allegory in play.

Readers who find "Three Movements" opaque generally go to A. Norman Jeffares's *A New Commentary on the Poems of W. B. Yeats* (1984) for help. Some readers resent the necessity of going outside the poems, even for the boon of enlightenment. Hugh Kenner, who did not

---

[3] Rosemond Tuve, *Elizabethan and Metaphysical Imagery: Renaissance Poetic and Twentieth-Century Critics* (University of Chicago Press, 1947, ninth impression 1972), pp. 143–144.
[4] Yeats, *Variorum Edition of the Poems*, p. 485.

resent having to decipher Pound's *Cantos*, apparently thought it more than flesh could bear when the necessity of annotating Yeats's difficult poems arose. "The unspoken premise of Yeats criticism," he claimed, "is that we have to supply from elsewhere – from his life or his doctrines – a great deal that didn't properly get into the poems: not so much to explain the poems as to make them rich enough to sustain the reputation."[5] I don't recall that Professor Jeffares expressed any reluctance on the matter. I give his report on "Three Movements" in full:

Yeats wrote a prose version of this poem in his White Manuscript book and dated it 20 January 1932; the poem is dated 26 January 1932 by [Richard] Ellmann (*The Identity of Yeats*, p. 267). It first appeared in *Words for Music Perhaps*.

1. *Shakespearean fish*: the prose draft reads: "Passion in Shakespeare was a great fish in the sea, but from Goethe to the end of the Romantic movement the fish was in the net. It will soon be dead upon the shore." There is a kindred sentiment in the essay on Bishop Berkeley which begins, "Imagination, whether in literature, painting, or sculpture, sank after the death of Shakespeare." (*Essays and Introductions*, p. 396).
2. *Romantic fish*: Shakespeare lived from 1564 to 1616; the romantic movement began in the late eighteenth century and continued in the nineteenth. Yeats described Lady Gregory and himself as "the last romantics." (*The Poems: A New Edition*, ed. Richard J. Finneran (1984) p. 254.[6]

Jeffares's aim was to help readers to construe the poem by removing the main obstacles. He did not recommend any particular interpretation. It was his practice to place selected relevancies in the vicinity of each poem, often companionable passages from Yeats's poems, essays, speeches, and reviews, sometimes from *A Vision*. It was as if he said: "you will find it helpful if you let these correlative passages inhabit your mind while you're reading the poem. Of course these readings will not interpret it for you." It is a mark of Yeats's books of poetry that one book often replies to its predecessor, corrects its extravagance, and speaks up for a rival set of values. Jeffares was alert to these nuances, but first he tried to guide Yeats's readers across the rough places of particular poems before letting them walk ahead on their own. In the present case, he did not think it his

[5] Hugh Kenner, "The Sacred Book of the Arts," reprinted in John Unterecker (ed.), *Yeats: A Collection of Critical Essays* (Englewood Cliffs, NJ: Prentice-Hall, 1963), pp. 13–14.
[6] A. Norman Jeffares, *A New Commentary on the Poems of W. B. Yeats* (London: Macmillan, 1984), pp. 279–280.

business to expound the differences between the poem and its prose version. Differences such as these: in the prose, two sentences imply one fish; in the verse, "fish" is evidently plural throughout the three lines. In the verse, we have parallel lines, each of twelve syllables and seven spoken stresses. A masculine, monosyllabic end-rhyme binds the three lines, and the meter in each coincides with the syntax. There are no run-on lines. Each of the first two lines delivers a perception deemed to be beyond question. The first lines are in the indicative mood, past tense and present continuous respectively. The last line, as often in Yeats's poems, brings the poem to a formal but alarming end on a rhetorical question. The syntactical form that is least an ending – the rhetorical question – confounds the insistences that have preceded it. A rudimentary paraphrase might run: "Shakespeare's heroes lived, acted, and suffered in conditions commensurate with the freedom of their passion. Romantic heroes (as in Goethe, Byron, Blake, and Shelley) lived their passion, subject entirely to the genius of their authors. In Romanticism the creative force posits itself at the centre of experience and goes out to the natural world from that certitude. What, I ask you, is happening to such passion now, in social and political conditions apparently lethal to it?" Even after this paraphrase, the poem remains to be read as a poem, not as a truncated essay.

The passage from Yeats's essay on Berkeley that Jeffares quotes is too brief to be decisive, but when readers read the whole essay, they sense amid further opacities that at least a few sentences clarify the decline, as Yeats saw it, from the Renaissance to modernity. The paragraph that Jeffares quotes in part reads in full:

Imagination, whether in literature, painting, or sculpture, sank after the death of Shakespeare; supreme intensity had passed to another faculty; it was as though Shakespeare, Dante, Michelangelo, had been reborn with all their old sublimity, their old vastness of conception, but speaking a harsh, almost unintelligible, language. Two or three generations hence, when men accept the inventions of science as a commonplace and understand that it is limited by its method to appearance, no educated man will doubt that the movement of philosophy from Spinoza to Hegel is the greatest of all works of intellect.[7]

Yeats meant Idealism, the philosophy that tries to make one's consciousness account for the whole of one's experience. In Cassirer's version: "Idealists want to transform the passive world of mere *impressions*, in

---

[7] W. B. Yeats, "Bishop Berkeley," in *Essays and Introductions* (London: Macmillan, 1961), p. 396.

which the spirit seems at first imprisoned, into a world that is pure *expression* of the human spirit."[8] It was the only force that Yeats thought capable of resisting the Empiricism he hated and feared:

When I speak of idealist philosophy I think more of Kant than of Berkeley, who was idealist and realist alike, more of Hegel and his successors than of Kant, and when I speak of the romantic movement I think more of Manfred, more of Shelley's Prometheus, more of Jean Valjean, than of those traditional figures, Browning's Pope, the fakir-like pedlar in *The Excursion*.[9]

As for modernity, those fish gasping on the strand:

The romantic movement with its turbulent heroism, its self-assertion, is over, superseded by a new naturalism that leaves man helpless before the contents of his own mind. One thinks of Joyce's *Anna Livia Plurabelle*, Pound's *Cantos*, works of an heroic sincerity, the man, his active faculties in suspense, one finger beating time to a bell sounding and echoing in the depths of his own mind; of Proust who, still fascinated by Stendhal's fixed framework, seems about to close his eyes and gaze upon the pattern under his lids.[10]

The only cure for this helplessness, Yeats thought, was a philosophy of the Act, adumbrated by the later Berkeley and articulated – though Yeats doesn't name him in this essay – by Giovanni Gentile. "Only where the mind partakes of a pure activity can art or life attain swiftness, volume, unity; that contemplation lost, we picture some slow-moving event, turn the mind's eye from everything else that we may experience to the full our own passivity, our personal tragedy . . . ."[11]

II

What then does "Shakespeare" mean in Yeats's structure of values? Even if we have some notion of "Shakespearean fish" – but how securely have we got this notion? – we can hardly eke it out to the extent of gaining access to Yeats's Shakespeare. We should try another way.

Scholars of Yeats seem to agree that Yeats received his first sense of Shakespeare from his father, John Butler Yeats, presumably in early conversations with him in Dublin and London. Our main authority for this conclusion is William M. Murphy, who maintains in *Prodigal Father: The Life of John Butler Yeats (1839–1922)* (1978) that the ideas expressed in

---

[8] Ernst Cassirer, *The Philosophy of Symbolic Forms*, trans. Ralph Manheim (4 vols., New Haven: Yale University Press, 1953), Vol. I, p. 81.
[9] Yeats, *Essays and Introductions*, p. 405.   [10] Ibid., p. 405.   [11] Ibid., p. 409.

Yeats's essay on Shakespeare, "At Stratford-on-Avon," "are completely his father's, though not specifically acknowledged."[12] John Kelly and Ronald Schuchard, the editors of *The Collected Letters of W. B. Yeats: Volume Three 1901–1904*, agree with Murphy that Yeats's views on Shakespeare, "and especially on *Richard II*, are almost identical with those his father had advanced in an argument with [Edward] Dowden in 1874."[13] I demur at Murphy's word "completely," and remain unappeased by the editors' concessive "almost." Murphy also says that in the dispute with Dowden "JBY passed his judgments on to his son, who assimilated them so completely that when he expressed them publicly a couple of decades later he forgot where he had received them."[14] This is not quite true. Murphy himself notes that Yeats wrote, in John Quinn's copy of *Ideas of Good and Evil* (the 1908 edition), "I think the best of these Essays is that on Shakespeare. It is a family exasperation with the Dowden point of view which rather filled Dublin in my youth. There is a good deal of my father in it, though nothing is just as he would have put it."[15] But there is much evidence for Murphy's initial claim. Building on Phillip L. Marcus's *Yeats and the Beginning of the Irish Literary Renaissance* (1970), he elucidates further the context of Yeats's sense of Shakespeare in early disputes between John Butler Yeats and his friend Dowden, the young Professor of English at Trinity College, Dublin, and later an eminent scholar of Shakespeare, Shelley, and other writers. They disagreed first about Wordsworth, then about Shakespeare. In later years J. B. Yeats thought his friend a provincial and let the communications lapse.

I give the dispute in its main outline. In March 1874, hearing of the success of Dowden's lectures on Shakespeare, J. B. Yeats wrote to congratulate him. In reply, on March 17, Dowden made the mistake of giving him the gist of his next lecture, on *Richard II*:

In K[ing] Richard II Shakspere [as Dowden spelled his name] represents the man with an artistic feeling for life who isn't an artist of life. The artist of life is efficient and shapes the world and his destiny with strong creative hands. Richard likes graceful combinations, a clever speech instead of an efficient one, a melodious passion instead of one which achieves the deed. . . . If things can be arranged

---

[12] William M. Murphy, *Prodigal Father: The Life of John Butler Yeats (1839–1922)* (Ithaca and London: Cornell University Press, 1978), p. 563n.

[13] John Kelly and Ronald Schuchard (eds.), *The Collected Letters of W. B. Yeats, Vol. III: 1901–1904* (Oxford: Clarendon Press, 1994), p. 74n.

[14] Murphy, *Prodigal Father*, p. 100.

[15] Ibid., pp. 589–590n, referring to Allan Wade, *A Bibliography of the Writings of W. B. Yeats*, third edition revised by Russell K. Alspach (London: Rupert Hart-Davis, 1968), no. 80, p. 90.

so as to appeal gracefully or touchingly to his esthetic sensibility, he doesn't concern himself much more about them. And so all of life becomes unreal to him through this dilettantism with life.[16]

The word "dilettantism" may have struck a nerve in J. B. Yeats, who had reason to fear that he himself was a dilettante by comparison with the prolific, efficient Dowden. J. B. Yeats immediately denounced Dowden's values, in relation to *Richard II*, as "a sort of splenetic morality that would be fitter in the mouth of the old gardener." He maintained, in effect, that lost causes are invariably the better ones. Bolingbroke was only "stronger in prudence" than Richard. Richard "had a more mounting spirit, his disdain was nobler, his mirth more joyous, his happiness had a more untiring wing."[17] Not that J. B. Yeats had any hope of changing Dowden's mind. Dowden already believed that "for [JBY] the ethical disappears in the aesthetic."[18] Gratified by that disappearance, he did not feel impelled to reconsider his view of the history plays. In *Shakspere – A Critical Study of His Mind and Art* (1875) he described Richard as boyish, unreal, lacking in authority and "executive power," a mere aesthete, an amateur in the mode of self-presentation:

Life is to Richard a show, a succession of images; and to put himself into accord with the aesthetic requirements of his position is Richard's first necessity. He is equal to playing any part gracefully which he is called upon by circumstances to enact. But when he has exhausted the aesthetic satisfaction to be derived from the situations of his life, he is left with nothing further to do. He is an amateur in living; not an artist.

Dowden conceded Richard's charm of person and presence: "Hotspur remembers him as 'Richard, that sweet, lovely rose'." "But a king who rules a discontented people and turbulent nobles needs to be something more than a beautiful blossoming flower."[19] It followed that Henry V "is Shakspere's ideal of the *practical* heroic character." But this character is not "the highest ideal of Shakspere, who lived and moved and had his being not alone in the world of limitation, of tangible, positive fact, but also in a world of the soul, a world opening into two endless vistas – the vista of meditation and the vista of passion." For these vistas, we must go to the tragedies and *The Tempest*.

---

[16] Quoted in Murphy, *Prodigal Father*, pp. 98–99.   [17] Ibid., p. 99.
[18] Edward Dowden, *Fragments from Old Letters E. D. to E. D. W: 1869–1892* (London: Dent, 1914), p. 55.
[19] Edward Dowden, *Shakspere – A Critical Study of His Mind and Art* (New York: Harper, 1875; third edition, 1918), pp. 172 ff.

In these Shakspere is engaged in a series of studies not concerning success in the mastery of events and things, but concerning the higher success and the more awful failure which appear in the exaltation or the ruin of a soul.

So in *Macbeth, Antony and Cleopatra, Othello, Coriolanus,* and *Timon of Athens*:

And, after exhibiting the absolute ruin of a life and of a soul, Shakspere closed the wonderful series of his dramatic writings by exhibiting the noblest elevation of character, the most admirable attainment of heart, of intellect, of will, which our present life admits, in the person of Prospero. What more was left for Shakspere to say?[20]

If J. B. Yeats had two or three reasons for being angry with Dowden, his son had ten. After a first period of social amenity, WBY became convinced that Dowden was his enemy, an obstacle to his cultural and national motives. Dowden was a Unionist, an Imperialist, the most visible image of the deplorable Trinity College, a famous scholar-critic ostentatiously indifferent to the work of Irish cultural nationalism to which Yeats had set himself. Dowden liked one or two Celtic legends, that of Deirdre for instance, and he was on visiting terms with some Irish writers, but he told Aubrey de Vere, in a letter of September 13, 1882, that he was "infinitely glad that I spent my early enthusiasm on Wordsworth and Spenser and Shakespeare, and not on anything that Ireland ever produced."[21] He also committed the indelicacy of urging the young poet Yeats to read George Eliot. Like Matthew Arnold, Dowden thought that Irish writers should be content to find their destiny by submerging themselves in the greater literature of England, where their small voices would be heard to advantage. In this respect as in his work on Shakespeare, Dowden was immensely influential. John Eglinton wrote of him, "he may even be said to have imposed his conception of Shakespeare on modern criticism."[22] It is no surprise, then, that Yeats attacked Dowden in several essays, speeches, and letters to the Editor. The attack was unfair, because Dowden was not entirely the hot gospeller of success that Yeats made him out to be. It is much to his credit that he was one of the first readers of Whitman in Europe. But Yeats was not deflected from rebuke. "The more I read the worse does the Shakespeare criticism become," he told Lady Gregory, "and Dowden is about the climax of it.

[20] Ibid., pp. 66–67.
[21] Edward Dowden, *Letters of Edward Dowden and His Correspondents* (London: Dent, 1914), p. 184
[22] John Eglinton, Preface, *Letters of Edward Dowden and His Correspondents,* p. xiii.

I[t] came out [of] the middle class movement & I feal (sic) it my legitimate enemy."[23] In "Ireland after Parnell" – the second book of "The Trembling of the Veil" (1922) – Yeats took the freedom of Dowden's death to list some of the grievances he cherished against him:

Edward Dowden, my father's old friend, with his dark romantic face, the one man of letters Dublin Unionism possessed, was withering in that barren soil. Towards the end of his life he confessed to a near friend that he would have wished before all things to have been the lover of many women; and some careless lecture, upon the youthful Goethe, had in early life drawn down upon him the displeasure of the Protestant Archbishop. And yet he turned Shakespeare into a British Benthamite, flattered Shelley but to hide his own growing lack of sympathy, abandoned for like reason that study of Goethe that should have been his life-work, and at last cared but for Wordsworth, the one great poet who, after brief blossom, was cut and sawn into planks of obvious utility.[24]

Two sources of grievance can be added. Dowden refused to help the Irish literary movement even to the extent of conceding that others might take it seriously. And when Wilde fell into disgrace and Yeats asked various Irish writers for letters of sympathy, "I was refused by none but Edward Dowden, who gave me what I considered an irrelevant excuse – his dislike for everything that Wilde had written."[25]

III

On April 22, 1901, Yeats went up to Stratford-on-Avon and lodged at the Shakespeare Hotel for a week so that he could attend the Benson Festival of Shakespeare's History Plays. He saw six of the eight: *King John*, *Richard II*, *Henry IV Part II*, *Henry V*, *Henry VI Part II*, and *Richard III*. In his spare time in the Library he read enough Shakespeare criticism to keep him exasperated. He had looked for an opportunity to write an essay on Shakespeare. While the experience of the history plays was fresh in his mind, he wrote "At Stratford-on-Avon" and published it in two parts in *The Speaker*, on May 11 and 18. The essay is in six sections. The first is in praise of Stratford, its "quiet streets, where gabled and red-tiled houses remember the Middle Ages" and one reads in the Library "with its oak-panelled walls and leaded windows of tinted glass." The second part

---

[23] W. B. Yeats, *The Collected Letters, Vol. III: 1901–1904*, ed. John Kelly and Ronald Schuchard (Oxford: Clarendon Press, 1994), p. 61 (Letter of April 25, 1901).

[24] Yeats, *Autobiographies*, ed. William H. O'Donnell and Douglas N. Archibald (New York: Scribner, 1999), p. 193.

[25] Ibid., pp. 224–225.

disapproves of the "half-round theatre" and the Naturalism of its sets, and, for contrast and exemplification, speaks warmly of Gordon Craig's scenery for the Purcell Operatic Society's production of *Dido and Aeneas* in London a month or so previously. In the theatre of Naturalism, Yeats says, "illusion comes to an end, slain by our desire to increase it." In the third section, he moves closer to his disapprovals, embodied for the moment in George Eliot and the Utilitarian critics of Shakespeare who worked in her shadow. He has not yet named Dowden, but the word "efficiency" indicates that he has him in view:

Because reason can only discover completely the use of those obvious actions which everybody admires, and because every character was to be judged by efficiency in action, Shakespearian criticism became a vulgar worshipper of success.[26]

Yeats is writing as a scholar of Blake. He is also, instructed by Symons's *The Symbolist Movement in Literature* (1899), an adept of the vision according to which the palpable world is no longer a reality, and the unseen world no longer a dream. In Yeats's version:

In *La Peau de chagrin* Balzac spends many pages in describing a coquette, who seems the image of heartlessness, and then invents an improbable incident that her chief victim may discover how beautifully she can sing. Nobody had ever heard her sing, and yet in her singing, and in her chatter with her maid, Balzac tells us, was her true self. He would have us understand that behind the momentary self, which acts and lives in the world, and is subject to the judgment of the world, there is that which cannot be called before any mortal judgment seat, even though a great poet, or novelist, or philosopher be sitting upon it.[27]

Reading a few books on Shakespeare – or at least turning them over in the Library – Yeats concluded that they conspired in an antithesis, "which grew in clearness and violence as the century grew older, between two types, whose representatives were Richard II, 'sentimental,' 'weak,' 'selfish,' 'insincere,' and Henry V, 'Shakespeare's only hero'." Gervinus was guilty, but Dowden was closer to the scene and could not be left out of the rebuke:

I know that Professor Dowden, whose book I once read carefully, first made these emotions eloquent and plausible. He lived in Ireland, where everything has failed, and he meditated frequently upon the perfection of character which had, he thought, made England successful, for, as we say, "cows beyond the water have long horns." He forgot that England, as Gordon has said, was made by her adventurers, by her people of wildness and imagination and eccentricity; and

---

[26] Yeats, "At Stratford-on-Avon," *Essays and Introductions*, p. 103.   [27] Ibid., p. 102.

thought that Henry V, who only seemed to be these things because he had some commonplace vices, was not only the typical Anglo-Saxon, but the model Shakespeare held up before England; and he even thought it worth while pointing out that Shakespeare himself was making a large fortune while he was writing about Henry's victories.[28]

In Dowden's successors, the celebration of Henry V went further, "and it reached its height at a moment of imperialistic enthusiasm, of ever-deepening conviction that the commonplace shall inherit the earth, when somebody of reputation, whose name I cannot remember, wrote that Shakespeare admired this one character alone out of all his characters."[29]

"I cannot believe," Yeats says in the fourth part of the essay, "that Shakespeare looked on his Richard II with any but sympathetic eyes." Richard is shown to fail, "a little because he lacked some qualities that were doubtless common among his scullions, but more because he had certain qualities that are uncommon in all ages." To suppose that Shakespeare preferred the men who deposed his king "is to suppose that Shakespeare judged men with the eyes of a Municipal Councillor weighing the merits of a Town Clerk." On the contrary:

[Shakespeare] saw indeed, as I think, in Richard II the defeat that awaits all, whether they be artist or saint, who find themselves where men ask of them a rough energy and have nothing to give but some contemplative virtue, whether lyrical fantasy, or sweetness of temper, or dreamy dignity, or love of God, or love of His creatures.[30]

Shakespeare meditated "as Solomon, not as Bentham meditated, upon blind ambitions, untoward accidents, and capricious passions, and the world was almost as empty in his eyes as it must be in the eyes of God." To support this sad, beautiful verdict, Yeats quoted in full sonnet 66, "Tir'd with all these, for restful death I cry."

In the fifth part of the essay, Yeats brings forward the notion that "there is some one myth for every man, which, if we but knew it, would make us understand all he did and thought." Shakespeare's myth, "it may be, describes a wise man who was blind from very wisdom, and an empty man who thrust him from his place, and saw all that could be seen from very emptiness." The myth can be found, he thinks, in "Richard III, that unripened Hamlet, and [in] Henry V, that ripened Fortinbras." Henry's purposes "are so intelligible to everybody that everybody talks of him as if he succeeded, although he fails in the end, as all men great and little

---

[28] Ibid., p. 104.   [29] Ibid., pp. 104–105.   [30] Ibid., p. 106.

fail in Shakespeare." It is not clear how Shakespeare's myth is fulfilled in this antithesis, but we may as well take Yeats's word for it.

In the last part of the essay Yeats refers, evidently with some misgiving, to the stories that came into English literature from Italy in the Renaissance:

And yet, could those foreign tales have come in if the great famine, the sinking down of popular imagination, the dying out of traditional fantasy, the ebbing out of the energy of race, had not made them necessary? . . . Shakespeare wrote at a time when solitary great men were gathering to themselves the fire that had once flowed hither and thither among all men, when individualism in work and thought and emotion was breaking up the old rhythms of life, when the common people, sustained no longer by the myths of Christianity and of still older faiths, were sinking into the earth.[31]

Before concluding the essay, Yeats inserted two sentences of explanatory intention that could only be speculative, lacking evidence in their favor. He was not scholar enough to verify them; he could only posit them because of his great desire that they would be found true:

The courtly and saintly ideals of the Middle Ages were fading, and the practical ideals of the modern age had begun to threaten the unuseful dome of the sky; Merry England was fading, and yet it was not so faded that the poets could not watch the procession of the world with that untroubled sympathy for men as they are, as apart from all they do and seem, which is the substance of tragic irony.[32]

Yeats returned to the motif a few months later in his essay on Spenser, where he tried to keep Shakespeare and Spenser in Merry England, an England mostly Norman, Angevin, and officially French, and in which there is a quarrel to the death "with that new Anglo-Saxon nation that was arising amid Puritan sermons and Marprelate pamphlets." The new nation "had driven out the language of its conquerors, and now it was to overthrow their beautiful haughty imagination and their manners, full of abandon and willfulness, and to set in their stead earnestness and logic and the timidity and reserve of a counting-house."[33] Chaucer, Shakespeare, and – equivocally, because he wanted to justify himself to his new masters – Spenser were on the merry side, Langland and Bunyan on the Puritan side. Shakespeare, his commitment to the Tudor myth a strained sentiment far short of conviction, gave his heart to the defeated side and found for its poor victims the most poetic lines, Richard II the most blessed in that respect.

---

[31] Ibid., pp. 109–110.   [32] Ibid., p. 106.   [33] Ibid., pp. 364–365.

IV

Yeats's sense of Shakespeare was equivocal. Shakespeare was indisputably a great writer, but he was born too late, he should have come into the world with Chaucer. Yeats writes, in "The Trembling of the Veil":

> [William] Morris had never seemed to care greatly for any poet later than Chaucer and though I preferred Shakespeare to Chaucer I begrudged my own preference. Had not Europe shared one mind and heart, until both mind and heart began to break into fragments a little before Shakespeare's birth? ... If Chaucer's personages had disengaged themselves from Chaucer's crowd, forgot their common goal and shrine, and after sundry magnifications became each in turn the centre of some Elizabethan play, and had after split into their elements and so given birth to romantic poetry, must I reverse the cinematograph?[34]

Each of these sundry magnifications becomes a great character in a play by Shakespeare – Lear, Hamlet, Macbeth, Ophelia – but there is loss, too. In Phase 20 of *A Vision* – Shakespeare's phase – "Unity of Being is no longer possible, for the being is compelled to live in a fragment of itself and to dramatise that fragment."[35] As he put it in the first *Vision*:

> Like the phase before it, and those that follow it immediately, [it is] a phase of the breaking up and subdivision of the being. The energy is always seeking those facts which being separable can be seen more clearly, or expressed more clearly, but when there is truth to phase there is a similitude of the old unity, or rather a new unity, which is not a Unity of Being but a unity of the creative act. He no longer seeks to unify what is broken through conviction, by imposing those very convictions upon himself and others, but by projecting a dramatization or many dramatizations. He can create, just in that degree in which he can see these dramatizations as separate from himself, and yet as an epitome of his whole nature.[36]

Phase 20 is exemplified by Shakespeare, Napoleon, and Balzac, but mostly by Shakespeare. It is some consolation to Yeats that the groundlings in Shakespeare's theatre could still "remember the folk-songs and the imaginative folk-life,"[37] but their sense of those communal experiences could only be residual. Shakespeare's fools and their songs are, as Peter Ure pointed out, "the vestiges of the old world of unity before the

---

[34] Yeats, *Autobiographies*, pp. 165–166.   [35] Yeats, *A Vision* (1937, corrected 1962), p. 148.

[36] W. B. Yeats, *A Vision: The Original 1925 Version*, ed. Catherine E. Paul and Margaret Mills Harper (New York: Scribner, 2008), pp. 70–71.

[37] W. B. Yeats, *Plays and Controversies* (New York: Macmillan, 1924), p. 86.

Renaissance scatterings,"[38] but they are desperate with a sense of loss and dread: that is why the heroic figures they pester can't abide their pointed nonsense. Meanwhile the hero's imagination – the "violence within" as Stevens called it – responds with force nearly equal and opposite to the external violence it has to endure: nearly, but not quite, there is always the winner, death. "Shakespeare's persons, when the last darkness has gathered about them, speak out of an ecstasy that is one-half the self-surrender of sorrow, and one-half the last playing and mockery of the victorious sword before the defeated world."[39] The ecstasy is a play of mind and spirit. Yeats assimilates these beautiful defeated heroes to the tragic joy of "The Gyres" and "Lapis Lazuli," but they still issue from a broken time. In 1906 Yeats wrote:

One of the means of loftiness, of marmorean stillness, has been the choice of strange and far-away places for the scenery of art, but this choice has grown bitter to me, and there are moments when I cannot believe in the reality of imaginations that are not inset with the minute life of long familiar things and symbols and places. I have come to think of even Shakespeare's journeys to Rome or to Verona as the outflowing of an unrest, a dissatisfaction with natural interests, an unstable equilibrium of the whole European mind that would not have come had John Palaeologus cherished, despite that high and heady look, copied by Burne-Jones for his Cophetua, a hearty disposition to fight the Turk.[40]

v

None of these sentiments is beyond the range of J. B. Yeats's rhetoric. I am willing to believe that father and son had many conversations leading to father's assertion many years later – long after "At Stratford-on-Avon" – on the subject of "Elizabethan ways":

There is another thing to be noted about Elizabethan ways. Getting a living was then a comparatively easy thing; they had not that absorption to interrupt their dreams, and here again let me add, that a people who do not dream never attain to inner sincerity, for only in his dreams is a man really himself. Only for his dreams is a man responsible – his actions are what he must do. Actions are a bastard race to which a man has not given his full paternity.[41]

---

[38] Peter Ure, *Yeats and Anglo-Irish Literature*, ed. C. J. Rawson (Liverpool University Press, 1974), pp. 212–213.

[39] Yeats, *Essays and Introductions*, p. 254.   [40] Ibid., p. 297.

[41] John Butler Yeats, *Letters to His Son W. B. Yeats and Others 1869–1922*, ed. Joseph Hone (London: Faber and Faber, 1944), p. 189.

Otherwise put, in the poet's terms: "In dreams begins responsibility."[42]

But two other influences are demonstrable: Emerson's essay on Shakespeare in *Representative Men* (1876) and Pater's "Shakespeare's English Kings" in *Appreciations* (1889). Yeats alludes to each in different essays. Emerson's Shakespeare is the genius of universality; there is no talk of the Tudor myth, Queen Elizabeth, or Henry V, but much brooding on the symbolic reach of entities:

Shakespeare, Homer, Dante, Chaucer, saw the splendor of meaning that plays over the visible world; knew that a tree had another use than for apples, and corn another than for meal, and the ball of the earth, than for tillage and roads: that these things bore a second and finer harvest to the mind, being emblems of its thoughts, and conveying in all their natural history a certain mute commentary on human life. Shakespeare employed them as colors to compose his picture. He rested in their beauty; and never took the step which seemed inevitable to such genius, namely to explore the virtue which resides in these symbols and imparts this power: what is that which they themselves say? He converted the elements which waited on his command, into entertainments. He was master of the revels to mankind.[43]

In his essay on Spenser, Yeats says that Spenser should not have occupied himself with moral and religious questions: "he should have been content to be, as Emerson thought Shakespeare was, a Master of the Revels to mankind."[44] As such a master, Shakespeare would be impartial in his performances, not a propagandist for this or that regime but sympathetic to all, the victorious and the defeated alike.

Pater's essay was more pervasive than Emerson's in Yeats's meditations at Stratford. He must have been turning over the pages of *Appreciations* or recalling a paragraph from an early reading. Yeats's sentence that I have in part quoted reads in full:

I cannot believe that Shakespeare looked on his Richard II with any but sympathetic eyes, understanding indeed how ill-fitted he was to be king, at a certain moment of history, but understanding that he was lovable and full of capricious fancy, a "wild creature" as Pater has called him.[45]

Pater called him that in one of the several passages in which he maintains that Shakespeare's concern is not with kingship but with the irony of it:

---

[42] Yeats, Epigraph to *Responsibilities*, in *Variorum Edition of the Poems*, p. 269.

[43] Ralph Waldo Emerson, *Representative Men* (Boston and New York: Houghton Mifflin, 1930 reprint), pp. 216–217.

[44] Yeats, "Edmund Spenser", in *Essays and Introductions*, p. 368.   [45] Ibid., p. 105.

the irony of kingship – average human nature, flung with a wonderfully pathetic effect into the vortex of great events; tragedy of everyday quality heightened in degree only by the conspicuous scene which does but make those who play their parts there conspicuously unfortunate; the utterance of common humanity straight from the heart, but refined like other common things for kingly uses by Shakespeare's unfailing eloquence.[46]

The refining act of consciousness makes space, I assume, for the unofficial, antinomian values that would otherwise be suppressed by the official ones. Pater speaks of "the person and story of Richard the Second, a figure – 'that sweet lovely rose' – which haunts Shakespeare's mind, as it seems long to have haunted the minds of the English people, as the most touching of all examples of the irony of kingship."

  Toward the middle of "Shakespeare's English Kings" Pater breaks into an expostulation, a tone unusual for him:

No! Shakespeare's kings are not, nor are meant to be, great men: rather, little or quite ordinary humanity, thrust upon greatness, with those pathetic results, the natural self-pity of the weak heightened in them into irresistible appeal to others as the net result of their royal prerogative. One after another, they seem to lie composed in Shakespeare's embalming pages, with just that touch of nature about them, making the whole world akin, which has infused into their tombs at Westminster a rare poetic grace. It is that irony of kinship, the sense that it is in its happiness child's play, in its sorrows, after all, but children's grief, which gives its finer accent to all the changeful feeling of these wonderful speeches: the great meekness of the graceful, wild creature, tamed at last –
  "Give Richard leave to live till Richard die!"[47]

VI

Yeats's Shakespeare, it begins to appear, is an antinomian at heart and on principle, even if by force of necessity he is enough of a Tudor mythographer to satisfy the authorities. According to the *OED*, an antinomian is a person who believes that the moral law is not binding on Christians, under the "law of grace." In *The Renaissance* and again in *Gaston de Latour* Pater explains what he takes the word to mean:

One of the strongest characteristics of that outbreak of the reason and the imagination, of that assertion of the liberty of the heart, in the middle age, which I have termed a medieval Renaissance, was its antinomianism, its spirit of rebellion and revolt against the moral and religious ideas of the time. In their

---

[46] Walter Pater, *Appreciations with an Essay on Style* (London: Macmillan, 1944 reprint), p. 193.
[47] Ibid., p. 207.

search after the pleasures of the senses and the imagination, in their care for beauty, in their worship of the body, people were impelled beyond the bounds of the Christian ideal; and their love became sometimes a strange idolatry, a strange rival religion.

He associates it with the survival of the pagan gods, such as "that ancient Venus, not dead, but only hidden for a time in the caves of the Venusberg, [and] those old pagan gods still going to and fro on the earth, under all sorts of disguise":

And this element in the middle age, for the most part ignored by those writers who have treated it preeminently as the "Age of Faith" – this rebellious and antinomian element, the recognition of which has made the delineation of the middle age by the writers of the Romantic school in France, by Victor Hugo for instance in *Notre-Dame de Paris*, so suggestive and exciting – is found alike in the history of Abelard and the legend of Tannhäuser. More and more, as we come to mark changes and distinctions of temper in what is often in one all-embracing confusion called the middle age, that rebellion, that sinister claim for liberty of heart and thought, comes to the surface.

Aucassin and Nicollete contains the most complete example of this antinomian spirit, according to Pater, but it is also found in the Albigensian movement, "connected so strangely with the history of Provençal poetry," in the Franciscan order, "with its poetry, its mysticism, its 'illumination,' from the point of view of religious authority, justly suspect," and in "the thoughts of those obscure prophetical writers, like Joachim of Flora, strange dreamers in a world of flowery rhetoric of that third and final dispensation of a 'spirit of freedom,' in which law shall have passed away."[48] Pater also ascribed the antinomian disposition to his own Marius the Epicurean, who discovers that to move in the outer world of other people, as though taking it at their estimate, would be possible only as a kind of irony.

In Shakespeare the antinomian element may be found, if one considers the plays under the guidance of J. B. Yeats and Pater, in his sympathy for the defeated, the distinctive poetry and pathos he writes for them, his tenderness toward lost causes known to be lost, certain traces of his Catholic associations, and the fact – which Pater notes in "Shakespeare's English Kings" – that while Shakespeare "was not wanting in a sense of the magnanimity of warriors" and records monumentally enough "the

[48] Walter Pater, *The Renaissance: Studies in Art and Poetry: The 1893 Text*, ed. Donald L. Hill (Berkeley: University of California Press, 1980), pp. 18–19.

grandiose of war" as in Vernon's speech in the first part of *Henry IV*
(IV.i.97–106) –

> All furnish'd, all in arms;
> All plum'd like estridges that with the wind
> Bated like eagles having lately bath'd;
> Glittering in golden coats, like images;
> As full of spirit as the month of May,
> And gorgeous as the sun at midsummer;
> Wanton as youthful goats, wild as young bulls.
> I saw young Harry, with his beaver on,
> His cuisses on his thighs, gallantly arm'd,
> Rise from the ground like feathered Mercury...

– there is always the afterthought, the figure of tragic irony, this time from
Hotspur –

> No more, no more: worse than the sun in March,
> This praise doth nourish agues. Let them come;
> They come like sacrifices in their trim.[49]

VII

But a question arises: were not J. B. Yeats, Emerson, and Pater superseded
in the end, as presences in Yeats's sense of Shakespeare, by Nietzsche? In
September 1902, eighteen months or so after Stratford, John Quinn sent
Yeats his own copy of *Thus Spake Zarathustra* and impersonal copies of
The Case of Wagner and *The Genealogy of Morals*. For several months Yeats
appears to have read no one but Nietzsche, "that strong enchanter," as he
called him in a letter to Lady Gregory. Nietzsche entered upon Yeats's
stream of consciousness, and never left it. When death and dying came
into his imagination – as it inescapably did in his late years – Nietzsche
was never far off, summoned to help him transform his fear into ecstasy.
We can be sympathetic toward this device or not. Eliot said that
"Nietzsche is the most conspicuous modern instance of cheering oneself
up," a remark provoked by Eliot's reflection on Othello's last speech,
"Soft you; a word or two before you go." Cheering oneself up seemed to
Eliot a symptom of *bovarysme*, "the human will to see things as they are

---

[49] Pater, *Appreciations*, p. 199.

not," a stoical attitude "the reverse of Christian humility."[50] A more sympathetic reader of Yeats would report, without adjudicating the point, that what appealed to Yeats most powerfully was Nietzsche's figure of the hero, adept of risk, bringing to bear upon his circumstances sufficient intensity of consciousness to defeat them or to be greatly defeated by them. In *The King's Threshold* he has Seanchan, dying, say:

> I need no help,
> He needs no help that joy has lifted up
> Like some miraculous beast out of Ezekiel. ...
> Dead faces laugh.[51]

In his last poems Yeats brought Shakespeare and Nietzsche together, as if talk of the will-to-power and the tragic hero found fulfillment only in Shakespearean tragedy. In these poems, Nietzsche displaces Pater and Emerson: companioned by Blake and Heraclitus, he dominates the scene. Yeats's Shakespeare is still antinomian, finding in that doom enough resilience and intensity – it could not be held without them – to confront whatever violence life might enforce. In "Lapis Lazuli" the words "gay" and "gaiety" have to do most of the heroic, Nietzschean work of insistence, building castles on Vesuvius:

> All perform their tragic play,
> There struts Hamlet, there is Lear,
> That's Ophelia, that Cordelia;
> Yet they, should the last scene be there,
> The great stage curtain about to drop,
> If worthy their prominent part in the play,
> Do not break up their lines to weep.
> They know that Hamlet and Lear are gay;
> Gaiety transfiguring all that dread ....[52]

Jeffares, elucidating "Lapis Lazuli," draws attention to a passage in Yeats's "A General Introduction for My Work." I quote part of it:

The heroes of Shakespeare convey to us through their looks, or through the metaphorical patterns of their speech, the sudden enlargement of their vision, their ecstasy at the approach of death; "She should have died hereafter," "Of many thousand kisses, the poor last," "Absent thee from felicity awhile." They have become God or Mother Goddess, the pelican, "My baby at my breast," but

[50] T. S. Eliot, "Shakespeare and the Stoicism of Seneca," in *Selected Essays: New Edition* (New York: Harcourt, Brace, and World, 1964), p. 132.
[51] W. B. Yeats, *Collected Plays* (London: Macmillan, 1952), p. 141.
[52] Yeats, *Variorum Edition of the Poems*, p. 565.

all must be cold; no actress has ever sobbed when she played Cleopatra, even the shallow brain of a producer has never thought of such a thing. The supernatural is present, cold winds blow across our hands, upon our faces, the thermometer falls, and because of that cold we are hated by journalists and groundlings.[53]

"Cold" corresponds in the audience to "gay" in Shakespeare's heroes and heroines, a sense amounting to a conviction of "the sudden enlargement of their vision, their ecstasy at the approach of death"; or the approach of a vision of death, mimed indeed but still to be believed in – lived through – for as long as the play lasts. There are at least two ways of interpreting "Gaiety transfiguring all that dread." It can mean that the momentary self, as Yeats called it, passes beyond its worldly state into a hidden or sublime form, perhaps the form of wisdom. In October 1909 Yeats wrote of this in his journal:

Saw *Hamlet* on Saturday night, except for the chief "Ophelia" scenes; missed these, as I had to be away for a while at the Abbey, without regret. I know not why, but their pathos, as it [is] played, always leaves me cold. I came back for Hamlet at the grave, where my delight begins again. I feel in *Hamlet*, as always in Shakespeare, that I am in the presence of a soul lingering on the storm-beaten threshold of sanctity. Has not that threshold always been terrible, even crime-haunted? Surely Shakespeare, in those last seeming idle years, was no quiet country gentleman, enjoying, as men like Dowden think, the temporal reward of an unvalued toil. Perhaps he sought for wisdom in itself at last, and not in its passionate shadows. Maybe he had passed the threshold, and none the less for Jonson's drinking bout. Certainly one finds here and there in his work – is it not at the end of *Henry VI*, for instance – praise of country leisure sweetened by wisdom.[54]

This may entail no more, and no less, than the conversion of passion into the skill of music, as Pater says in "Shakespeare's English Kings":

As in some sweet anthem of Handel, the sufferer, who put finger to the organ under the utmost pressure of mental conflict, extracts a kind of peace at last from the mere skill with which he sets his distress to music.[55]

Or it may mean that the momentary self, by sublime negligence, achieves what Giorgio Agamben calls "a self-forgetting in the proper" – which I construe as the proper of the tragic form, the whole in which every part – every part of feeling and dread – is at once lost and saved.[56]

---

[53] Yeats, *Essays and Introductions*, pp. 522–523.
[54] W. B. Yeats, *Memoirs*, transcribed and ed. Denis Donoghue (London: Macmillan, 1972), p. 233.
[55] Pater, *Appreciations*, p. 208.
[56] Giorgio Agamben, *The End of the Poem: Studies in Poetics*, trans. Daniel Heller-Roazen (Stanford University Press, 1999), p. 98.

The conversion of passion into music, fear into ecstasy, was a late accomplishment in Yeats. When Edmund Wilson published *Axel's Castle: A Study in the Imaginative Literature of 1870–1930* in 1931, he was justified in saying that "even the poetry of the noble Yeats, still repining through middle age over the emotional miscarriages of youth, is dully weighted, for all its purity and candor, by a leaden acquiescence in defeat."[57] But in the few remaining years of Yeats's life, and with the provocation of Nietzsche, he transfigured that dread. Not without cost: some of these poems rant and rage more than is good for them, but the best of them – "The Statues" and "Cuchulain Comforted" – are justly Nietzschean.

VIII

In "The Tragic Theatre" (1910) Yeats wrote that "there is an art of the flood, the art of Titian when his *Ariosto*, and his *Bacchus and Ariadne*, give new images to the dreams of youth, and of Shakespeare when he shows us Hamlet broken away from life by the passionate hesitations of his reverie."[58] Reverie is Yeats's word for the mind when it is attending to its own business, indifferent to the world's. It occurred to him often and most tellingly on September 26, 1937 when he attended a performance of *Richard II* at the Queen's Theatre in London. Displeased with it – although John Gielgud played Richard, Michael Redgrave Bolingbroke, and Peggy Ashcroft Queen Isabel – he complained to Dorothy Wellesley that "the modern actor can speak to another actor, but he is incapable of reverie." "On the advice of Bloomsbury he has packed his soul in a bag and left it with the bar-attendant." And then he put a question to Lady Dorothy: "Did Shakespeare in *Richard II* discover poetic reverie?"[59]

The question comes as close as we are likely to come to Yeats's Shakespeare. In effect, it anticipates by more than sixty years Harold Bloom's claim, in *Shakespeare: The Invention of the Human* (1999), that Shakespeare invented us by inventing "human inwardness," "personality," and the ability to change by overhearing ourselves thinking. "Overhearing his own reverie," Bloom says of Richard II in a marginal tribute to Yeats's reading of that pathetic king and dazzling metaphysical poet, "Richard

---

[57] Edmund Wilson, *Literary Essays and Reviews of the 1920s and 30s*, ed. Lewis M. Dabney (New York: Library of America, 2007), p. 835.

[58] Yeats, *Essays and Introductions*, p. 242.

[59] *The Letters of W. B. Yeats*, ed. Allan Wade (London: Rupert Hart-Davis, 1954), p. 899. Letter of September 27, 1937.

undergoes a change."[60] The human quality that Bloom adds to Yeats on reverie is that of a character's listening to himself and completing, sometimes in action, sometimes in failure, his own rhetoric. Listening to oneself and turning the listening into theatre make a nuance in the understanding of reverie. Yeats's sense of reverie makes it an intrinsic form of consciousness: it is never clear what the mind in reverie is thinking about, except that it has exempted itself from conditions and circumstances. Yeats described it most fully in "The Irish Dramatic Movement," where he distinguished it from the common understanding of thought as the efficient form of cognition. He referred to a man who had in mind, when he spoke of thought, "the shaping energy that keeps us busy." The obstinate questionings this man had most respect for "were how to change the method of government, how to change the language, how to revive our manufactures, and whether it is the Protestant or the Catholic that scowls at the other with the darker scowl." Another man had in mind "thought as Pascal, as Montaigne, as Shakespeare, or as, let us say, Emerson, understood it – a reverie about the adventures of the soul, or of the personality, or some obstinate questioning of the riddle." "Many who have to work hard," Yeats continued, "always make time for this reverie, but it comes more easily to the leisured, and in this it is like a broken heart, which is, a Dublin newspaper assured us lately, impossible to a busy man."[61] Reverie is Yeats's word for the antinomian form of thinking. In Shakespeare, as in Yeats, it is invariably found where the conditions it faces are the wrong ones, such that in weak spirits or in especially difficult times it makes the mind feel ashamed of itself. It achieves itself only when the conditions of its thinking are transcended. If we were to change "broken away," in that quotation from "The Tragic Theatre," from the passive to the active voice, we would think again of Yeats's Nietzsche and give Yeats's Pater an edge he rarely had. Common to these several comparisons is Yeats's determination not to have Shakespeare – or himself – coincide with his time or act as its spokesman. Yeats considered himself, as he considered Shakespeare and to some extent Spenser, as a man born too late to find his proper companionship. "If we would find a company of our own way of thinking, we must go backward to turreted walls, to Courts, to high rocky places, to little walled towns, to jesters like that jester of Charles V who made mirth out of his own death; to the Duke Guidobaldo in his sickness, or Duke Frederick in his strength, to all those who understood that life is not lived, if not lived for

---

[60] Harold Bloom, *Shakespeare: The Invention of the Human* (London: Fourth Estate, 1999), p. 268.
[61] Yeats, *Plays and Controversies*, pp. 87–88.

contemplation or excitement."[62] Sometimes the excitement was in a turn of phrase, as in one that often occurred to Yeats – his father read it to him in Dublin – when he thought of reverie or of its companion, style: Coriolanus's answer to one of the impudent servants in Aufidius's house who demands, "Where dwellest thou?", to which Coriolanus answers: "Under the canopy." Reference to the canopy, the sky, rebukes the servant with an irony he could not be expected to appreciate. "Under the canopy!" the servant repeats, "Where's that?" The *OED* cites this to mean "the overhanging firmament" and also gives Hamlet's "this most excellent canopy, the air, look you, this brave o'erhanging firmament, this majestical roof fretted with golden fire." Yeats referred to the episode in "Reveries over Childhood and Youth." "I have seen *Coriolanus* played a number of times since then, and read it more than once, but that scene is more vivid than the rest, and it is my father's voice that I hear and not Irving's or Benson's."[63] John Butler Yeats's voice, reading high passages from *Coriolanus* and other plays and poems to his son in Dublin, stayed in the poet's mind even when other considerations entered to qualify his sense of Shakespeare.

IX

In "Shakespeare and the Stoicism of Seneca" (1927) Eliot noted that "the last few years have witnessed a number of recrudescences of Shakespeare." Three of them held his attention:

There is the fatigued Shakespeare, a retired Anglo-Indian, presented by Mr. Lytton Strachey; there is the messianic Shakespeare, bringing a new philosophy and a new system of yoga, presented by Mr. Middleton Murry; and there is the ferocious Shakespeare, a furious Samson, presented by Mr. Wyndham Lewis in his interesting book, *The Lion and the Fox.*[64]

It seemed to Eliot that "one of the chief reasons for questioning Mr. Strachey's Shakespeare, and Mr. Murry's, and Mr. Lewis's, is the remarkable resemblance which they bear to Mr. Strachey, and Mr. Murry, and Mr. Lewis respectively." "I have not a very clear idea of what Shakespeare was like," he claimed, "but I do not conceive him as very like either Mr. Strachey, or Mr. Murry, or Mr. Wyndham Lewis, or myself."[65]

It would be proper to add Yeats's name to these scholars of Shakespeare, and to say that Yeats's Shakespeare bears a resemblance, remarkable or not,

---

[62] Yeats, "Poetry and Tradition," in *Essays and Introductions*, p. 252.
[63] Yeats, *Autobiographies*, p. 80. [64] Eliot, *Selected Essays*, p. 126. [65] Ibid.

to Yeats. Like Shakespeare, Yeats was born out of his time: unity of the creative act had to make up for an impossible Unity of Being:

I see in Shakespeare a man in whom human personality, hitherto restrained by its dependence on Christendom or by its own need for self-control, burst like a shell. Perhaps secular intellect, setting itself free after five hundred years of struggle has made him the greatest of dramatists, and yet because an *antithetical* art could create a hundred plays which preserved – whether made by a hundred hands or by one – the unity of a painting or of a Temple pediment, we might, had the total works of Sophocles survived – they too born of a like struggle though with a different enemy – not think him greatest.[66]

Yeats did not think of Shakespeare, as he thought of Blake and Shelley, as kin to himself; though he claimed that Shakespeare's imagination, like Blake's and his own, was Celtic and had the Celtic susceptibilities. He would not concede to Dowden that Shakespeare was a comfortable Tudor. The aspects of Shakespeare which I have called antinomian – Pater's word – were also aspects of Yeats when he thought of himself as by native genius outside the law. Yeats and his Shakespeare moved, like Pater's Marius, in the external world and among other people only as a kind of irony. For that reason, Shakespeare was to Yeats "always a tragic comedian."[67] And for that reason, I think, *Hamlet* and *Richard II* touched him more acutely than the other plays, each of their heroes being, as he said of Hamlet, "a soul jagged & broken away from the life of its world."[68]

---

[66] Yeats, *A Vision* (1925), p. 169.
[67] Yeats, *Letters*, ed. Wade, p. 549. Letter of February 23, 1910 to John Butler Yeats.
[68] Yeats, letter of October 25, 1909 to John Martin Harvey, quoted in R. F. Foster, *W. B. Yeats: A Life, Vol. I: The Apprentice Mage 1865–1914* (Oxford University Press, 1997), p. 413.

CHAPTER 7

Yeats: Trying to be modern

I

In March 1935 Yeats was contracted by Oxford University Press to compile an *Oxford Book of Modern Verse* for the period 1900 to 1935. He was evidently pleased by the invitation: perhaps it would allow him to set the choice poems in a persuasive order. On July 4 he asked the publisher if he might start the book at 1892, the year of Tennyson's death, so that he might bring in Hopkins, Ernest Dowson "and some others who belong to the Modern Movement, though they died before 1900."[1] This was agreed without fuss, and the anthology was indeed called *The Oxford Book of Modern Verse 1892–1935*. At one stage of preparation it was meant to include American poets, but in the event it hardly did, only Eliot and Pound being featured. No Frost, no Stevens. In 1935 Auden was still an English poet. Yeats wrote to Olivia Shakespear: "My problem this time will be: 'How far do I like the Ezra [Pound], Eliot, Auden school and if I do not, why not?'"[2] He set to work and finished the job by the end of November: he must have known most of the poems he liked and intended to include. It took several months to deal with problems of copyright, permissions, refusals, and fees, but the book was published a year later, on November 19, 1936, though it was dated 1937.

Yeats refers to "the Modern Movement" as if such a thing existed and he knew its members. His reference to the Pound, Eliot, Auden school indicates that his understanding of these writers was limited; there was no such school. By the Modern Movement he can only have meant the

---

* Lecture to the Yeats International Summer School, Sligo, July 26, 2010.

[1] Quoted in Jon Stallworthy, "Yeats as Anthologist," in A. Norman Jeffares and K. G. W. Cross (eds.), *In Excited Reverie: A Centenary Tribute to William Butler Yeats 1865–1939* (New York: Macmillan, 1965), p. 176.

[2] Quoted in Stallworthy, "Yeats as Anthologist," p. 175. Also in *The Letters of W. B. Yeats*, ed. Allan Wade (London: Rupert Hart-Davis, 1954), p. 833.

Rhymers' Club which he founded with Ernest Rhys in 1890, a loose company of poets who met every week or so in the Old Cheshire Cheese chop-house in Fleet Street, London, to read their poems to one another and drink some wine. Yeats also had in mind the publication of the first *Book of the Rhymers' Club* in 1892; the second one appeared in 1894. *The Wanderings of Oisin and Other Poems* was published in 1889 and reissued in 1892. *The Countess Kathleen and Various Legends and Lyrics* was also published in 1892. His edition of Blake was published in 1893. But probably the death of Tennyson seemed to Yeats a turning point in poetry as the death of Parnell in 1891 was a turning point in Irish politics. As late as 1935, apparently, he wanted to pay tribute to his sad, desperate friends of the Nineties, the "tragic generation." The year 1900 would have been too late as a starting point. In that year, as he reported, "everybody got down off his stilts; henceforth nobody drank absinthe with his black coffee; nobody went mad; nobody committed suicide; nobody joined the Catholic church; or if they did I have forgotten."[3]

The one conviction or prejudice common to the members of the Rhymers' Club, according to Yeats, was the rejection of all ideas, "all generalizations that can be explained and debated." These, I think, were mainly the ideas propounded by positivism, empiricism, naturalism, and realism. Yeats saw, or thought he saw, that "Swinburne in one way, Browning in another, and Tennyson in a third, had filled their work with what I called 'impurities,' curiosities about politics, about science, about history, about religion; and that we must create once more the pure work." By "once more" I think he remembered the Coleridge of "The Ancient Mariner" and "Kubla Khan" and Dante Gabriel Rossetti's poems, the work of poets who made, as he writes in "The Tragic Generation," "what Arnold has called that 'morbid effort,' that search for 'perfection of thought and feeling, and to unite this to perfection of form,' sought this new, pure beauty and suffered in their lives because of it."[4] They suffered because –

> What portion in the world can the artist have
> Who has awakened from the common dream
> But dissipation and despair?[5]

[3] W. B. Yeats (ed.), *The Oxford Book of Modern Verse 1892–1935* (New York: Oxford University Press, 1937), pp. xi–xii.
[4] W. B. Yeats, *Autobiographies* (London: Macmillan, 1966), p. 313.
[5] W. B. Yeats, "Ego Dominus Tuus," in *The Variorum Edition of the Poems*, ed. Peter Allt and Russell K. Alspach (New York: Macmillan, 1957), p. 369.

The common dream is the assumption that reality is as it is supposed to be, according to the dictates of common sense and science. Meanings, in that prosaic sense, are the most insidious impurities; they must be got rid of. To awaken from the common dream is to gain an occult form of wisdom, but it entails having nothing to lean on in the ordinary world. Yeats's most gifted colleagues among the Rhymers were also the most defeated – Arthur Symons, Lionel Johnson, and Ernest Dowson. One night, when more poets than usual turned up, Yeats remarked, "None of us can say who will succeed, or even who has or has not talent. The only thing certain about us is that we are too many."[6]

For a time, Symons was Yeats's ideal Rhymer. He brought the good news from Paris and, in 1899, wrote a book called *The Symbolist Movement in Literature* – dedicated to Yeats, appropriately – in which he maintained that the literature he was expounding was "a literature in which the visible world is no longer a reality and the unseen world no longer a dream."[7] That was a tall order of displacement, even if it had the authority of Blake to sustain it, and the lesser authorities of Poe's "The Man of the Crowd," Baudelaire's "The Painter of Modern Life," Mallarmé's "*Crise de Vers*," and Valéry's "Introduction to the Method of Leonardo da Vinci." Yeats found that version of Symbolism entirely congenial, at least for a few years. For the first fourteen years of his poetic life, from 1889 to 1903, he did his best to keep his poetry clear of any acknowledgement of daily life, the oppressive commonplace of things. Better to assume with Blake that the true world was that of one's dreams and visions. Yeats reported that he had dreamed the story of "The Cap and Bells" "exactly as I have written it."[8] There is no reason to doubt his word. Dreams and visions gave him not only the symbolic stories he needed but license to use words in occult ways. "Words alone are certain good," according to Yeats's happy shepherd, but those were not the words of ordinary transactions and conversations: they were not devoted to the delivery of meanings or other currencies of communication, they had a more rarefied aim, the "exchange of dynamisms in the ecology of language," a phrase I am happy to accept from Hugh Kenner.[9] The general context of this poetics includes revulsion against the ordinary world – a common sentiment in

---

[6] Yeats, *Autobiographies*, pp. 167, 171.
[7] Arthur Symons, *The Symbolist Movement in Literature* (New York: E. P. Dutton, revised and enlarged edition, 1919), p. 4.
[8] Yeats, *Variorum Edition of the Poems*, p. 808.
[9] Hugh Kenner, *The Pound Era* (Berkeley: University of California Press, 1971), p. 126.

French, English, and Irish poetry at this time. Valéry writes, in one of his *Tel Quel* reflections:

The Self is distinct from every created thing. It withdraws from negation to negation. What we call "the Universe" might be defined as everything in which the Self declines to recognize itself.[10]

But there was one great exception to that severe rule: language, which has the merit of being an entirely human creation. It is also quite capable of declaring its independence: in that spirit it aspires to the condition of music and dance. Language in that respect does not imitate or transcribe worldly appearances: rather, it enables the human imagination to construct poems from its own creative resources – figures of speech, syllables, words, rhymes, assonance, sonority, repetition. At the end of his poem "La Pythie" Valéry proclaims the honor of language – sainted Language:

> Honneur des hommes, Saint LANGAGE,
> Discours prophétique et paré,
> Belles chaînes en qui s'engage
> Le dieu dans la chair égaré,
> Illumination, largesse!

– in Elizabeth Sewell's translation: "Honour of men, sainted Language, discourse prophetic and adorned, fair chains in which the god lost in the flesh is content to be taken; illuminations, bounty!" The poem continues:

> Voici parler une Sagesse
> Et sonner cette auguste Voix
> Qui se connaît quand elle sonne
> N'être plus la voix de personne
> Tant que des ondes et des bois![11]

– "Here speaks a Wisdom, here sounds that august voice which when it sounds knows itself to be no more the voice of a person than that of the waters and the woods."[12] This, too, was part of the Symbolist programme, to set voices astir which are not merely those of individual, isolated men and women but of life in the natural world.

But the Symbolist program comes at a price. When you read Yeats's "He Remembers Forgotten Beauty" – a Symbolist poem of twenty-four

---

[10] Paul Valéry, *Analects*, trans. Stuart Gilbert, Bollingen Series 14 (Princeton University Press, 1970), p. 280.

[11] Paul Valéry, *Poésies* (Paris: Gallimard, 1958 reprint), p. 82.

[12] Elizabeth Sewell, *Paul Valéry: The Mind in the Mirror* (Cambridge: Bowes and Bowes, 1952), p. 56.

lines, one that Stephen Dedalus recalled, if only to reject its lesson – you think the syntax of the first three lines will keep you safe:

> When my arms wrap you round I press
> My heart upon the loveliness
> That has long faded from the world.

The rest of the poem is an inventory of those lovely things, complicated for a while by the play of sense in units of three lines against that of rhyme in two end-rhymes. But by the ninth and tenth lines the sense has begun to coincide with the rhyming couplets. At this point the syntax drifts away, so much so that the final seven lines are left to fend for themselves:

> And when you sigh from kiss to kiss
> I hear white Beauty sighing, too,
> For hours when all must fade like dew,
> But flame on flame, and deep on deep,
> Throne over throne where in half sleep,
> Their swords upon their iron knees,
> Brood her high lonely mysteries.[13]

If you wonder who is talking to whom, the answers are various. In one printing, O'Sullivan Rua is talking to Mary Lavell; in another, Michael Robartes is talking to his beloved, and in the third and final version the speaker is an anonymous He talking to an anonymous You. I learn from Allen Grossman that the last five lines "represent the transcendental worshipers of Beauty in the form of the hierarchy of the angels who are Yeats's way of referring to the cherubic guardians of the Heavenly Eden: all will 'fade' at the anticipated Last Judgment but the celestial guardians. They remain."[14] One gets little satisfaction from asking what Beauty's "high lonely mysteries" are or why they are mysteries, high and lonely. The only help we get from Yeats, outside the poem, is that Michael Robartes is "fire reflected in water" and "the pride of the imagination brooding upon the greatness of its possessions."[15] What the lines I've quoted mainly give are events internal to the English language, such as the closed couplets, the monosyllabic rhymes, except for the final rhyme of "knees" and "mysteries." The syntax is rudimentary, and the words "For" and "But" are hard pressed to keep the verses going.

---

[13] Yeats, *Variorum Edition of the Poems*, p. 156.

[14] Allen R. Grossman, *Poetic Knowledge in the Early Yeats: A Study of "The Wind Among the Reeds"* (Charlottesville: University Press of Virginia, 1969), p. 118.

[15] Yeats, *Variorum Edition of the Poems*, p. 803.

The title I've chosen for this lecture comes from a sentence in Yeats's Introduction to the *Oxford Book of Modern Verse* which remains obscure to me after several readings. After some of those readings, I have almost been persuaded that the sentence is casual, perhaps flippant, almost a joke. But the next reading makes me think that Yeats is just as serious here as on other occasions. He has undertaken to say what is modern about modern poetry, and who the really modern poets are or have been. I'll quote the opaque passage without comment in a moment. Yeats has been saying that certain poets, Cecil Day-Lewis, Charles Madge, and Louis MacNeice, for instance, "are modern through the character of their intellectual passion." He does not indicate what an intellectual passion is or how it differs, in these poets, from other or earlier manifestations of it, or from other kinds of passion. Then he continues:

We have been gradually approaching this art through that cult of sincerity, that refusal to multiply personality which is characteristic of our time. They may seem obscure, confused, because of their concentrated passion, their interest in associations hitherto untravelled; it is as though their words and rhythms remained gummed to one another instead of separating and falling into order. I can seldom find more than half a dozen lyrics that I like, yet in this moment of sympathy I prefer them to Eliot, to myself – I too have tried to be modern. They have pulled off the mask, the manner writers hitherto assumed, Shelley in relation to his dream, Byron, Henley, to their adventure, their action. Here stands not this or that man but man's naked mind.[16]

The questions that arise from this passage are more obvious than the answers. What does Yeats mean by "modern"? Is it a term of praise or not? Why and when did he try to be modern? What did the effort entail? Does he think there are several ways of being modern, or does one way exclude the other ones? By "I too" does he mean himself in addition to Day-Lewis, Madge, and MacNeice and other poets who wrote in ways similar to theirs? How does "man's naked mind" differ from "this or that man"? Is it plausible that Yeats, even for a moment of sympathy, preferred the poems of Day-Lewis, Madge, and MacNeice to his own?

It has generally been assumed that when Yeats uses the word "modern," he is practicing an irony, and that the word is his way of indicating "the

---

[16] W. B. Yeats, "Introduction," *The Oxford Book of Modern Verse*, p. xxxvi.

emptiness of *this* moment in history."[17] The only cultural and political ages he regularly praised were the eighteenth century in which the Protestant Ascendancy flourished in Ireland, the Italian Renaissance of the sixteenth century, and, if we take his poems of Byzantium seriously, an age several centuries earlier still. But irony was only one of his tones in using the word "modern." In February 1926, when he visited St. Otteran's school in Waterford – a school run by the Sisters of Mercy who practiced the Montessori method of teaching – he was so pleased with it that, as he wrote in the first stanza of "Among School Children,"

> I walk through the long schoolroom questioning;
> A kind old nun in a white hood replies;
> The children learn to cipher and to sing,
> To study reading-books and history,
> To cut and sew, be neat in everything
> In the best modern way –[18]

Some readers find an irony in "be neat in everything/In the best modern way," but I don't: it seems to me entirely praise. But in "The Statues" Yeats spits out the word, disgusted as he is by the leveling force of democracy in the twentieth century:

> We Irish, born into that ancient sect
> But thrown upon this filthy modern tide
> And by its formless spawning fury wrecked,
> Climb to our proper dark, that we may trace
> The lineaments of a plummet-measured face.[19]

Presumably the tide is filthy because it is modern, socially indiscriminate, as distinct from the ancient sect that was supposedly governed by noble rules and hierarchy. The opportune rhyme of "sect" and "wrecked" enforces the political point. The verb in "Climb to our proper dark" seems to be in the imperative mood, demanding that "we Irish," even now at the eleventh hour, return to the Greek proportions upon which alone a genuine culture may be composed.

Some other uses of the word are neutral. In "Vacillation" "the body of a modern saint" refers to Saint Teresa, named a few lines earlier. In "Blood and the Moon," the question – "Is every modern nation like the tower,/ Half

---

[17] Allen Grossman, *The Long Schoolroom: Lessons in the Bitter Logic of the Poetic Principle* (Ann Arbor: University of Michigan Press, 1997), p. 97. Cf. Donald T. Torchiana: "'Among School Children' and the Education of the Irish Spirit," in Jeffares and Cross (eds.), *In Excited Reverie*, p. 141.
[18] Yeats, *Variorum Edition of the Poems*, p. 443. [19] Ibid., p. 611.

dead at the top?" – is straightforward, though it might become contentious in other contexts. So is "modern" in the third stanza of "A Model for the Laureate" –

> The Muse is mute when public men
> Applaud a modern throne:
> Those cheers that can be bought or sold,
> That office fools have run,
> That waxen seal, that signature,
> For things like these what decent man
> Would keep his lover waiting,
>   Keep his lover waiting?[20]

– which evidently means to say that King Edward VIII acted decently in abdicating the throne rather than keep Mrs. Simpson waiting. In "The Municipal Gallery Revisited" the reference to Lady Gregory, Synge, and Yeats himself as "we three alone in modern times" is again a simple claim. "High Talk" is more pointed, since it nearly maintains that Yeats is the best modern poet:

> Processions that lack high stilts have nothing that catches the eye.
> What if my great granddad had a pair that were twenty foot high,
> And mine were but fifteen foot, no modern stalks upon higher .... [21]

But there is a passage in "Ego Dominus Tuus" in which "modern" calls for slow reading.

This poem is one of Yeats's dialogues, a conversation between two old friends, as they might be, who differ in every respect except in their mutual regard. Yeats calls them Hic and Ille. I'll call them the first and the second. The first begins by rebuking the second for being enslaved to "the unconquerable delusion," meaning presumably that he is still infatuated with his moonlit visions, which he traces as "magical shapes" on the strand. The second, whom we can identify with Yeats if we want to, answers:

> By the help of an image
> I call to my own opposite, summon all
> That I have handled least, least looked upon.

This is a version of a motive well-established in Yeats, which he expounds in several essays and poems. It is a theory common to poets who would speak not directly in their own voices, but obliquely as if they determined

---

[20] Ibid., pp. 597–598.   [21] Ibid., p. 623.

to put a safe distance between themselves and their feelings. We find it in Eliot and Pound, who invent figures different from themselves and speak through them: Prufrock, Gerontion, Marina, Hugh Selwyn Mauberley. Gradually we come to recognize as Eliot's voice a voice that is not heard directly or resoundingly, but only as a murmur among the dramatic words. Gradually, too, in the *Cantos* we hear Pound's voice behind the voices of figures we often know only by remote name or not at all. We find this obliquity, indeed, in the dramatic monologue from Browning to Pound. I recall John Crowe Ransom saying that we should read every poem as if it were a dramatic monologue, even when it appears not to be. Such a reading would be rather artificial, I'm afraid, in taking up a poem that begins, "I walk through the long schoolroom questioning." But Yeats favored a corresponding aesthetic of distance so often – the doctrine of the mask and the anti-self – that we must accept his injunctions. In "The Death of Synge" he writes:

I think that all happiness depends on the energy to assume the mask of some other self; that all joyous or creative life is a rebirth as something not oneself, something which has no memory and is created in a moment and perpetually renewed. We put on a grotesque or solemn painted face to hide us from the terrors of judgment, invent an imaginative Saturnalia where one forgets reality, a game like that of a child, where one loses the infinite pain of self-realization.[22]

This procedure, we see now, is not quite the same as Eliot's or Pound's. Hugh Selwyn Mauberley, J. Alfred Prufrock, Gerontion, and Marina, whether we call them figures or by some other noun, are confined to their implied situations. Eliot and Pound bear responsibility for them and their predicaments, and must take care of them. But when Yeats says that the something which takes the form of a mask "has no memory and is created in a moment and perpetually renewed," he seems to mean that it is part of the creative force in life that goes by any number of names: genius, vision, creativity, Daimon, inspiration, the Muses. When he uses masks or half-masks in his plays – inspired by Gordon Craig – he refuses to let us think that they are persons or personages; they are impersonal forces at large, forms of energy that constitute life but do not respect human laws. They are metaphors which give new life and freedom to our otherwise mere selves. Yeats said of Aedh and Hanrahan, in his early poems, that he used them "more as principles of the mind than as actual personages."[23]

---

[22] Yeats, *Autobiographies*, pp. 503–504.   [23] Yeats, *Variorum Edition of the Poems*, p. 803.

Yeats does not say, in "Ego Dominus Tuus" or elsewhere, how an image helps him to summon up his opposite, unless he means – as perhaps he does – that an image at the furthest remove from oneself is likely to bring forth one's greatest imaginative effort. Coleridge noted, as a mark of Shakespeare's genius on the evidence of his characters, "the utter *aloofness* of the poet's own feelings, from those of which he is at once the painter and the analyst."[24] At this point in Yeats's poem, the first speaker interrupts to say:

> And I would find myself and not an image

and the second rejoins –

> That is our modern hope, and by its light
> We have lit upon the gentle, sensitive mind
> And lost the old nonchalance of the hand;
> Whether we have chosen chisel, pen or brush,
> We are but critics, or but half create,
> Timid, entangled, empty and abashed,
> Lacking the countenance of our friends.[25]

The distancing begins with "our" – "our modern hope" – which denotes with fitting irony not an active fellowship but the little we have been compelled to settle for. It is decent of Yeats to include himself in that diminished state, but there is no escaping his implication that while "the gentle, sensitive mind" is a worthy thing to have, it is merely the best quality that modern bourgeois life has achieved: he regards it as one of the small virtues, enough for ordinary people to be going along with. It is neither heroic nor tragic. And to acquire it, we have had to lose "the old nonchalance of the hand." I take this phrase as a reference to a passage in Castiglione's *Il Cortegiano* which Yeats read in Sir Thomas Hoby's translation in 1903 or thereabouts: he consulted other translations as well. Castiglione gives as an attribute of the ideal courtier – indeed the ideal man – a certain *sprezzatura*, which Hoby translates as "recklessness" and L. E. Opdycke as "nonchalance."[26] It is a virtue, a freedom the courtier can take when he is fully possessed of the courtly qualities. Yeats has toned it down a little in moving from "recklessness" to "nonchalance," but I have no doubt he had the princely qualities of the Italian Renaissance in view. The old nonchalance of the hand is an attribute of the power that

[24] Samuel Taylor Coleridge, *Biographia Literaria*, ed. James Engell and W. Jackson Bate, Bollingen Series 75 (2 vols., Princeton University Press, 1983), Vol. II, p. 22.
[25] Yeats, *Variorum Edition of the Poems*, p. 368.
[26] Cf. Corinna Salvadori, *Yeats and Castiglione: Poet and Courtier* (Dublin: Allen Figgis, 1965), p. 14.

made Urbino and Ferrara. "Lacking the countenance of our friends": because they have the composure we lack. In "Anima Hominis" Yeats says that "our culture, with its doctrine of sincerity and self-realization, made us gentle and passive, and that the Middle Ages and the Renaissance were right to found theirs upon the imitation of Christ or of some classic hero":

Saint Francis and Caesar Borgia made themselves overmastering, creative persons by turning from the mirror and meditating upon a mask .... If we cannot imagine ourselves as different from what we are, and try to assume that second self, we cannot impose a discipline upon ourselves though we may accept one from others. Active virtue, as distinguished from the passive acceptance of a code, is therefore theatrical, consciously dramatic, the wearing of a mask.[27]

In "Ego Dominus Tuus" Yeats gives the second speaker the last word, invoking a second or third or fourth self, his Muse or Daimon:

> I call to the mysterious one who yet
> Shall walk the wet sands by the edge of the stream,
> And look most like me, being indeed my double,
> And prove of all imaginable things
> The most unlike, being my anti-self,
> And, standing by these characters, disclose
> All that I seek; and whisper it as though
> He were afraid the birds, who cry aloud
> Their momentary cries before it is dawn,
> Would carry it away to blasphemous men.[28]

These men are blasphemous because they mock "our secret discipline," the occult traditions of Wisdom which Yeats never ceased to avow.

The awkward word, in the passages I've been quoting, is "sincerity." Whatever Yeats thought of sincerity as a private virtue, or as a social and moral practice, he did not proclaim it in his poetics. I remember Donald Davie, in Dublin a long time ago, calling Yeats the most histrionic of modern poets, with a strong implication that that was not, in a moral perspective, the best kind of poet to be. Yeats, in his first meetings with Oscar Wilde, didn't know how seriously to take Wilde's conversations in which the wizard turned conventional values upside down. Sometimes he took Wilde's words for play, as on one occasion when Wilde called insincerity "'a mere multiplication of the personality' or some such words."[29] But these plays of words tended to

---

[27] W. B. Yeats, *Mythologies* (London: Macmillan, 1961), p. 334.
[28] Yeats, *Variorum Edition of the Poems*, p. 371.   [29] Yeats, *Autobiographies*, p. 285.

lodge in Yeats's mind, and he brought them out when he began to turn his notions of mask, self, and anti-self into an aesthetic theory or at least a working prejudice. In the passage I've quoted about "that cult of sincerity," Yeats immediately glosses it as "that refusal to multiply personality which is characteristic of our time." If you refuse to multiply personality, even for the gratification of seeing your energy take many different forms, it must be because you treasure your own self and would not have another. You have probably been reading Rousseau, Emerson, and Hawthorne. But how can you be sure that what you regard as your treasure is really your own, not someone else's which you have borrowed or appropriated; or merely a personality much the same as the common run of personalities that coincide with your time? Yeats was dismayed when he thought of such a fate. "One thinks of Joyce's *Anna Livia Plurabelle*, Pound's *Cantos*, works of an heroic sincerity, the man, his active faculties in suspense, one finger beating time to a bell sounding and echoing in the depths of his own mind . . . ."[30] The first speaker in "Ego Dominus Tuus" says, in this bewildered spirit: "And I would find myself and not an image." At least he concedes that he would have to "find" himself; he couldn't just reach into his pocket and bring it out.

Yeats came close to this issue again in his BBC broadcast on modern poetry when he quoted a passage from Eliot's "Preludes" and commented:

We older writers disliked this new poetry, but were forced to admit its satiric intensity. It was in Eliot that certain revolutionary War poets, young men who felt they had been dragged away from their studies, from their pleasant life, by the blundering frenzy of old men, found the greater part of their style. They were too near their subject-matter to do, as I think, work of permanent importance, but their social passion, their sense of tragedy, their modernity, have passed into young influential poets of to-day: Auden, Spender, MacNeice, Day-Lewis, and others.[31]

This poetry, Yeats said, "is supported by critics who think it the poetry of the future – in my youth I heard much of the music of the future – and attack all not of their school."[32]

In the Introduction to the *Oxford Book* he gave those poets a larger showing. The first entry in the book is a famous sentence from Walter Pater's essay on Leonardo da Vinci, one of those that meditate on the Mona Lisa and develop an elaborate fantasy in her presence. Yeats misquotes it a little and turns it into *vers libre*, to "show its revolutionary importance":

---

[30] W. B. Yeats, *Essays and Introductions* (London: Macmillan, 1961), p. 405.   [31] Ibid., p. 500.
[32] Ibid., p. 500.

She is older than the rocks among which she sits;
Like the Vampire,
She has been dead many times,
And learned the secrets of the grave;
And has been a diver in deep seas,
And keeps their fallen day about her;
And trafficked for strange webs with Eastern merchants;
And, as Leda,
Was the mother of Helen of Troy,
And, as St Anne,
Was the mother of Mary;
And all this has been to her but as the sound of lyres and flutes,
And lives
Only in the delicacy
With which it has moulded the changing lineaments,
And tinged the eyelids and the hand.[33]

Pater's aim is not Matthew Arnold's, "to see the object as in itself it really is," but "to know one's own impression as it really is, to discriminate it, to realize it distinctly."[34] Impressionism, either Pater's or the French version of it in painting, was at one with Symbolism in privileging the imagination, whether it was called subjectivity or vision. The object in view is merely the occasion – if not the excuse – for one's impression, and it may be allowed to disappear into it. Several pages later in the Introduction, having recalled Pater's sentence in an obscure relation to W. J. Turner's poetry, Yeats says:

Yet one theme perplexes Turner, whether in comedy, dialogue, poem. Somewhere in the middle of it all da Vinci's sitter had private reality like that of the Dark Lady among the women Shakespeare had imagined, but because that private soul is always behind our knowledge, though always hidden it must be the sole source of pain, stupefaction, evil.[35]

Normally when Yeats refers to "soul," we may expect to find "self" nearby, in an antithetical relation to "soul" if not one of outright conflict. But here the private soul is always "behind our knowledge," not in opposition to it but to complete it on its dark side. She may have dire messages to deliver, as distinct from the more accommodating forms of knowledge we enjoy by day, and there may be occasions on which she keeps her secrets, but she has "private reality," probably occult by comparison with her day-time self.

---

[33] Yeats, *Oxford Book of Modern Verse*, p. 1. Cf. Walter Pater, *The Renaissance: Studies in Art and Poetry: The 1893 Text*, ed. Donald L. Hill (Berkeley: University of California Press, 1980), p. 99.
[34] Pater, *The Renaissance*, p. xix.   [35] Yeats, *The Oxford Book of Modern Verse*, pp. xxx–xxxi.

This is supported by Yeats's reference to the Dark Lady of Shakespeare's sonnets, a force of presence, sinister or not, among the more ascertainable ladies of the sonnet-sequence.

The poets who have "pulled off the mask" – Auden, Spender, Day-Lewis, MacNeice – are determined to be sincere. They have perhaps attended to one of the axioms of that motive, Polonius's advice to his son Laertes on his going back to France:

> This above all: to thine own self be true,
> And it must follow, as the night the day,
> Thou canst not then be false to any man.   (*Hamlet*, I.iii.78–80)

– though that hardly means much more than: "I have reared you to be a true Dane; keep that constantly in mind when you're among the fleshpots of Paris." Auden and his associates intend to be sincere, to speak their experience in their realized voices, each his own self; when their verse gains resonance, it is because self in each of them has his private soul behind his knowledge. When Yeats says, "I too have tried to be modern," I think he is recalling the occasions on which he felt impelled to put aside the aesthetic of mask and anti-self and speak from his mere self. As in "Pardon, Old Fathers," from which I quote the final lines:

> Pardon that for a barren passion's sake,
> Although I have come close on forty-nine,
> I have no child, I have nothing but a book,
> Nothing but that to prove your blood and mine.[36]

These are great lines, as Eliot testified when he went on to say that Yeats's naming of his age is significant: "more than half a lifetime to arrive at this freedom of speech. It is a triumph."[37]

Yeats does not define sincerity, unless we take his late commitment to "the foul rag-and-bone shop of the heart" as sufficient definition. Lionel Trilling takes the word to mean "a congruence between avowal and actual feeling."[38] Yeats would have accepted that definition. There is no evidence that he thought of authenticity or any other moral sentiment in an antithetical relation to sincerity. Trilling describes authenticity as suggesting "a more strenuous moral experience than 'sincerity' does, a more exigent conception of the self and of what being true to it consists in, a wider reference to the universe and man's place in it, and a less acceptant

---

[36] Yeats, *Variorum Edition of the Poems*, p. 270.
[37] T. S. Eliot, *Selected Prose*, ed. Frank Kermode (London: Faber and Faber, 1975), pp. 251–252.
[38] Lionel Trilling, *Sincerity and Authenticity* (Cambridge, Mass.: Harvard University Press, 1972), p. 2.

and genial view of the social circumstances of life."[39] I think Yeats was so surprised to find himself talking about the modern success of sincerity that he let the word stand without interrogation. But the cult of sincerity in modern poetry has its dangers. It would be painful if we were to discover that Yeats was not close on forty-nine when he wrote that poem. In truth, he was; we need not have worried. But if we look ahead from that moment, we have to worry and occasionally to be dismayed, as in reading his rant, sincere no doubt, in "Under Ben Bulben." The sincerity of Robert Lowell in *Life Studies* and of Allen Ginsberg in *Howl* also raises a question – even if an answerable question – of shamelessness. If those confessions are true, we feel that we might have been spared them, we are embarrassed by their audacity; but then we are to feel that the poet showed great nobility of heart in confessing them.

It seems clear, then, that Yeats recognized two kinds of modern poetry: the poetry of sincerity and the poetry of distance, the dramatic monologue. Mostly, he committed himself to the dramatic monologue, but he often felt misgiving – as in saying "I too have tried to be modern" – and turned to the poetry of sincerity. We normally mark a change in the development of his poetry in 1903 – not indeed the only change – with the publication of *In the Seven Woods*. The title-poem in that book lets the bad world in because it can't be kept out any longer. Yeats was susceptible to being exasperated by local and international events, at whatever cost to his Symbolism. After 1903, his poems become an extraordinary play of words that can't help acknowledging what Wallace Stevens called "the journalism of subjects," good and bad, private and public, accredited and occult. I associate this development with Yeats's quietly retiring from Symons's Symbolism and putting himself to school with Nietzsche, at the turn of the century. Words may aspire toward the condition of music and dance, but in the end they can't achieve those states of being; they are worldly instruments, they insist on dragging into every context the "impurities" the Symbolist Yeats deplored.

III

If Yeats recognized at least two kinds of modern poetry, is it necessary to posit some high entity that contains them while allowing for their differences? That is where the question of Modernism comes in, whatever we take the word to mean. In June 1924 John Crowe Ransom wrote: "The

---

[39] Ibid., p. 11.

arts generally have had to recognize Modernism – how should poetry escape?" He thought it had not escaped, on the evidence of Imagism and Free Verse, neither of which he welcomed: he had evidently decided not to mention Whitman's *Leaves of Grass* and Eliot's *The Waste Land*. He continued to hold that poetry, as one of the formal arts, "has for its specific problem to play a dual role with words: to conduct a logical sequence with their meanings on the one hand, and to realize an objective pattern with their sounds on the other." Poems that fulfilled the dual role seemed to him little miracles, and he hoped that such felicities would continue to occur:

Now between the meanings of words and their sounds there is ordinarily no discoverable relation except one of accident: and it is therefore miraculous, to the mystic, when words which make sense can also make a uniform objective structure of accents and rhymes. It is a miracle of harmony, of the adaptation of the free inner life to the outward necessity of things.[40]

But he was not sanguine about the future of poetry: it might not be "immense," as Matthew Arnold promised it would be. "One is not so sure in these days," Ransom acknowledged, since poetry "has felt the fatal irritant of Modernism." He thought that poetry might have to yield to prose, for the sense of it, and might have to lay aside its ambition altogether in regard to the sounds. As for his own poetry, he settled for the few occasions on which the little miracle of sense and sound seemed yet again to present itself. He decided not to be intimidated by the examples of Imagism and Free Verse and to take comfort from the unimpeachable poetic traditions.

So did Yeats, who continued to practice the old metres, especially the *ottava rima*, as Helen Vendler has shown in *Our Secret Discipline*. Having separated himself from the poetries of Tennyson, Swinburne, and Arnold, Yeats was ready to think of himself as modern, a poet of his time. That time began for him in 1892. But when he came to choose fourteen poems of his own for the *Oxford Book*, he chose only one from as early as 1913: most of them came from the years 1929 to 1932. *Words for Music Perhaps and Other Poems* (1932) seems to have been his favorite book. "Vacillation" from that book may have been his favorite poem, and the poem in which he comes closest to acknowledging one of the ways of Modernism, "juxtaposition without copula," as we have become used to calling it,

---

[40] John Crowe Ransom, "The Future of Poetry," *The Fugitive*, February 1924, reprinted in Ransom, *Selected Essays*, ed. Thomas Daniel Young and John Hindle (Baton Rouge and London: Louisiana State University Press, 1984), p. 26.

with the spliced assertions of Cubism in mind. Yeats included the eighth section of "Vacillation" – the riposte to Baron Von Hügel – in the *Oxford Book* as if it were his last will and testament:

> Homer is my example and his unchristened heart.
> The lion and the honeycomb, what has Scripture said?
> So get you gone, Von Hügel, though with blessings on your head.[41]

Some early drafts of those lines had "Homer and Shakespeare sang original sin," but in the end Homer was enough.[42] What Scripture said in Judges was that sweetness comes from strength, with Samson to prove it.

Would we gain anything by assuming that Yeats participated in the large, ramifying movement – if it was such – that goes under the name of Modernism? I have heard it argued that Modernism "as a notion is the emptiest of all cultural categories. Unlike the terms Gothic, Renaissance, Baroque, Mannerist, Romantic or Neo-Classical, it designates no describable object in its own right at all: it is entirely lacking in positive content."[43] But that charge may be explained by the disappointment of finding that the art we think of as Modernist, in architecture, music, painting, and literature, did not bring about a transformation of social and economic practices. Unlike those other terms, Modernism seemed to hold out a promise of such transformation, a promise canceled by the dominance of advanced capitalism.

I am inclined to hold that Yeats was modern, but not Modernist. In music, you know that Debussy, Schoenberg, Alban Berg, and Webern made different sounds than did Rachmaninov, Mahler, Richard Strauss, or even Stravinsky. In *The Philosophy of Modern Music* Adorno gave reasons for approving the difference. In painting, if you want to understand what you are looking at in a work by Manet or Cézanne, T. J. Clark's *The Painting of Modern Life* points you in a good if not necessarily the right direction. But literature can't get rid of words and their standard meanings quite as easily as sounds can be distributed across an orchestra or paint applied to canvas without comment. Efforts to apply to literature the considerations that have proved useful in trying to define Modernism in painting, architecture, and music have not been successful. We hear a good deal these days about "material" and the materiality of language. But language isn't material as canvas and paint are: words are

---

[41] Yeats, *Variorum Edition of the Poems*, p. 503.

[42] W. B. Yeats, *Words for Music Perhaps and Other Poems: Manuscript Materials*, ed. David R. Clark (Ithaca and London: Cornell University Press, 1999), p. 63.

[43] Perry Anderson, *A Zone of Engagement* (London: Verso, 1992), p. 45.

sounds, creative events in speech and writing. Meaning is a more oppressive nuisance in literature than in any other art; it is like a poor relation we're responsible for and can't contemplate getting rid of. Meanwhile we should be content to think of "the modern" – as distinct from "the Modernist" – as a sufficient context for Yeats's work: it allows for many possibilities, without making any promises. Better still, it does not intimidate, as the ideology of Modernism does.

PART IV

On Joyce

CHAPTER 8

A plain approach to Ulysses

Sometime in 1904 James Joyce, much given to drink and dissipation but not to violence, stumbled into a fracas in Dublin. Providentially he was rescued by a man named Alfred H. Hunter. Sobered up, Joyce conceived the notion of turning the episode into a short story and calling it "Ulysses." It is not clear how the title would have suited the story or how the story might have been developed to answer the title. Homer's Odysseus was commonly thought of as a man of the world, a voyager, "the interminable adventurer," as Wallace Stevens calls him in "The World as Meditation." He was also admired as a man of parts, endlessly resourceful. But he was rarely identified with the Good Samaritan. Joyce intended to include the story in a book called *Dubliners*. He knew little about Hunter, except that he was reputed to be a Jew and to have an unfaithful wife. In the event, Joyce didn't write the story. On February 6, 1907 he told his brother Stanislaus that it "never got any forrader than the title." But the matter didn't end there. Several years later and long after the publication of *Dubliners*, the unwritten story became chapter 16 ("Eumaeus") of a long novel, *Ulysses*. In that chapter Leopold Bloom rescues Stephen Dedalus "in orthodox Samaritan fashion" from a bad night on the town and brings him to the cabman's shelter under the Loop Line Bridge, near Butt Bridge and the Custom House. The scene is Dublin, the hour 1 a.m., time to go home if one had a home.

Joyce started work on the book in 1914, declared it finished on October 29, 1921, and saw it published, copiously error-ridden, on his fortieth birthday, February 2, 1922. Alfred H. Hunter remained as an element in the hero of *Ulysses*, Leopold Bloom, but merely one of many. Leopold Paula Bloom, to give him his full name, is a Jew by race, but he is not a religious man. His mother was Ellen Higgins, his father Lipoti Virag or Virag Lipoti, who left his native Hungary about 1852, played Wandering

---

* Introduction, without footnotes, written for an unpublished edition of *Ulysses*.

157

Jew for many years, turned up in London in 1865, moved to Dublin, converted to the Church of Ireland upon the persuasion of the Society for Promoting Christianity among the Jews, changed his name to Rudolph Bloom, and fathered upon Ellen a child, Leopold, born about May 6, 1866 at 52 Clanbrassil Street. The child was baptized a Protestant in the Church of St. Nicholas Without, the Coombe. Twenty-two years later the same Leopold Paula Bloom was baptized a Catholic in the Church of the Three Patrons, Rathgar, Dublin, preparatory to his marrying Marion Tweedy, four years and four months his junior. So, yes, he is a Jew. And he has a wife who, at least on the afternoon of June 16, 1904, is unfaithful to him. But Leopold Bloom is not merely Alfred H. Hunter, transcribed. Several other gentlemen in their early-middle years contributed to his plenitude: notably Charles Chance, a canvasser for advertisements, whose wife was the soprano Madame Marie Tallon, and Ettore Schmitz, a friend of Joyce's in Trieste, better known as Italo Svevo, novelist. In addition, there is the not-to-be-forgotten Ulysses, Latinized name of Homer's wanderer, who departs from his residence in Ithaca, undergoes sundry torments and temptations, and returns home at length to his patient wife Penelope.

But let us start with a young man far gone in drink and vanity and call him Stephen Dedalus, making him twenty-two, two years older than he was when last heard of in *A Portrait of the Artist as a Young Man*. He is still in practice as a promising young man, an impending poet, man of letters, employed for the time being by Mr. Deasy to teach the upper-middle-class youth of Dalkey and its environs. In one version Stephen is "the young poet who found a refuge from his labours of pedagogy and metaphysical inquisition in the convivial atmosphere of Socratic discussion." His father is Simon Dedalus, but the relation in Greek mythology between Daedalus (so spelt) and his son Icarus is taken somewhat loosely in *Ulysses*. In the myth, Daedalus has constructed a labyrinth for Minos; he has helped Ariadne in providing Theseus with a ball of thread which enables him to escape. Imprisoned in the labyrinth for this treachery, Daedalus devises a pair of wings, made of wax, by which he and Icarus effect their escape. But Icarus, like Stephen Dedalus too vain for his good, flies close to the sun, the wax is melted, and he falls into the sea. No wonder Stephen is a hydrophobe. "You were going to do wonders, what?" he taunts himself in the third chapter of *Ulysses*, his flight to Paris by way of Newhaven and Dieppe having resulted in many books read but none written. He has returned to Dublin with little to show of Paris but his Latin-quarter hat. The telegram that summoned him was conspicuously deformed: "Nother dying come home father."

Add to these constituents Leopold Bloom, thirty-eight years old though he sounds older, 5 feet 9 1/2 inches tall, 11 st. 4 lbs in weight, by profession for the moment a "staid agent of publicity," by prudence and calculation "holder of a modest substance in the funds." He is an outsider in Dublin, though born there; partly because he is a Jew, more to the point because he is reluctant to spend money on the provision of drink for idle Dubliners. Add, too, an unfaithful wife Marion or Molly, and her partner in sexual congress on this Thursday June 16, 1904, one Hugh ("Blazes") Boylan – "He's coming in the afternoon." "Think no more about that," Bloom admonishes himself while thinking about little else. "Stop. Stop. If it was it was. Must." An hour later: "Pub clock five minutes fast. Time going on. Hands moving. Two. Not yet." So Bloom beguiles the time that declines to be beguiled: he wanders the streets of Dublin, absenting himself from the homestead at 7 Eccles Street, Molly's assignation with Boylan having been arranged to begin at 4 p.m. and to be adjourned at an unstated hour. "Then about six o'clock I can. Six. Six. Time will be gone then. She." If all goes well for Boylan, and evidently it does, this Thursday tryst will lead to another visit the following Monday, same time, same warm place. But sufficient for the day: Bloom has many hours to kill before he can assume that the coast is clear and he can go home and slip without interrogation or fuss into Molly's bed. Six o'clock comes and goes. Bloom leaves Barney Kiernan's public house, visits Mrs Dignam in Sandymount, and masturbates upon watching a girl on the Strand. Meanwhile he has much on his mind besides Molly and Boylan: his father, who poisoned himself in the Queen's Hotel, Ennis; his son Rudy, born December 29, 1893 – "He would be eleven now if he had lived" – who died eleven days later, January 9, 1894; his daughter Milly, born June 15, 1889, now fifteen and apprenticed to a photographer in Mullingar, where she is attracting the sexual attention of one Alec Bannon – "a young student comes here some evenings named Bannon his cousins or something are big swells" – from whom no good is expected.

Joyce's method was always the same: keep the structure of the story simple – he was not given to complex plotting – but enhance its texture, the spaces between the events. On September 21, 1920 he explained in a letter to Carlo Linati what he had in view with *Ulysses*:

It is an epic of two races (Israelite-Irish) and at the same time the cycle of the human body as well as a little story of a day (life). The character of Ulysses always fascinated me – even when a boy. Imagine, fifteen years ago I started writing it as a short story for *Dubliners*! For seven years I have been working at this book – blast it! It is also a sort of encyclopaedia. My intention is to transpose the myth *sub specie temporis nostri.* Each adventure (that is, every hour, every organ, every art being interconnected and interrelated in the structural scheme of the whole) should not only condition but even create its own technique. Each adventure is so to say one person although it is composed of persons – as Aquinas relates of the angelic hosts.

Sub specie temporis nostri means telling an old story as if it were new. A myth is a story told for the benefit of the community to which it is addressed: it enables the members of the community to ascribe names and deeds to the otherwise opaque forces that beset them. Wishing to transpose the events of the *Odyssey* into a day in the life of early twentieth-century Dublin, Joyce necessarily domesticates his heroes and villains, but he retains shadowings of the epic deeds they don't know they're miming. Instead of a battle, we have a row in Barney Kiernan's pub; instead of a sword, Bloom wields a cigar. Still, shadows are tokens of substances. The old myths are still there to be alluded to and reinterpreted, as in Camus's *The Myth of Sisyphus*, Valéry's "Mon Faust," and Mann's *Doctor Faustus*.

Before writing *Ulysses* Joyce had the Homeric figure of Telemachus in his head, too, the Stephen Dedalus of the *Portrait*, a book that ends with Stephen's invocation to "Old father, old artificer" to "stand me now and ever in good stead." It was an easy thing, except for the writing, to have Odysseus (Ulysses: Bloom) search for a son, and a son (Telemachus: Daedalus: Dedalus) search for a father. No, that would be naive. Let father search for son without knowing that that is what he is doing; let son spend his substance avoiding his biological father and every spiritual father. They must meet, father and son, but equivocally, in the end.

Except for the title – but that is a big exception – it would be possible to read *Ulysses* without adverting to the *Odyssey*. Little is to be gained by consulting the latter to resolve difficulties in the former. In certain chapters a recollection of the Prodigal Son or the Good Samaritan is more helpful. But Joyce instructed his first readers to think of Homer. At least two of his most influential devotees obeyed him. Ezra Pound thought the *Odyssey* was useful to Joyce as scaffolding: the house once built, he could let readers take it down by ignoring it. Pound didn't contest the matter. Once he had accepted that Joyce was a superb writer and that his works must be helped into publication, he took the author's word for the details. If there was a chapter or a paragraph that Pound didn't like, no matter. "The excuse for parts of *Ulysses* is the whole of *Ulysses*," he told Joyce.

T. S. Eliot was a more systematic reader. When he read the early chapters of *Ulysses* in the *Little Review*, he was confused, but the more he thought of the book as it was developing, the more convinced he became not only that it was a great work but that it was a liberating event in modern literature. Reviewing the book in the *Dial* for November 1923 he presented it as a work of Einsteinian significance, not because it enabled writers to write about anything without equivocation or euphemism but because it showed how the meaninglessness of mere events might be redeemed. An event, considered merely in itself, may be nothing: it becomes significant only when it is construed in relation to a larger perspective, a "higher dream," a grander story in which it participates. This interpretation has been immensely influential, even though it tells us more about Eliot's needs as the author of *The Waste Land* than about the structure of *Ulysses*. Eliot talked to Pound about the book in those terms. Pound wasn't especially interested. He had already decided that *Ulysses* was good, so he didn't feel obliged to supply an elaborate reason for its merit. He thought Joyce went to excess with the lavatory paragraphs. Leopold Bloom at stool was not a consideration of endless interest. No matter. Joyce was a good writer in a tradition Pound thought of as French: Stendhal and Flaubert were his masters. Eliot also talked about *Ulysses* to Virginia and Leonard Woolf. Mrs. Woolf was repelled by it at first and thought Joyce merely low-bred, but eventually Eliot persuaded her that *Ulysses* was a major work.

In the *Dial* review of *Ulysses* Eliot distinguishes between "the narrative method" and Joyce's "mythical method." By "narrative method" Eliot means the procedures of the realistic novel, in which the novelist invents characters and situations and confines his attention to the level of being on which they are plausibly to be found: there is presumably no other level to be alluded to. These characters and events have whatever value the novelist succeeds in giving them, but they have no other mode of existence than that of being recognizable and therefore persuasive. For the moment and under the impact of *Ulysses*, Eliot thought that realism had come to an end with Flaubert and James: he later recanted that notion. In 1923 he convinced himself that modern research in ethnology, comparative mythology, and anthropology had made it possible to find the significance of characters and events on a level of being other than that on which they are ordinarily found. If certain myths are still alive in certain communities, they maintain that life by being repeated day by day. An ordinary event becomes significant in the light of the myth it enacts, however residually. It acquires a halo of significance when it is seen under a higher perspective, or when it can be shown to participate in a form, a pattern of being, at a certain remove from the level on which otherwise it is merely an event like any other. This possibility was a matter of moment to Eliot when he was intuiting a form for *The Waste Land* and trying to find a principle of order to give shape and significance to what, lacking such a principle, could only be local instances of futility and anarchy. The role of Tiresias in that poem corresponds, in a measure, to that of the Homeric myth in *Ulysses*. Tiresias, adept of sexual experience male and female, is qualified to bring to bear upon the events of the poem a perspective cognitively more comprehensive than that on which otherwise they proceed. In later poems Eliot summons to attend on the events certain figures – from Dante, St. John of the Cross, Dame Juliana of Norwich and other holy sources – which bring a higher perspective to bear on the local figures, such as they are. That is what Eliot's becoming a Christian (Anglican) meant to the poetry.

But I should not make this matter seem merely pious. Eliot knew that the method, adumbrated by Yeats as he deemed it to be, does not commit its exponent to piety. In the poems to which I assume Eliot is referring – "No Second Troy," for instance – Yeats is not claiming that the unnamed woman (Maud Gonne, let us say) is identical in scale, historical consequence, or even in beauty with Helen of Troy. He is proposing a relation, its terms and value to be determined upon consideration, between the "she" of the modern poem and Homer's Helen. "Was there another Troy for her to burn?" he asks. Readers are free to respond to that question as they please. Some may regard it as absurd; in that event the poem can't survive. But there is a certain latitude for Yeats and for his readers. A relation is proposed between a great epic figure and a modern correlative instance. The significance of the modern instance is in that relation, not merely in herself or her local historical conditions. But acts of reverence are not required.

Similarly Joyce's relation to Homer, like Dante's, is respectful but quizzical. He doesn't enforce the myth as stringently as Eliot does, or Yeats: there is no intention of exerting critical or moral pressure upon Bloom as Eliot directs Tiresias's age-old irony upon the "young man carbuncular" and the typist he seduces. Joyce doesn't invite us to stand in judgment upon Bloom or find him guilty of harboring trivial images. Bloom is a canvasser for advertisements, catering to the induced desires of the petit-bourgeois world he himself exemplifies. It is not our business to condescend to him. In the *Inferno* Dante treats Odysseus severely: he regards him as a busy fool, twitchingly curious about the world; his mind should have been directed to first and last things. Joyce makes that curiosity one of Bloom's charming qualities. We find it endearing that

Bloom is so undemanding, so willing to be interested in the parade as it passes and in the associations his mind makes as it goes along. Joyce doesn't ask us, on Bloom's behalf, for anything more than to be interested. The quality of the interest or the nature of the feelings on show is not interrogated. By contrast with Stephen, who regards the world as mostly beneath his notice, Bloom is content with the fate of being ordinary. He doesn't claim that he was made for higher things or resent the mundane quality of the issues he is obliged to have on his mind. In this he resembles his creator. Joyce once said of himself that he had the mind of a grocer's assistant. As a writer, he asked only that he be allowed to write what he wanted, to have his sources and to obey them or play fast and loose with them. On the whole, his relation to Homer is genial rather than ironic. I call Bloom the hero of *Ulysses* because he shadows the more substantial hero, Odysseus. Bloom doesn't set out to do anything or to go anywhere; he is merely passing the time, going to a funeral, trying to get an advertisement placed, conducting a mild affair of the heart by means of pseudonymous letters. His homecoming is the achievement of having stayed out long enough to find Boylan gone and the coast clear. On December 10, 1920 Joyce writing to Frank Budgen said:

A point about Ulysses (Bloom). He romances about Ithaca (Oi want teh gow beck teh the Mawl Enn Road, s'elp me!) and when he gets back it gives him the pip.

Not that Bloom expected to find Penelope waiting up for him: in the last chapter, before falling asleep, she is exciting herself with old memories and the new possibility of taking Stephen Dedalus to bed. As for Stephen: our Telemachus is mainly burdened with wrecked teeth, a bad conscience about his dead mother, unfulfilled literary ambition, and resentment directed upon his associates.

Joyce withholds his irony from Homer's Odysseus, only to turn it upon the several institutions that encompass him, including Ireland, the British Empire, the Roman Catholic Church, and Yeats's Irish Literary Revival, the latter a project embodied in the Abbey Theatre. The Ireland that Joyce mocks is the one that Yeats and his associates invented, compounded of Celtic lore, intimations of the folk, myths that have the disadvantage of not being Greek, an Ireland rural, primitive, illiterate, and garrulous. In his doggerel poems, as in *Ulysses,* Joyce ridiculed the Irish Literary Revival, the Gaelic League, and the strivings that led to the founding of the Abbey. His own Ireland, he took care not to admit, is equally an invention, it does not come with the authority of History or Natural Law, it is a construction like any other. Unlike Yeats's and opposed to that, it is predicated upon a city,

Dublin, and upon social classes which have meaning chiefly in a city. Yeats, too, wrote of Dublin, but mainly to remark "the daily spite of this unmannerly town": his spiritual home was rural, pre-industrial Ireland, Coole Park and Innisfree, the lovely West. If Yeats invented that Ireland, Lady Gregory, Synge, AE (George Russell) and Douglas Hyde adorned the invention and are suitably teased in *Ulysses*. But Yeats isn't mocked. He is Joyce's great antagonist. One of Yeats's poems, "Who Goes with Fergus?" – set to music – stays in Stephen's mind throughout the book and is recalled in poignant association with his dead mother:

> And no more turn aside and brood
> Upon love's bitter mystery
> For Fergus rules the brazen cars.

When Joyce tilts at the Empire, it is not because he has suddenly aligned himself with nationalists and patriots, but because the Empire is an instrument of power. Nationalism and patriotism also get a wretched press in *Ulysses*, presented as they are in the person of the Citizen in chapter 12, a boor, a barbarian. Every reference to the Irish language is mockery, only partly mitigated by the fact that the mocker is usually Buck Mulligan, to whom nothing is sacrosanct. In the *Portrait* Joyce allowed Stephen to resent the fact that the language spoken in Ireland was imposed by foreigners, but little of that sentiment has been retained in *Ulysses*. Joyce was not prepared to honor the Irish language as if it were French or Italian. Oddly, *Ulysses* suggests that Bloom may have been associated with Arthur Griffith, founder of Sinn Féin, who may have explained to him that Hungary achieved its independence from the Austro-Hungarian Empire by maintaining passive resistance. Griffith's thoughts on the resurrection of Hungary were published in 1904. For many years, readers of Joyce assumed that he had no political convictions, being preoccupied with an art that in his practice had no need of them. He was known to have certain sentiments, among them devotion to Parnell and affection for Griffith. But when it was noted that Joyce's shelves contained many books of vaguely socialist or anarchist persuasion, the earlier assumption was amended. He had a politics, it was decided, even if it wasn't a feasible one in any foreseeable world. Meanwhile he had no great affection for the British Empire or its imposition of pink upon the map of the known world.

He had no affection for the Roman Catholic Church, either, at least in its Irish manifestation. Joyce was born into a Catholic household and brought up – so far as he could be said to have been brought up – as a Catholic, and therefore he was marked for life. He left the Church, but the Church never left him, he never let it alone. Its theology appealed to him, especially in the form of the *Summa* of Aquinas, and he greatly admired Newman. The intellectual structure of *Ulysses* is founded upon Aristotle and Aquinas. Trained in a Jesuit school, Joyce never escaped from the Order. Chapter 17, weird as it is, becomes lucid when we read it as an extreme development of Jesuit catechetical procedures. Chapter 15, the "Nighttown" chapter, is a phantasmagoria, but what it mainly expresses, as E. R. Curtius observed, is "the choking despair of the apostate."

But the institution upon which Joyce directed his most persistent irony was narration itself. "Each adventure ... should not only condition but even create its own technique." What could that admonition mean? In practice it meant that Joyce used all the available narrative procedures without committing himself to the epistemological stance implied by any of them. He appropriated every available style of English to the point at which he could be said to have no style of his own but only an inordinate knack of appropriation. Some passages of the book are direct quotation: "O my! Puddeny pie! protested Ciss. He has his bib destroyed." Some are instances of apparently objective narration: "Mr Bloom stooped and turned over a piece of paper on the strand. He brought it near his eyes and peered." Some are "interior monologue," as if the character were musing to himself; so the passage after the one about Bloom and the piece of paper reads:

Letter? No. Can't read. Better go. Better. I'm tired to move. Page of an old copybook. All those holes and pebbles. Who could count them? Never know what you find.

Some parts of the narrative are handed over to a figure, nameless as in the scene in Barney Kiernan's, where the comedy arises from the inadequacy of the "point of view" to report the matters assigned to it, trivial as many of them are. It is a parody of Henry James's procedure, since James invariably entrusted the point of view to a character well qualified for the job. In *Ulysses* many passages are conveyed in the style – "indirect free style," as critics call it – the character in the case would use, were he or she narrating it. As if Gertrude MacDowell, for instance, were in charge, lifting her head from a favorite fiction:

Miss puny little Edy's countenance fell to no slight extent and Gerty could see by her looking as black as thunder that she was simply in a towering rage though she hid it, the little kinnatt, because that shaft had struck home for her petty jealousy and they both knew that she was something aloof, apart, in another sphere, that she was not of them and never would be and there was somebody else too that knew it and saw it so they could put that in their pipe and smoke it.

"In another sphere" and "in a towering rage" come, like the contents of Emma Bovary's mind, from magazines and books of a certain kind; but there are many passages which don't observe any of these conventions of style, passages in which the words in their sequence can't be ascribed to a character or even to an omniscient, silent witness. To make sense of these, we have to think of the invention of the printing press, and of one of the possibilities it disclosed, that of separating words from any hypothetical speaker. Anonymous or pseudonymous publication was the first beneficiary, crucial to pamphleteers in times of licensing laws and paper wars. A further possibility was a new linguistics, founded not upon the "speech acts" of an individual but upon those of a society, a "collective assemblage" as it has been called. According to that linguistic theory, when I open my mouth and say something, I enjoy a concession permitted by the collective assemblage of which I am a part: enjoy, subject to certain constraints of meaning, communication, and interpretation. The words I speak are the words I've learnt by growing up in, say, Dublin. The language spoken is the language heard and repeated, day by day. Call it hearsay: not "you took the words out of my mouth," but "you put the words into my mouth." Or as Bloom says to himself, "Never know whose thoughts you're chewing." Communal memory retains such utterances, and the printing press dispenses them upon request. If in 1904 the English language in Dublin had been analyzed, it would have been found to contain many idiolects, signs of class distinction, trade lore, street locutions, formal terms to be discovered in newspapers, advertisements, printed invitations, agendas, committee reports, letters to the Editor. Joyce took most of his information for *Ulysses* from his memory, newspapers, family lore, and *Thom's Directory*. Not only did he commit to paper several passages which defeat the elocutionist, but he capitalized upon the fact that print will wait till you come to it, and will stay in place when your attention has wandered off. If you've missed something, you can come back to it. So the first two pages of chapter 11 are meaningless for the time being, while you're reading them, but the meaning is restored to them in every detail a page or two later. Since the "art" of the chapter is music, more specifically nineteenth-century opera, these first pages are an overture, separated in the first edition by a blank page from the opera that ensues. What we hear, in those first pages of "Sirens," is a rigmarole of motifs, but wait, all will be revealed in time. Hence the first two lines of the chapter:

> Bronze by gold heard the hoofirons, steelyringing.
> Imperthnthn thnthnthn.

Patience – hard thing: two pages later all is clear. The two barmaids in the Ormond Hotel, bronze-haired Lydia Douce and gold-haired Mina Kennedy, are adverting to the Viceregal party going by, having issued from the great Lodge in Phoenix Park. To be precise:

Bronze by gold, miss Douce's head by miss Kennedy's head, over the crossblind of the Ormond bar heard the viceregal hoofs go by, ringing steel.

As for the printable but unspeakable words beginning with "I" and "t," these turn out to be the saucy boots's mocking imitation of Miss Douce's threat to report him to Mrs. de Massey for his "impertinent insolence."

Enjoying latitude available from the printing press, Joyce often presents us with a problem: how do we know, especially in some later chapters, what has "really" happened as if it were in a standard novel, and what is fantasy, phantasmagoria, as in much of chapter 15? Short answer: an event is something witnessed by two or more people independently. Thus a Viceregal cavalcade proceeds from Phoenix Park through the city and back again. Alec Bannon lives in Mullingar. At a certain moment a cloud covers the sun and turns Dublin Bay greenish. There has been an outbreak of foot-and-mouth disease. How do we know these things? Because several people have borne witness to them. Matters become more doubtful in chapters of hallucination caused by drink, exhaustion, and debauchery: verification can't occur. Readers deal with this doubt in various ways. Eliot thought that the later chapters showed "a turning from the visible world to draw rather on the resources of phantasmagoria," perhaps as a consequence of Joyce's failed eyesight. Other readers think we have two fictions for the price of one: a fairly straightforward realistic, psychological novel for the first ten chapters, followed by six chapters in which Joyce's language declares itself independent of characters and iden- tities, and brought to a conclusion by two chapters in which the book returns to veridical satisfactions. My own view: I believe in the printing press and the collective assemblage to which it corresponds. We are reading one book, therefore, not two; each chapter is its own master. In chapter 15, set in a brothel in Mecklenburgh Street, Stephen is drunk but still orderly enough to speculate that "gesture, not music not odour, would be a universal language, the gift of tongues rendering visible not the lay sense but the first entelechy, the structural rhythm." To which his companion-at-arms Lynch replies: "Pornosophical philotheology. Meta- physics in Mecklenburgh Street!" Not decisive, but worth making a note of.

Ulysses is a book big enough to move about in and to recall certain chapters with particular affection. My favorite chapter comes early on.

Stephen is teaching at Mr. Deasy's school in Dalkey: the subjects ramble from ancient history to Milton's "Lycidas." After class, one of the boys, Cyril Sargent, defeated by the mysteries of arithmetic, brings his lesson to Stephen, and Stephen helps him with the sums. Before the instruction begins, several images float into Stephen's mind: the boy, his mother, Stephen's own mother, and a riddle about a fox burying his grandmother under a hollybush. Then he looks at Cyril:

Ugly and futile: lean neck and thick hair and a stain of ink, a snail's bed. Yet someone had loved him, borne him in her arms and in her heart. But for her the race of the world would have trampled him underfoot, a squashed boneless snail. She had loved his weak watery blood drained from her own. Was that then real? The only true thing in life? His mother's prostrate body the fiery Columbanus in holy zeal bestrode. She was no more: the trembling skeleton of a twig burnt in the fire, an odour of rosewood and wetted ashes. She had saved him from being trampled underfoot and had gone, scarcely having been. A poor soul gone to heaven: and on a heath beneath winking stars a fox, red reek of rapine in his fur, with merciless bright eyes scraped in the earth, listened, scraped up the earth, listened, scraped and scraped.

This passage removes the difference in general attitude between Stephen and Leopold. When we say, as a generalization, that Stephen thinks the world not good enough for his attention and Bloom would not think of raising that question, we have to forget such moments as this one. Later, Stephen demands to escape from conditions and to flee to first entelechies, but for the moment he is patient. As Joyce is. Where Yeats is always reaching for mastery, a style of command, Joyce is reaching for many styles, reflecting many differences. Not because he was himself indifferent, but because he loved the multiplicity of the world and wanted only to imagine its forms. Nothing very much happens in *Ulysses*, if we think of major occasions and an intricate plot. A man leaves his home and, many painful hours later, returns to a bed still warm from the conjunction of his wife and an interloper. He brings with him a younger man who may or may not accept his hospitality. So much, or so little, for plot. The day and much of the night are occupied by notions, images, and talk. The city traversed during those long hours is not a place of work or efficiency. Mr. Deasy runs a school, Stephen Dedalus teaches there – but not for long; Barney Kiernan runs a public house, someone drives cattle to the North Wall, there are doctors and nurses in the Holles Street Maternity Hospital. But *Ulysses* doesn't convey the impression of a society preoccupied with work, trade, and getting on in the world. In 1904 Ireland was a country of thirty-two counties still part, if a neglected part, of the British

Empire. Dublin was a city, but not a thriving one: it was the result of sluggish and haphazard development since the Famine of the 1840s. It is no wonder that a reader of *Ulysses* believes that the Dublin trams ran on talk and reverie. History is not the history of consciousness, loose association, and habit, but a reader of *Ulysses* is inclined to think it might be. Paddy Dignam dies, and Molly Bloom copulates with Blazes Boylan: these events are not to be thought away. But the reality of Dublin for the most part seems to consist of talk, rumination, old songs, the drift of associations idly held in someone's mind. The chapters are replete, but indiscriminate, as if Joyce saw no good reason for preferring one motif to another, one style to another. Whatever comes into Bloom's mind has as much right to be there as anything else: no consideration of relevance is allowed to assert itself.

CHAPTER 9

Joyce, Leavis, and the revolution of the word

I

I would like to raise two related questions about literary criticism. The first is: does it make sense to invoke, as a critical consideration, the "spirit" of a language – the English language, for instance, or the American language, or Spanish, French, or any other? If it does, is this spirit to be construed essentially or historically: does it float free of its conditions or is it found only among those conditions? And again: is it pertinent for a critic to maintain, literary evaluation being in question, that a particular work of literature does or does not acknowledge the "spirit" of the language in which it is written? Does this matter? I'll refer to two occasions on which a critic apparently assumed that there is indeed a "spirit of the English language," that it has certain qualities – socially and historically acquired – and that the work in question is perverse for having transgressed that spirit.

In September 1933 F. R. Leavis published in *Scrutiny* a review of several items from Joyce's workshop and its vicinity: *Anna Livia Plurabelle*, fourteen issues of the journal *transition*, *Haveth Childers Everywhere*, *Two Tales of Shem and Shaun*, Eugene Jolas's *The Language of Night*, and *Our Exagmination Round his Factification for Incamination of Work in Progress*, ascribed to "Samuel Beckett and Others." Leavis admired *Ulysses*, or at least parts of it, notably the "Proteus" chapter – Stephen Dedalus walking along Sandymount Strand – but he had nothing warm to say of *Work in Progress* and he rejected the arguments in its favor put forward in the *Exagmination*. He was particularly exasperated by Jolas's contribution to that book – "The Revolution of Language and James Joyce" – and by his claim that "in developing his medium to the fullest, Mr. Joyce is after all doing only what Shakespeare has done in his later plays, such as *The*

* *The Sewanee Review*, Vol. 112, No. 3 (Summer 2004).

Winter's Tale and *Cymbeline*."[1] To enforce that claim, Jolas quoted three short passages from the first Act of *Cymbeline* and three from the fifth. From the first, he quoted a few lines of conversation between "two Gentlemen" in which one of them says that while the King is distressed by his daughter's marriage, she has in fact chosen an incomparable man:

> FIRST GENTLEMAN: I do not think
> So fair an outward and such stuff within
> Endows a man but he.
> SECOND GENTLEMAN: You speak him far.
> FIRST GENTLEMAN: I do extend him, sir, within himself,
> Crush him together rather than unfold
> His measure duly.[2]

The verbal murmuring from "fair" to "far" to "extend" is hardly worth the labor. As Frank Kermode says: "The struggle with the idea that in straining to praise him the Gentleman has managed to diminish rather than exaggerate Posthumus's virtues seems to be simply a waste of energy – evidence, perhaps, that there was a nervous excess of energy to be wasted."[3] It's not clear whether Kermode means a nervous excess of energy in the Gentleman or in the play at large which might have wasted itself in any character but happens to start the wasting with the First Gentleman. In the chapter of *Shakespeare's Language* on *Macbeth* Kermode refers again to "an excess of energy," this time on Shakespeare's part, resulting in verse "that sometimes makes so much trouble for itself," complicating what might well have been simple.[4] Jolas didn't comment on the First Gentleman's lines, but presumably he quoted them to show that Shakespeare, like Joyce in *Work in Progress*, was willing to exceed the strict requirements of narration and description and to give the language unlimited freedom. In one of the passages that Jolas quoted from the fifth Act, Iachimo tells Cymbeline about Posthumus –

> sitting sadly,
> Hearing us praise our loves of Italy
> For beauty that made barren the swell'd boast
> Of him that best could speak, for feature, laming

---

[1] Eugene Jolas, "The Revolution of Language and James Joyce," in *Our Exagmination Round his Factification for Incamination of Work in Progress* (London: Faber and Faber, second impression, 1961), pp. 86–87.

[2] *Cymbeline*, I.i.22–27, in Hardin Craig and David Bevington (eds.), *The Complete Works of Shakespeare* (Glenview, Ill.: Scott, Foresman and Company, 1973), p. 1182.

[3] Frank Kermode, *Shakespeare's Language* (New York: Farrar, Straus, Giroux, 2000), p. 265.

[4] Ibid., p. 207.

> The shrine of Venus, or straight-pight Minerva,
> Postures beyond brief nature, for condition,
> A shop of all the qualities that man
> Loves woman for, besides that hook of wiving,
> Fairness which strikes the eye.[5]

It is high talk, but Shakespeare's first audiences probably took it in their stride. The style is formulaic, a standard version of hyperbole with a few local encrustations. A common member of the audience was unlikely to ask himself the questions an adept of conceits would linger on: precisely how the shrine of Venus could be lamed or why Minerva is called "straight-pight." In such passages, according to Jolas, Shakespeare "obviously embarked on new word sensations before reaching that haven of peacefulness mirrored in the final benediction speech from the latter play [*Cymbeline*]." But Jolas doesn't recognize that Shakespeare provided something for everybody and gave the groundlings enough to get the drift of what was going on. Cultivated members of the audience got, in addition, more-than-enough verbal subtlety to stretch their minds. The King himself is irritated with Iachimo's speech, but not because he can't keep up with its intricacies. "I stand on fire," he says to Iachimo: "come to the matter." It is hard to see why Jolas invoked this speech to endorse Joyce's procedures in *Work in Progress*, unless he thought that any instance of the ornate style in Shakespeare would help to make his case. Leavis rejected the comparison:

Mr. Joyce's liberties with English are essentially unlike Shakespeare's. Shakespeare's were not the product of a desire to "develop his medium to the fullest," but of a pressure of something to be conveyed. One insists, it can hardly be insisted too much, that the study of a Shakespeare play must start with the words; but it was not there that Shakespeare – the great Shakespeare – started: the words matter because they lead down to what they came from. He was in the early wanton period, it is true, an amateur of verbal fancies and ingenuities, but in the mature plays, and especially in the late plays stressed above, it is the burden to be delivered, the precise and urgent command from within, that determines expression – tyrannically. That is Shakespeare's greatness: the complete subjection – subjugation – of the medium to the uncompromising, complex and delicate need that uses it. Those miraculous intricacies of expression could have come only to one whose medium was for him strictly a medium; an object of interest only as something that, under the creative compulsion, identified itself with what insisted on being expressed: the linguistic audacities are derivative.[6]

---

[5] *Cymbeline*, V.v.160–168.
[6] F. R. Leavis, *For Continuity* (Cambridge: The Minority Press, 1933), p. 208.

Joyce's style in *Work in Progress* seemed to Leavis to have taken a wrong turn. The interest in words and their promiscuous relations evidently came first: more and more possibilities of stratification and complication then proposed themselves. The organization that Joyce achieved in *Work in Progress*, according to Leavis, was "external and mechanical." To justify such a procedure, Joyce would have had to have "a commanding theme, animated by some impulse from the inner life capable of maintaining a high pressure." He had a sufficient theme in *Ulysses* and the earlier books, where "the substance is clearly the author's personal history and the pressure immediately personal urgency." The historical particularity in those books, Leavis said, "is explicit enough and it is hardly impertinent to say that *Ulysses* is clearly a catharsis." But Leavis found no such theme in *Work in Progress*. If one asks, he says, "what controls the interest in technique, the preoccupation with the means of expression, in the *Work in Progress*, the answer is a reference to Vico; that is, to a philosophical theory."[7]

Leavis takes it for granted, in that review as elsewhere, that there is a before-and-after in expression. What comes first in a great writer is a creative compulsion, silent, insistent, irrefutable. The words come later, though in a writer of Shakespearean power not much later. The apparent immediacy of the expression testifies to the force of the "impulse from the inner life" that achieved its form in those words. Leavis's assumption of the necessary sequence of feeling and words seems reasonable, but it is not decisive. The inner life is not the only source. Writers often discover perceptions in the transactions of one word, image, or figure with another, perceptions prompted by something as fortuitous as an acoustic similarity. Macbeth's "If th' assassination/Could trammel up the consequence, and catch/With his surcease, success" may have come from his inner life, but it is more probable that it came from Shakespeare's feeling for the latencies of expression in words alike and different: surcease, success. These perceptions could be claimed to have come ultimately from Macbeth's imagined inner life, but ultimately is a long way down. It is enough that the whole speech is convincing as Macbeth's.

I've said that the words come later, though in a writer of Shakespearean power not much later. The critic and psychologist D. W. Harding maintained that what distinguishes a creative writer from other people is that the writer brings language to bear upon expression at a remarkably early stage in the cognitive process. Ordinary people have feelings and look about for ways of expressing them, searching patiently or not among the

---

[7] Ibid., pp. 211–212.

words at hand, but creative writers bring the medium – the available words, grammars, and syntaxes – to bear upon the expressive need at the earliest possible moment in its demand. Harding made the case most explicitly in an essay on the poems of Isaac Rosenberg:

Usually when we speak of finding words to express a thought, we seem to mean that we have the thought rather close to formulation and use it to measure the adequacy of any possible phrasing that occurs to us, treating words as servants of the idea. "Clothing a thought in language," whatever it means psychologically, seems a fair metaphorical description of much speaking and writing. Of Rosenberg's work it would be misleading. He – like many poets in some degree, one supposes – brought language to bear on the incipient thought at an earlier stage of its development. Instead of the emerging idea being racked slightly so as to fit a more familiar approximation of itself, and words found for *that*, Rosenberg let it manipulate words almost from the beginning, often without insisting on the controls of logic and intelligibility.[8]

In another essay, "The Hinterland of Thought," Harding showed that there are passages in Shakespeare – notably the "Pity, like a naked new-born babe" passage in *Macbeth* – which reveal "not disorder but a complex ordering of attitude and belief achieved a stage earlier than discursive statement."[9] The difference between Harding's theory and Leavis's is not immense, but it is a difference that issues in Leavis's rejection of *Work in Progress*. Leavis uses his theory of creative sequence – the compulsion first, then the words – to make a comprehensive distinction between Shakespeare's methods and Joyce's. Harding's theory would make it more difficult to enforce the distinction, and might make it impossible, the temporal gap between feeling and words being in his version nearly closed. An adequate account of the difference would bring in William Empson's meditations on ambiguity and on various examples of complex feelings expressed by their not being entirely or discursively specified.

At this point in Leavis's review it becomes clear that he is not merely rejecting Jolas's comparison of the later Joyce with the later Shakespeare: he is making a far larger critical and cultural case. He starts with the conditions that made Shakespeare possible:

He represents, of course, the power of the Renaissance. But the power of the Renaissance could never so have manifested itself in English if English had not already been there – a language vigorous enough to respond to the new influx, ferment and literary efflorescence, and, in so doing, not lose, but strengthen its

---

[8] D. W. Harding, *Experience into Words* (New York: Horizon Press, 1964), p. 99.   [9] Ibid., p. 182.

essential character. The dependence of the theatre on both Court and populace ensured that Shakespeare should use his "linguistic genius" – he incarnated the genius of the language – to the utmost. And what this position of advantage represents in particular form is the general advantage he enjoyed in belonging to a genuinely national culture, to a community in which it was possible for the theatre to appeal to the cultivated and the populace at the same time.[10]

Such a culture, such a community, in Leavis's view, no longer exists. "The strength of English," he claims, "belongs to the very spirit of the language – the spirit that was formed when the English people who formed it was predominantly rural." When England was a configuration of villages and parishes, the people lived by mutualities of recognition – it is Leavis's theme, and L. C. Knights's – that did not, as a social norm, survive the Industrial Revolution. Dickens is an equivocal figure in this context. *Dombey and Son* finds both good and ill in the new railways. But "the modern suburban world," as Leavis calls it, testifies to an order that is gone, "and there are no signs of its replacement by another":

The possibility of one that should offer a like richness of life, of emotional, mental and bodily life in association, is hardly even imaginable . . . If the English people had always been what they are now there would have been no Shakespeare's English and no comparable instrument.[11]

Leavis's conclusion was rueful but not entirely dispirited:

At any rate, we still have Shakespeare's English: there is indeed reason in setting great store by the "word" – if not in the revolutionary hopes of Mr. Jolas and his friends. With resources of expression that would not have existed if Shakespeare's England had not been very different from his own, Gerard Manley Hopkins wrote major poetry in the Victorian Age. We have poets in our own day, and James Joyce wrote *Ulysses*. For how long a cultural tradition can be perpetuated in this way one wonders with painful tension. Language, kept alive and rejuvenated by literature, is certainly an essential means of continuity and transition – to what?[12]

Leavis felt that he must at least put the question forward, and give the necessary evidence.

The spirit of the English language – the genius of it – is the value to which Leavis appeals in repudiating *Work in Progress*. Shakespeare is supremely its embodiment and proof that the language available to him was strong enough not only to survive the continental immigrations but to thrive on them. If Jolas had not offered the challenge of a comparison

---

[10] Leavis, *For Continuity*, pp. 215–216.   [11] Ibid., p. 218.   [12] Ibid., p. 218.

of Joyce and Shakespeare, I don't think Leavis would have risen to the
occasion in that way. Jolas seemed to be claiming not that Joyce was as
great as Shakespeare but that Joyce's method in *Work in Progress* was
comparable to Shakespeare's in the last plays, and just as valid. Leavis, in
reply, insists that the spirit of the English language necessarily took the
form of Shakespeare's mature plays and could not have been adequately
fulfilled by any other manifestation. In a sarcastic sentence, he brushed
aside two linguistic ventures that seemed to be seriously on offer in 1933:

The "internationalization of language" acclaimed by Joyce's apostles is a comple-
mentary phenomenon to Basic English; indeed, we note with a surprised and
pleased sense of fitness that Mr. C. K. Ogden has shown an active interest in the
Work in Progress.[13]

Each of these inventions, Leavis implies, is mechanical, a mere device,
lacking roots in a national culture. Each could be proposed only in default
of the necessary community of values and at a time when there seemed to
be a desperate reaching out for stratagems.

   In the same number of *Scrutiny* in which the review of Joyce appeared
there also appeared Leavis's essay on Milton's verse, an essay that appeals
even more explicitly to the spirit or genius of the English language as a
decisive critical consideration. Leavis makes appropriate acknowledgement to T. S. Eliot and John Middleton Murry, and might well have
thanked Ezra Pound, writers who preceded him in the attempted dislodg-
ment of Milton. His own contribution to that end is his insistence that
Paradise Lost is for the most part characterized by "the routine gesture, the
heavy fall, of the verse ... the foreseen thud that comes so inevitably, and
at last irresistibly."[14] Leavis quotes a passage from Book III and another
from Book VI to enforce his judgment. But he also quotes, for praise and
grateful contrast, a passage from Comus's temptation of the Lady:

> Wherefore did nature pour her bounties forth
> With such a full and unwithdrawing hand,
> Covering the earth with odors, fruits, and flocks,
> Thronging the seas with spawn innumerable,
> But all to please and sate the curious taste?
> And set to work millions of spinning worms
> That in their green shops weave the smooth-hair'd silk
> To deck her sons; and that no corner might
> Be vacant of her plenty, in her own loins

---

[13] Ibid., p. 215.   [14] F. R. Leavis, "Milton's Verse," *Scrutiny*, Vol. 2, No. 2 (September 1933), p. 124.

She hutched th'all worshipped ore and precious gems
To store her children with. If all the world
Should in a pet of temperance feed on pulse,
Drink the clear stream, and nothing wear but frieze,
Th' all-giver would be unthanked, would be unpraised,
Not half his riches known, and yet despised,
And we should serve him as a grudging master,
As a penurious niggard of his wealth,
And live like nature's bastards, not her sons,
Who would be quite surcharged with her own weight,
And strangled with her waste fertility;
Th'earth cumbered, and the winged air darkened with plumes,
The herds would over-multitude their lords,
The sea o'er-fraught would swell, and th'unsought diamonds
Would so emblaze the forehead of the deep,
And so bestud with stars, that they below
Would grow inured to light, and come at last
To gaze upon the sun with shameless brows.[15]

Leavis regarded that passage as exhibiting "the momentary predominance in Milton of Shakespeare." The verse, he says, is "richer, subtler and more sensitive than anything in *Paradise Lost, Paradise Regained* or *Samson Agonistes*." More specifically:

The texture of actual sounds, the run of vowels and consonants, with the variety of action and effort, rich in subtle analogical suggestion, demanded in pronouncing them, plays an essential part, though this is not to be analysed in abstraction from the meaning. The total effect is as if words as words withdrew themselves from the focus of our attention and we were directly aware of a tissue of feelings and perceptions.[16]

Colin MacCabe has interpreted this passage as indicating Leavis's "distrust of words which in their materiality prevent the experience of the author (life) shining through." The passage, he claims, shows in Leavis the opposition between the supposed truth of the voice and the alleged falsity of writing.[17] There are sentences in Leavis's essay which justify this interpretation. In the passage he quotes from Book VI of *Paradise Lost*, Leavis says, "Milton seems here to be focusing rather upon words than upon perceptions, sensations or things." He exhibits "a feeling *for* words rather than a capacity for feeling *through* words." Further:

---

[15] Quoted in ibid., pp. 126–127.   [16] Ibid., pp. 127–128.
[17] Colin MacCabe, *James Joyce and the Revolution of the Word* (London: Palgrave Macmillan, second edition, 2003), pp. 78–79.

The extreme and consistent remoteness of Milton's medium from any English that was ever spoken is an immediately relevant consideration. It became, of course, habitual to him; but habituation could not sensitize a medium so cut off from speech – speech that belongs to the emotional and sensory texture of actual living and is in resonance with the nervous system; it could only confirm an impoverishment of sensibility.[18]

It is also true that Leavis appeals, both in the essay on Milton and the review of Joyce, to a time in English culture when speech was "a popularly cultivated art," when people talked "instead of reading or listening to the wireless."[19] But MacCabe doesn't remark that Leavis's insistence on the creative force of English speech and English idiom is propelled by his conviction that the spirit or genius of the English language is there to be appealed to and that he knows what it is. Leavis does not anticipate Derrida's invidious contrast between the axioms of speech and of writing: he does not advert to logocentrism, nor does he question the privileging of voice with its aura of personal presence. Milton is culpable in Leavis's view because the Grand Style he developed "renounced the English language, and with that, inevitably, Milton being an Englishman, a great deal else."[20] Milton Latinized, not only by writing in Latin, but by trying to turn English into Latin, cultivating "a callousness to the intrinsic nature of English." Shakespeare supremely incarnated the genius of the English language. So, too, on a different scale, did Donne. Quoting a few lines from Donne's third Satire –

> . . . . On a huge hill,
> Cragged, and steep, Truth stands, and he that will
> Reach her, about must, and about must go;
> And what the hill's suddenness resists, win so;
> Yet strive so, that before age, death's twilight,
> Thy soul rest, for none can work in that night –[21]

Leavis commented:

This is the Shakespearean use of English; one might say that it is the English use – the use, in the essential spirit of the language, of its characteristic resources.[22]

He then quoted the lines in Milton's "Lycidas" about the "stormy Hebrides" –

> For so to interpose a little ease,
> Let our frail thoughts dally with false surmise.
> Ay me! Whilst thee the shores, and sounding Seas

---

[18] Leavis, "Milton's Verse," pp. 129–130.   [19] Leavis, *For Continuity*, p. 217.
[20] Leavis, "Milton's Verse," p. 130.   [21] Quoted in ibid., p. 132.   [22] Ibid., p. 133.

Wash far away, where ere thy bones are hurld,
Whether beyond the stormy Hebrides,
Where thou perhaps under the whelming tide
Visit'st the bottom of the monstrous world ....[23]

– and maintained that while the words in "Lycidas" "are doing so much less work than in Donne," they seem to value themselves more highly: "they seem, comparatively, to be occupied with valuing themselves rather than with doing anything."[24]

If we go back to an early quotation from Leavis's essay on Milton's verse, we may be able to connect his observations on Milton and on Joyce in a way compatible with Colin MacCabe's interpretation, but without recourse to a Derridean emphasis. You will recall that Leavis, praising the passage from "Comus," said: "The total effect is as if words as words withdrew themselves from the focus of our attention and we were directly aware of a tissue of feelings and perceptions."[25] I would interpret that sentence as saying more generally that words as words in any work of literature should withdraw themselves – or should at least seem to do so – and disappear among the feelings and perceptions they have produced. That is the proper destiny of words – to die into the further human life they have created. It may be wise not to call this further life "presence," lest that word enforce a stronger ontological claim than we need.

Leavis's assumptions appear to entail such a sequence as this one. Since the invention of movable type, we start with graphic signs, words on a page. (Manuscript is another question.) The reader construes these as signs of someone's speech, and takes for granted voice, articulation, and audibility. Inevitably, each event of the speech is displaced by the next, while a tissue of feelings and perceptions is forming in the reader's or the listener's mind; and so on till the end of the speech when every word has disappeared into silence. The best analogies for this process are performances of music and dance. At the end, nothing remains but the silence in which the experience of the work has been, one hopes, resolved. The work can be recovered now only by having the performance repeated or a new interpretation disclosed. Partial recovery is possible by an act of one's memory. I do not need to read again Yeats's "The Folly of Being Comforted" to recall "The fire that stirs about her, when she stirs,/Burns but more clearly," or Eliot's "La Figlia che Piange" to recall "Sometimes these cogitations still amaze/The troubled midnight and the noon's

---

[23] Quoted in ibid.   [24] Ibid.   [25] Ibid., p. 128.

repose." In that sense, not all of the words have disappeared into silence. And in every act of reading or listening there are differences of response. Sir Philip Sidney allows for these differences when he has Philisides, in the third book of the *Arcadia*, sing one of his songs, "As I my Little Flock on Ister Bancke." When the twenty-three stanzas are over, Sidney tells us that "According to the Nature of dyvers Eares, dyvers Judgmentes streight followed, some praysing his voice, others the wordes, Fitt, to frame a Pastorall style, others the straungenes of the Tale, and scanning what hee should meane by yt." And one listener, old Geron, accused Philisides of bad taste in telling a tale of "hee knewe not what Beastes at suche a Banquett when rather some Songe of Love or matter for Joyfull melody was to bee broughte forthe."[26] That sequence, or something like it, is implied by the kind of writing and reading that Leavis approves. It follows that the scandal of Milton and Joyce, in Leavis's view, is that in their later work they resorted to uses of words that would not withdraw. Milton's words would not disappear – as speech does and should – into the silence that surrounds them. That is what his Latinizing allegedly comes to. Joyce's words in *Work in Progress* and later in the complete *Finnegans Wake* are devised in such forms that they cannot withdraw from the context they enforce. There is nowhere for them to go. They have to remain on the page in the graphic state of what Leavis calls "words as words." No wonder so many of them defeat the attention of the elocutionist and can only be read in the sense of being looked at. Even in passages that reward reading aloud, we are often left wondering what the pleasure of doing so has entailed, as in this little passage from Jaun's sermon to a group of girls:

I've a hopesome's choice if I chouse of all the sinkts in the colander. From the common for ignitious Purpalume to the proper of Francisco Utramare, last of scorchers, third of snows, in terrorgammons howdydos.[27]

It is possible to make sense of this, as Fritz Senn has done by making a loose assemblage of names in the vicinities of St. Ignatius Loyola and St. Francis Xavier.[28] But even if "in terrorgammons howdydos" may be

---

[26] Sir Philip Sidney, *The Countess of Pembroke's Arcadia*, ed. Albert Feuillerat (Cambridge University Press, 1926), p. 242. My attention was drawn to this passage by Lorna Hutson, "An Earlier Perspective," *Times Literary Supplement*, May 30, 2003, p. 4.

[27] James Joyce, *Finnegans Wake* (New York: Viking Press, 1939; London: Faber and Faber, 1939), pp. 432–433.

[28] Fritz Senn, *Joyce's Dislocations: Essays on Reading as Translation*, ed. John Paul Riquelme (Baltimore and London: The Johns Hopkins University Press, 1984), pp. 90–94.

derived from a moment in the Litany of the Saints – *te rogamus audi nos* – the main attribute of Joyce's locution is its refusal to withdraw either into the litany or the feelings and perceptions which the litany expresses. "The sinkts in the colander" may be deduced from "the saints in the calendar," but it is hard to be assured that the deduction constitutes a new perception.

II

It may be thought that Leavis's appeal to the spirit of the language is eccentric, but he was not alone in making it. George Eliot, in an essay on the natural history of German life, glances at the project of constructing a universal language:

> Suppose, then, that the effort which has been again and again made to construct a universal language on a rational basis has at length succeeded, and that you have a language which has no uncertainty, no whims of idiom, no cumbrous forms, no fitful shimmer of many-hued significance, no hoary archaisms "familiar with forgotten years" – a patent deodorized and non-resonant language, which effects the purpose of communication as perfectly as algebraic signs.[29]

This supposed language would be fine for science, George Eliot concedes, but not otherwise for life, "which is a great deal more than science." There is no substitute for historical language:

> With the anomalies and inconveniences of historical language, you will have parted with its music and its passion, with its vital qualities as an expression of individual character, with its subtle capabilities of wit, with everything that gives it power over the imagination .... The sensory and motor nerves that run in the same sheath are scarcely bound together by a more necessary and delicate union than that which binds men's affections, imagination, wit, and humour with the subtle ramifications of historical language.[30]

You could also appeal to the spirit of a language by considering what it might have been rather than what it turned out to be. Hopkins was in this sense a linguistic and cultural nationalist, sympathetic to the aims diversely represented by William Barnes, George P. Marsh, F. J. Furnivall, E. A. Freeman, and R. C. Trench, grammarians and linguists who thought that English had taken a wrong turn at the Renaissance and had thwarted its genius by

---

[29] George Eliot, "Natural History of German Life: Riehl," in *The Writings of George Eliot: Essays and Leaves from a Note-Book* (Boston and New York: Houghton Mifflin, 1909), p. 225.
[30] Ibid.

welcoming indiscriminate continental usages.[31] The founding of the Early English Text Society in 1864 activated the question of English, its rise and perhaps its fall. Hopkins imagined a better English having issued from Anglo-Saxon, a modern language that would not have been amenable, as Shakespeare's English was, to influxes from Latin, Italian, and French. He sympathized with Barnes and thought his project admirable except for the certainty that it must fail. As he wrote to Robert Bridges:

Talking of chronologically impossible and long words the Rev. Wm. Barnes, good soul, of Dorset-dialect poems (in which there is more true poetry than in Burns; I do not say of course vigour or passion or humour or a lot of things, but the soul of poetry, which I believe few Scotchmen have got) has published a "Speech craft of English Speech"= English Grammar, written in an unknown tongue, a sort of modern Anglosaxon, beyond all that Furnival in his wildest Forewords ever dreamed. He did not see the utter hopelessness of the thing. It makes one weep to think what English might have been; for in spite of all that Shakspere and Milton have done with the compound I cannot doubt that no beauty in a language can make up for want of purity. In fact I am learning Anglosaxon and it is a vastly superior thing to what we have now. But the madness of an almost unknown man trying to do what the three estates of the realm together could never accomplish! He calls degrees of comparison pitches of suchness: we *ought* to call them so, but alas![32]

In much the same tones Ezra Pound imagined what a better thing the English language would have become if Shakespeare and the Elizabethan poets had opened their ears to Cavalcanti rather than to Petrarch.

The spirit of the language was not only an English consideration. In 1899 Remy de Gourmont published *Esthétique de la langue française*, a tribute to the spirit of the French language and a plea that it should be kept up. There continue to be such appeals. In *Required Writing* and the *New Oxford Book of Modern Verse* Philip Larkin celebrated Hardy as incomparably the greatest twentieth-century poet in English, a tribute that could only have arisen from his sense of the genius of the language as Hardyesque and his conviction that the Modernism of Pound and Eliot was alien to that genius and therefore an aberration. Hugh Kenner has also proposed a distinction between the spirit of the English language and the spirit of the American language. In "Words in the Dark" he maintains that the English language received its definitive form and tone from its service to the Elizabethan theatre, an institution in

---

[31] Cf. Austin Warren, *Rage for Order: Essays in Criticism* (University of Chicago Press, 1948), pp. 61–63.
[32] *The Letters of Gerard Manley Hopkins to Robert Bridges*, ed. Claude Colleer Abbott (London: Oxford University Press, 1935), pp. 162–163. Letter of November 26, 1882. Barnes's *An Outline of English Speech-Craft* was published in 1878.

which words were required to direct one's imagination away from the penury of the stage and its appearances. "There are potentialities in Chaucer," Kenner says, "that have never been developed since, chiefly because the English drama had no use for them, and brought modern English to a working maturity without them." The incantation of Marlowe's writing for the stage didn't encourage the audience to examine what they could see but to "dream away from the visible." They were to imagine Helen of Troy, not by looking at the painted boy who crossed the stage, but by letting their minds inhabit for the duration of the words the evening air and "the beauty of a thousand stars." The sonorousness of Donne's "A bracelet of bright hair about the bone" has the theatre in its ears even though the line of verse was not written to be performed in that space. But the spirit of the American language has no theatre to escape from, no words to transcend the dark; it received its character from the eighteenth-century necessities of pamphlet and sermon. It was expected to acknowledge visible things and to help in administering them. Franklin, not Shakespeare, dominated its modes. There was no place for "majestic imprecision and incantation." Kenner offered this distinction between the spirit of the English language and the spirit of the American language in the hope of recommending to English readers the poetry of Pound, H. D., William Carlos Williams, Marianne Moore, and Louis Zukofsky, poets exempt from the Shakespearean echo and therefore free to make their words accompany the trajectory of things seen. They were also free to practice not just Imagism but translation, to isolate "the poetic effects that are not local and parochial, concocted out of the accidental sounds and colours of the language in which they are conceived."[33] English readers with Shakespeare in their ears should not expect to find in modern American Objectivist poetry the incantations and reverberations of "words in the dark." Kenner's further implication was that American writers who did not attend to the spirit of the American language – Stevens, notably, and Faulkner – did not know what they were doing and lost themselves in pastiches and mimicries.

These are instances of critics positing a spirit of a language and claiming that writers should act in an observant relation to it. Leavis implied that Joyce veered from such observance, perhaps because in Dublin, Paris, Trieste, and Zurich he did not have an adequate national culture or a community to belong to. Presumably he should have

[33] Hugh Kenner, "Words in the Dark," in E. V. Rieu (ed.), *Essays by Divers Hands Being the Transactions of the Royal Society of Literature*, new series, Vol. XXIX (London: Oxford University Press, 1958), p. 122.

committed himself, as Conrad, Henry James, and T. S. Eliot did, to the particles of an English national culture that still remained, and made the best of them; though Leavis eventually came to believe that Eliot remained an American of divided creative loyalties and made his commitment to the spirit of English only notionally and in questionable faith. Conrad and James made the most of their opportunities and found a place for themselves in the "great tradition" of English fiction with Jane Austen, George Eliot, and D. H. Lawrence.

III

Can one still appeal to the spirit or genius of a language as a critical value bearing on this new work or that? Linguists would not give much credence to the notion: they would regard Leavis's appeal to the spirit of the English language as a rhetorical gesture, the spirit being merely a trope standing for art and culture. They would also regard as foolish the effort to cultivate words of one quality or origin rather than another. Some linguists of an older time thought that particular languages might be characterized. Jespersen fancied that English and German are "masculine," and French and Italian "feminine." This seems a mystification. It is probably more reasonable to ascribe genius or spirit to writers, and to think of a language as a medium and nothing more. But I am not entirely convinced. Social scientists and cultural historians talk boldly about millennia, centuries, generations, and decades – the "Twenties," the "Sixties" – as if those times could be delineated by producing a few events and declaring them exemplary. They seem to feel no misgiving in attributing to such periods a *Zeitgeist* to which various adjectives may be appended. Personification is as rampant in these activities as in Pope's *Dunciad*. As soon as you argue that, say, English has certain qualities and that French has other qualities – an argument that Conrad was not alone in making – you can hardly avoid making further distinctions as if the languages distinguished were persons. Differences between historical or national English and the dialect of Dorset – Barnes's medium in many poems – can't be ignored; nor can they be described in strictly empirical or statistical terms. Spirit and genius, as terms of invocation, don't float higher above the rough ground than other words regularly used: nation, race, culture, Renaissance, Europe. I myself use these words.

I find no theoretical fault in Leavis's attempt to support his critical values by appeal to the spirit or genius of the English language, if I bear in mind that the device is rhetorical – designed to persuade – rather than probative. The attempt becomes more controversial when Leavis argues that the spirit of English is incarnated in Shakespeare and Donne rather than in Spenser and Milton; that it finds its life in the Elizabethan theatre or in language that is familiar with the theatre, rather than in epic poetry and pamphleteering; that it is at one with speech and the idioms of actual life rather than with graphic forms dependent on print and publication; and that it has not survived the lapse of a national culture. Leavis's rhetoric was persuasive in the years between the two World Wars when Eliot, too, presented English literature as predicated on Shakespeare, Donne, George Herbert, and the Jacobean dramatists. I think Leavis was also justified in correlating the power of English as an expressive and inventive medium with the centuries in which English life was predominantly rural. But that time is gone, as he conceded. If by a distinctive modern literature we mean the trajectory from Baudelaire to Eliot, that was an affair of cities, and the provocative emotion was the friction of urban life. Modern art did not arise from Dorchester or Mansfield Park but from London, Paris, New York, Dublin, Trieste, Prague, and Vienna. Eliot appealed – in what linguists might regard as another mystification – to a larger cultural entity than the genius of English:

[The poet] must be aware that the mind of Europe – the mind of his own country – a mind which he learns in time to be much more important than his own private mind – is a mind which changes, and that this change is a development which abandons nothing *en route*, which does not superannuate either Shakespeare, or Homer, or the rock drawing of the Magdalenian draughtsmen.[34]

Pound's understanding of tradition was predicated on a still larger set of recognitions, selected acts in the cultures of Italy, China, Greece, and America. But neither Eliot nor Pound had any aspiration toward "the internationalization of language" in the sense of *Work in Progress* and the *transition* project. *The Waste Land,* "Hugh Selwyn Mauberley," and the *Cantos* are poems in historical English, phrases from foreign languages being called upon to acknowledge that there are other cultures in the world.

There is indeed a "story of English," but it has culminated in the proliferation of a language throughout the world that is primarily devoted to money and power. English is the dominant international language of politics, war, finance, aviation, professional sport, and tourism. In that

[34] T. S. Eliot, *Selected Prose*, ed. Frank Kermode (New York: Harcourt Brace Jovanovich, 1975), p. 39.

sense it may be regarded as a cultural remnant of the Empire, but London is no longer its center, Westminster and the BBC are not its emblems. Shakespeare as supreme embodiment of the genius of the language has been dislodged not by Broadway or Hollywood but by American TV news programs and talk shows in their relation to the residue of common life.

IV

What critical value, then, can we bring to a reading of *Work in Progress* and its successor, *Finnegans Wake*, if these are scandals to Leavis and alien to the genius of the English language? Is *Finnegans Wake* a sport, the sole instance of its kind, a source of pleasure for a few professional readers, or a great work of English fiction? Northrop Frye thought that there were four forms of prose fiction and that *Finnegans Wake* was an example of an irregular but not unique fifth, a form "traditionally associated with scriptures and sacred books, [it] treats life in terms of the fall and awakening of the human soul and the creation and apocalypse of nature":

> The Bible is the definitive example of it; the Egyptian Book of the dead and the Icelandic Prose Edda, both of which have left deep imprints on *Finnegans Wake*, also belong to it.[35]

But this doesn't help in the detail of reading the *Wake*, even though it offers a majestic context in which the reading might be pursued. There is a special problem here.

I am persuaded by Fritz Senn that we have succeeded – or some scholars have – in reading the *Wake* in particles but not as a whole:

> But while we can usually make an instructive show of select passages, we ought not to confuse the *Wake*'s exemplary complaisance with our understanding of it. When I started out, some thirty years ago, in the juvenile flush of those euphoric first unravelings of meaning, I hoped that within some decades we might jointly arrive at sufficient basic understanding (at the modest level of Roland McHugh's helpful *Annotations*) that would enable us to go beyond those resistant details and to make statements of more general import and validity, perhaps even in a scholarly way. We obviously haven't.[36]

It may be that the work of annotation is the necessary ground work, the first act of reading, and that statements of more general import and validity may be made later. But the trouble with annotation is that the

---

[35] Northrop Frye, *Anatomy of Criticism: Four Essays* (Princeton University Press, 1957), p. 314.
[36] Senn, *Joyce's Dislocutions*, p. xi.

note, necessary and useful as it is, reduces Joyce's pages to their presumably normative origins. If I know the Irish language, I can report that "drawhure deelish" (455) means "dear sister." But the annotation stops when it has divined the source. When I read "Mades of ashens when you flirt spoil the lad but spare his shirt" (436), I place beside the rhyming "flirt" and "shirt" the rhyme of "Maid of Athens when we part, give oh give me back my heart" as well as the saw about sparing the rod and spoiling the child, but I don't get much gratification from putting these old tunes back where they seem to belong in Joyce's page.

There are other problems. I started reading *Ulysses* with the help of Eliot's review of it, and especially the sentence in which he says that Joyce's use of the Homeric myth "is simply a way of controlling, of ordering, of giving a shape and a significance to the immense panorama of futility and anarchy which is contemporary history."[37] I have sometimes thought that it might be possible to extend that sentence to illuminate *Finnegans Wake*. If it were, it would supply a critical value and perhaps take the place of Leavis's appeal to the genius of the English language. But it wouldn't help much. Whether we regard Joyce's recourse to the *Odyssey* in *Ulysses* as reverential, casual, or both, at least Homer's poem is there, and it exerts on the modern story something of the pressure that Eliot describes. But in *Finnegans Wake* no single story is invoked beyond that of HCE and ALP. There are many sources, including the *Egyptian Book of the Dead*. There are hundreds of stories, including one about an Irish soldier shooting at a Russian general during the Crimean War; but their multiplicity ensures that none of them has the authority (however we measure that) of the *Odyssey* in *Ulysses*. Wherever we find the normative origin of one of Joyce's "dislocutions," as Senn calls them, it does not impose a critical or cultural perspective: it does not do the work of Tiresias in *The Waste Land*. These dislocations disperse the positivism of words in relation to their local referents, and they set resonances astir, but they do not exert any cultural pressure on the narrative.

Senn's idea of metastasis is more useful: metastasis meaning, in rhetoric, a rapid move from one point to another – often called "the flitting figure." What Senn has in mind is Joyce's way of making a sudden change in a sentence or phrase, indicating that something unusual is going on. His prime example is "Chrysostomos" on the first page of *Ulysses*, in a passage about Buck Mulligan:

---

[37] Eliot, *Selected Prose*, p. 177.

He peered sideways up and gave a long slow whistle of call, then paused awhile in rapt attention, his even white teeth glistening here and there with gold points. Chrysostomos. Two strong shrill whistles answered through the calm.[38]

The word comes abruptly, it seems to have erupted on to the page from nowhere and to enforce a "rapid transition from one point of view to another."[39] You have to stop to ask what is happening, and you wonder whether Stephen Dedalus hasn't simply translated Buck Mulligan's gold-capped teeth into the Greek word meaning "golden-mouthed." Or maybe he is thinking of St. John Chrysostomos, divine and orator. We are given no syntactical help in deciding what the word is doing there; we have to work out something for ourselves: as in abstract art, where points of color and light are deployed in paintings which have no intent of reference or description. Without any syntax, we have to look at each painting and register its lines of force. Normative reduction is impossible: there is nothing to which the painting can be referred, there is no landscape, no face. It is the absence of syntax that makes such peremptory gestures comparable to metastases. Kenner claims that "juxtaposed objects render one another intelligible without conceptual interposition," and if I knew precisely what he means by "intelligible" I could be convinced.[40] Jackson Pollock's drip paintings appear to dream of freeing themselves from human volition, as if their paint insisted on having only material existence.[41] But the difference between metastases and juxtapositions without copula is that with metastases you try to supply a plausible copula and you may succeed at least to your own satisfaction. You can decide why "Chrysostomos" has broken into the paragraph. In the case of abstract paintings, there is no merit in guessing what the copula might have been, had there been one. Sometimes in *Finnegans Wake* the metastasis is so abrupt that you think you may be dealing with a misprint, as in a passage where the four masters are peering at Tristram and Iseult making love:

... drinking in draughts of purest air serene and revelling in the great outdoors, before the four of them, in the fair fine night, whilst the stars shine bright, by she light of he moon, we longed to be spoon, before her

---

[38] James Joyce, *Ulysses*, ed. Hans Walter Gabler with Wolfhard Steppe and Claus Melchior (3 vols., New York: Garland, 1984), p. 3.

[39] Senn, *Joyce's Dislocutions*, p. 139.

[40] Hugh Kenner, *The Poetry of Ezra Pound* (Norfolk, Conn.: New Directions, reprinted 1974), p. 39.

[41] Cf. T. J. Clark, *Farewell to an Idea: Episodes from a History of Modernism* (New Haven, Conn.: Yale University Press, 1999), pp. 166–167.

honeyoldloom, the plain effect being in point of fact their being in the whole, a seatuition so shocking and scandalous.[42]

The obvious allusion here is to Ed Madden's song of 1919: "By the light of the silvery moon/I want to spoon/To my honey I'll croon love's tune/ Honey moon, keep a shining in June/Your silv'ry beams will bring love dreams/We'll be cuddling soon/By the silvery moon." "By she light of he moon" looks like a mistake or a typographical joke, and instead turns out, I think, to be an invention, a metastasis. Joyce has carried the practice of metastasis into the otherwise normative structure of individual words: "honeyoldloom" and "seatuition" as cases in point. A change is seen to be possible and therefore desirable. No critical force is entailed. The voyeurs, "the big four, the four master waves of Erin" may be Matthew, Mark, Luke, and John, or any other quartet that comes to one's mind. Nothing is to be gained by going back to the New Testament. The technique of metastasis, as Joyce manages it, is akin to a stylistic device he practiced from as early as *Dubliners*. In *Joyce's Voices* Kenner has described it as a deliberate discrepancy between narrative and diction, or as I would prefer to say between one diction and another, one diction giving place to another within the same sentence. It is like a change of key within the melodic line.

But I should not give the impression that the idea of the genius or spirit of the English language has been entirely set aside in *Finnegans Wake* or that Leavis's being scandalized is the last event in the case. Leavis urged that a writer of English should acknowledge the spirit of the language and respect it. That was sufficient tradition for him. Eliot extended the idea of tradition and enlarged its contents, but he continued to emphasize that writers should submit themselves to the tradition, and establish themselves in a strong but devout relation to it. But it would also be possible to respect a tradition – or at least to take it seriously – while challenging it. Bakhtin is the critic we think of as recommending this stance, especially in his writings on Rabelais and in everything he has said about carnival and carnivalesque subversions of reality as officially prescribed. In "Discourse in the Novel" Bakhtin says:

The resistance of a unitary, canonic language, of a national myth bolstered by a yet-unshaken unity, is still too strong for heteroglossia to relativize and decenter literary and language consciousness. This verbal-ideological decentering will

---

[42] James Joyce, *Finnegans Wake* (New York: Viking Press, 1939: London: Faber and Faber, 1939), p. 385.

occur only when a national culture loses its sealed-off and self-sufficient character, when it becomes conscious of itself as only one among other cultures and languages.[43]

This is the situation of England or even of Britain as a "national culture," though Leavis was reluctant to admit it in 1933: it is one among other cultures and languages. The fact that English has become the dominant international language is not a consideration from which Leavis would have derived much satisfaction.

Still, it is hard to see *Finnegans Wake* as a politically subversive book or as the modern correlative to the third book of Rabelais's *Gargantua and Pantagruel.* It is a ludic book, though not a joke; at least it is more ludic than carnivalesque. The difference is that the carnivalesque needs a strong national or international culture to mock: there have to be laws to be obeyed, punishments to be meted out before the mockeries and saturnalia count. In 1939, when *Work in Progress* became *Finnegans Wake*, John Crowe Ransom welcomed it as a protest against the reality defined by science and positivism. It may still be that. Or, to bring things up to date and to think of inserting *Finnegans Wake* in our context rather than Joyce's, it may count as a protest against the forces which have turned science, positivism, banking, brokerage, and information technology into an omnivorous system. But when Joyce plays fast and loose with the English language, I recognize an impulse of play short of real subversion. He lacks an enemy that admits his existence. In the absence – or the intangibility, which amounts to the same thing – of an enemy, Joyce's revolution of the word is an extreme and beautiful instance of burlesque, of "the high language of low purpose,"[44] as R. P. Blackmur called burlesque, and it has whatever force of dissent we assign to it: little enough, I think, certainly not enough to make global institutions tremble. That is not Joyce's fault or his inadequacy, unless we think that a work of fiction must, to be any good, bring the house down. No houses will come down because of *Finnegans Wake*. It is enough that the spirit of play and dissent, a more comprehensive spirit than that of the English or any other language, be maintained. But I don't find Joyce and *Finnegans Wake* in association with Rabelais, Voltaire, and Swift, writers who brought houses down.

[43] M. M. Bakhtin, *The Dialogic Imagination: Four Essays*, trans. Caryl Emerson and Michael Holquist (Austin: University of Texas Press, 1981), p. 370.

[44] R. P. Blackmur, *Outsider at the Heart of Things*, ed. James T. Jones (Urbana and Chicago: University of Illinois Press, 1989), p. 199.

PART V

Other occasions

CHAPTER 10

Mangan

On February 15, 1902 James Joyce, aged twenty, read a paper on James Clarence Mangan to the Literary and Historical Society of what is now University College, Dublin. It was a brash performance. Joyce spoke as if he were introducing an unknown poet, and chose to ignore the fact that there were several collections of Mangan's poems at large and that writers as various as John Mitchel, Charles Gavan Duffy, D. J. O'Donoghue, Father Charles Meehan, Louise Imogen Guiney, Lionel Johnson, Francis Thompson, and W. B. Yeats had written of his life and work. "Mangan has been a stranger in his country," Joyce claimed, "a rare and unsympathetic figure in the streets, where he is seen going forward alone like one who does penance for some ancient sin."[1] Evidently more interested in Mangan's temperament than in his poems and essays, Joyce spoke of his reserve: "This purely defensive reserve is not without dangers for him, and in the end it is only his excesses that save him from indifference."[2] Reaching for a comparison, Joyce recalled the passage, already famous, in which Walter Pater completed his "imaginary portrait" of Watteau:

He has been a sick man all his life. He was always a seeker after something in the world that is there in no satisfying measure, or not at all.[3]

Swaying to Pater's cadences, Joyce described Mangan:

Weaker than Leopardi, for he has not the courage of his own despair but forgets all ills and forgoes his scorn at the showing of some favour, he has, perhaps for this reason, the memorial he would have had – a constant presence with those that love him – and bears witness, as the more heroic

---

* *London Review of Books*, March 17, 2005.
[1] James Joyce, *Occasional, Critical, and Political Writing*, ed. Kevin Barry (Oxford University Press, 2000), pp. 54f.
[2] Ibid., p. 56.
[3] Walter Pater, "A Prince of Court Painters," *Imaginary Portraits* (London: Macmillan, 1910, reprinted 1967), p. 40.

pessimist bears witness against his will to the calm fortitude of humanity, to a subtle sympathy with health and joyousness which is seldom found in one whose health is safe.[4]

Joyce's portrait of Mangan is entirely sympathetic, as if he saw in Mangan's life a companionable image of his own wretchedness in Dublin, falling from domestic comfort into a state close to destitution.

James Mangan – Clarence was a later addition – was born in Dublin on May 1, 1803, "amid scenes of blasphemy and riot,"[5] if we are to credit a fragment of autobiography he wrote in the last months of his life. As epigraph to that bizarre document, Mangan quoted two lines he claimed to have found in Philip Massinger, though no one else has found them there: "A heavy shadow lay/On that boy's spirit: he was not of his fathers."[6] Mangan was the second son of James Mangan and his wife Catherine. His father, for a time a hedge-school teacher, married into a fairly successful grocery and spirits business and soon put an end to its prosperity. In 1810 the boy started school at Saul's Court, a Jesuit estab-lishment, but he was soon moved from one school to another and yet another, probably because his parents thought he was eccentric, if not demented. In 1818, to support them, he was taken from school and apprenticed as a scrivener to the first of several law firms. In the *Autobiography* he blamed his father for his woes:

He was of an ardent and forward-bounding disposition, and, though deeply religious by nature, he hated the restraints of social life, and seemed to think that all feelings with regard to family connections, and the obligations imposed by them, were totally beneath his notice. Me, my two brothers, and my sister, he treated habitually as a huntsman would treat refractory hounds. It was his boast, uttered in pure glee of heart, that we "would run into a mouse-hole" to shun him .... To him I owe all my misfortunes.[7]

"And in the lowest deep a lower deep," to quote one of Mangan's favorite lines from *Paradise Lost*.

Mangan's father, it is clear, was hopelessly improvident: indiscrimin-ately open-handed to other people, he made no provision for wife and children. Every commercial venture he took up was a failure. Like the

[4] Joyce, *Occasional, Critical, and Political Writing*, p. 58.
[5] James Clarence Mangan, *Selected Writings*, ed. Sean Ryder (University College Dublin Press, 2004), p. 412.
[6] *The Collected Prose of James Clarence Mangan: Prose 1840–1882 and Correspondence*, ed. Jacques Chuto et al. (Dublin: Irish Academic Press, 2002), p. 226.
[7] Ibid., p. 418.

Joyces, the Mangans flitted from one miserable house to another. The misfortunes the poet suffered included illness of several kinds, debility, and in later years addiction to drink and, it may be, to opium. His employment was irregular. He started publishing verses in 1818, mostly acrostics and other word-puzzles which he published in almanacs: he was fascinated by charades, puns, parodies, burlesques, and travesties. Over the next years he made a few pounds by writing for more serious magazines. In 1838 he got a job in the Ordnance Survey office, and when the Survey was closed down three years later, he was taken on as a cataloguing clerk in the library of Trinity College, Dublin, full-time to begin with but lapsing to part-time after a while. For the last years of his life he depended on the generosity of friends and the hospitality of taverns. In 1849 he contracted cholera, was removed to a cholera shed, and on June 20 died of – it appears – malnutrition. Ellen Shannon-Mangan's *James Clarence Mangan: A Biography* (1996) removes the legendary aura that has enveloped Mangan's life and replaces it with evidence and good sense.

Some aspects of Mangan's life are hard to explain. His education was at best irregular, but he learned or taught himself several modern languages, and was particularly strong in German and French. He claimed to understand eight languages and, as Joyce said, he made a liberal parade of his learning: "he has read recklessly in many literatures, crossing how many seas, and even penetrated into Peristan, to which no road leads that the feet travel."[8] "About four-fifths of Mangan's poems purport to be translations," according to Jacques Chuto's count. He translated, as many modern poets do, from languages he did not know. Joyce remarked upon "this fury of translation in which he has sought to lose himself." There was always someone to provide a crib to start him off. Many of his poems are wayward versions of poems by Goethe, Schiller, Tieck, and poets real or fictitious: he often ascribed his own poems to poets who did not exist. In other moods he presented as his own compositions his translations or versions from unacknowledged sources. He wrote several essays on Persian and Turkish poetry, which he knew only at the double remove of German translations. It is doubtful that he knew any Irish: his most celebrated poems were written from literal translations of Irish poems supplied by James Hardiman, John O'Donovan, Eugene O'Curry, John O'Daly, Edward Walsh, Samuel Ferguson, and other sources. Ellen Shannon-Mangan elucidates nearly every question one might ask, but not how

[8] Joyce, *Occasional, Critical, and Political Writing*, p. 56.

Mangan could have written so many poems and essays in a few years beset by poverty, illness, drunkenness, and what he himself called "moral insanity."[9]

Mangan's place in Irish culture is secure but its terms are not agreed. He has been regarded as a major figure in the cultural nationalism that led to the Literary Revival at the end of the nineteenth century, and for that reason his poems have been taught in Catholic – and for all I know in Protestant – schools throughout the country. In 1938 or thereabouts a girl, a pupil in the Sisters of Charity Convent in Stanhope Street, Dublin, was urged by Sister Loreto to commit to memory Mangan's poem "A Vision of Connaught in the Thirteenth Century" and to perform it with appropriate gestures. Seventy years later, she can still recite its sixty lines with a little prompting. In the Christian Brothers School, Newry, at the same age I learned (under Brother Cotter) Mangan's most famous poem, "Dark Rosaleen," and (under Mr. Crinion) the Gaelic poem "Roisin Dubh," of which Mangan's is a loose translation or imitation. Nationalism ran a little higher in Newry than it did in Dublin, so Mangan's political prophecy, as I was taught to interpret that poem, spoke to me with irresistible authority. I do not recall bringing any irony to bear on Mangan's hyperboles. But I find I can recite only a few lines of the Irish poem and the first stanza of Mangan's:

> O, my Dark Rosaleen,
> 　Do not sigh, do not weep!
> The priests are on the ocean green,
> 　They march along the Deep.
> There's wine from the royal Pope,
> 　Upon the ocean green;
> And Spanish ale shall give you hope,
> 　My Dark Rosaleen!
> 　My own Rosaleen!
> Shall glad your heart, shall give you hope,
> Shall give you health, and help, and hope,
> 　My Dark Rosaleen![10]

Later, I sang the poem in a setting by a composer whose name I can't remember, though I remember the music.

Mangan's nationalism could not have been in doubt, especially since Yeats wrote in an early poem, "To Ireland in the Coming Times," that he himself sang "to sweeten Ireland's wrong":

---

[9] Mangan, *Selected Writings*, p. 419.　　[10] Ibid., p. 222.

Nor may I less be counted one
With Davis, Mangan, Ferguson,
Because, to him who ponders well,
My rhymes more than their rhyming tell
Of things discovered in the deep,
Where only body's laid asleep.[11]

That Yeats was a better poet than Davis, Mangan, or Ferguson has seemed less significant than that he put himself in their nationalist company and uttered with them the "spirit of the nation." But he wasn't much interested in Mangan otherwise and wrote two essays mainly to declare that he knew the name of the poet's lost love, Miss Stacpoole. Yeats told John Quinn, in a letter quoted by Terence Brown in his Foreword to *Selected Poems* (2003), that Mangan differed from the impersonal ballad writers of his time only in being miserable.

Mangan's relation to cultural nationalism is no longer as clear as it seemed in Newry. Joyce thought he was "little of a patriot."[12] David Lloyd has argued that Mangan's life "appears resistant to a nationalist typology, and it frames a body of work that is equally inassimilable to a nationalist aesthetic."[13] He doesn't deny that Mangan often wrote for the nationalist cause, especially when he took John Mitchel's side against the more accommodating Gavan Duffy. In the spring of 1846, appalled by the Famine, Mangan published in the *Nation* three "songs of hatred" denouncing the British "despots." "I hate thee, Djaun Bool [John Bull]" was the gist of them. In 1847 he wrote:

Slender as our talents are, we have become exceedingly desirous to dedicate them henceforward exclusively to the service of our country. For that country – and we now express ourselves merely in reference to its literature – we see a new era approaching. Ireland has been "for a certain term doomed to walk the night" of tribulation and ignorance. But that "night is far spent," and "the day is at hand." The better time is coming – approaching with chariot-like speed.[14]

Such a promise didn't go very far, but it meant something, especially in view of Mangan's sluggishness in patriotic zeal during the early years. Lloyd emphasizes how refractory Mangan was in relation to the Young Ireland movement, and how reluctant he was "to commit himself fully to

[11] W. B. Yeats, *The Variorum Edition of the Poems*, ed. Peter Allt and Russell K. Alspach (London: Macmillan, 1957), pp. 137–138.
[12] Joyce, *Occasional, Critical, and Political Writing*, p. 54.
[13] David Lloyd, *Nationalism and Minor Literature: James Clarence Mangan and the Emergence of Irish Cultural Nationalism* (Berkeley: University of California Press, 1987), p. 47.
[14] Mangan, *Collected Prose 1840–1882*, p. 160.

the nationalist cause."[15] The burden of his argument, to give a too summary account of it, is that Mangan wanted to establish himself in a critical rather than an enthusiastic relation to Irish nationalism; without the criticism, nationalism seemed to him, at least on many occasions, yet another illusion. There was a discrepancy between Mangan's overt intentions, when he wrote for nationalism, and the bias of his aesthetic. Lloyd makes much of his "refusal to find in his sufferings a source of identity with humanity."[16] No transcendent unity is allowed for. Mangan's writings, according to Lloyd, "play out the founding contradictions of an aesthetic that is fundamentally colonial in its terms and determinants."[17] He might have eluded the contradictions if he had been willing and able to make the leap, with Mitchel and Young Ireland, to the ideology of racial unity that is prior to mere history and belongs to an essentialist rhetoric and politics. Because he could not, Mangan had to remain, like Joyce, "in critical alienation,"[18] a parodist by necessity. Not that Lloyd blames him for the condition he brought on himself.

This is Susan Howe's justification, as I interpret it, for removing Mangan from history to typology. In a prose poem, "Melville's Marginalia" (1993), included in her *The Nonconformist's Memorial,* she claims that "the real James Clarence Mangan is the progenitor of fictional Bartleby."[19] But there is a problem of chronology. Melville wrote "Bartleby, the Scrivener: A Story of Wall Street" in the summer of 1853. He did not acquire his copy – second hand – of *Poems by James Clarence Mangan, with Biographical Introduction by John Mitchel* (1859) till February 15, 1862 – at least that is the day on which he wrote his name on it. He read through the book, drawing lines in the margin beside passages that especially interested him, such as Mitchel's assertion that Mangan "was a rebel politically, and a rebel intellectually and spiritually, – a rebel with his whole heart and soul against the whole British spirit of the age."[20] Apart from the marginal lines, Melville made no comments, or if he did they have been erased. But Howe notes that Mangan had American readers as early as 1851. From September to December 1851 Charles Carroll Leeds published four articles in the *United States Magazine and Democratic Review,* two of which dealt with Mangan. As Howe writes:

---

[15] Lloyd, *Nationalism and Minor Literature,* p. 78.   [16] Ibid., p. 190.   [17] Ibid., p. 209.
[18] Ibid., p. 210.
[19] Susan Howe, "Melville's Marginalia," *The American Poetry Review,* Vol. 22, No. 1 (January–February 1993), pp. 35f.
[20] Quoted in Walker Cowen (ed.), *Melville's Marginalia* (2 vols., New York: Garland, 1988), Vol. I, p. 202.

By the time Melville acquired Mitchel's edition of Mangan's poems in 1862, he was already familiar with the poet's life and work. False fleeting perjured Clarence.[21]

The rest of Howe's poem consists of a tissue of quotations from Mitchel's Introduction to Mangan, the lecture on Mangan that Joyce gave in Trieste in 1907, and Melville's marginalia on other writers. Her association of Mangan with Bartleby is not as fanciful as it may appear. It would not be hard to imagine a fiction called "Clarence, the Scrivener: A Story of Dublin Streets." Mangan often withdrew from his haunts and lived in barns or outhouses. It is not absurd to think that he might have said to his employer, as Bartleby said to his, "I would prefer not to." Or that he would have died of starvation in the Tombs, asleep with kings and counselors.

It is good to have a complete edition of Mangan's work, four volumes of poems and two volumes of prose, all helpfully annotated. Inevitably, the uniform character of the six volumes makes the work seem more coherent than it is. Not surprisingly, the poems tend to slip into our sense of Mangan as *le poète maudit*: we think first of his accursed state and only later of his poems. He wrote carelessly as the condition of his writing, and had no time to revise. It is surprising that some of his prose has the perspicuity he admired in other writers. Even when we suspect that he hardly knew what he was talking about, he often produced sentences worth making a note of, as in this passage on German poetry – it is strange that he found the leisure to write at such a thoughtful pace:

If we were asked what it is that constitutes the leading characteristic of German poetry, we should be disposed to answer – Too adventurous an attempt to assimilate the creations of the ideal with the forms of the actual world. Throughout that poetry we can trace a remarkable effort to render vivid and tangible and permanent those phantasmagoria of the mind which by the statutes of our nature are condemned to exhibit an aspect of perpetual vagueness and fluctuation.[22]

Mangan's relation to his themes was opportunistic; he could write on anything, the merits and defects of Tieck's poetry, the superiority of tongs to pokers, the provenance of ghostcraft in Germany. He wrote nearly a thousand poems. His poems on Irish or more-or-less Irish themes seem to me his best, but I value a few poems from other sources. My short list doesn't differ much from anyone else's: "Dark Rosaleen," "Siberia," "And Then No More," "Khidder," "Lament over the Ruins of

---

[21] Howe, "Melville's Marginalia," pp. 35f.   [22] Mangan, *Selected Writings*, p. 392.

the Abbey of Teach Molaga," "A Vision of Connaught in the Thirteenth Century," "Twenty Golden Years Ago," "The Nameless One," "The Woman of Three Cows," "An Elegy on the Tironian and Tirconnellian Princes Buried at Rome," "The Lamentation of Mac Liag for Kincora," "To the Ingleezee Khafir," and "O'Hussey's Ode to the Maguire." David Wheatley has chosen about sixty poems for his selection and added a perceptive introduction. Chuto and his colleagues have selected about two hundred and thirty poems and retained the notes from the four volumes of poetry. The sum is bewildering. Joyce noted that Mangan "wrote with no native tradition to guide him, and for a public which cared for matters of the day, and for poetry only so far as it might illustrate these."[23] He may be compared, in point of sensibility, with Coleridge and De Quincey, but the comparison can't be pushed very far. His poems often give an impression of haphazard, as if he stumbled into their eloquence and achieved their forms by default. But he had an astonishing if wayward lyric gift.

[23] Joyce, *Occasional, Critical, and Political Writing*, p. 56.

CHAPTER 11

Beckett in Foxrock

The philosopher E. M. Cioran knew Beckett in Paris, not very well but well enough to appreciate that he must keep his distance. When they met, he took care not to intrude: he allowed Beckett to lead the conversation, such as it was. Origins were not alluded to, either by a philosopher born in Romania or a dramatist and fiction-writer born in Ireland, both now resident in Paris. In 1976, thinking about those meetings, Cioran wrote:

Granted, our beginnings matter, but we make the decisive step toward ourselves only when we no longer have an *origin*, when we offer as little substance for a biography as God .... It is both important and utterly unimportant that Beckett is Irish.[1]

I'll try to take that admonition into account, short of knowing precisely what it entails.

On April 21, 1935 – Easter Sunday – Oliver Sheppard's sculpture "The Death of Cuchulain" was unveiled in the centre of the General Post Office in Dublin. It was not designed for the occasion or commissioned by a government to celebrate, the following year, the twentieth anniversary of the Easter Rising, 1916. Sheppard created the sculpture in 1911/1912 before there was any symbolic or political call for it. The sculpture depicts Cuchulain, the mythical Celtic warrior, dying, tied to a rock to help him stand up to face his enemies, his body limp, his head rolled to one side, his shield falling from his grasp. A raven, signifying death, sits on his shoulder. Sheppard exhibited the sculpture at the Royal Hibernian Academy in 1914 and again during Dublin Civic Week in 1927. When Eamon de Valera and his Fianna Fáil party won the general election in February 1932 and formed a government, one of his first thoughts, I infer,

---

* Lecture to the Program in Irish Studies, Princeton University, October 3, 2003.
[1] E. M. Cioran, *Anathemas and Admirations*, trans. Richard Howard (London: Quartet Encounters, 1992), p. 135.

was the desirability of celebrating with appropriate vigor the twentieth anniversary of Easter Week. Such a celebration would complete the electoral victory of 1932 and would take possession of the republican tradition after ten years of avoidance, blankness, and bad faith allegedly incurred by the Irish Free State. Looking about for an appropriate emblem, de Valera was brought by John L. Burke, a solicitor and art collector, to see Sheppard's sculpture in his studio. He approved of it and, as President of the Executive council, ordered a bronze cast to be made for installation in the Post Office in 1935 in good time for the anniversary. The statue was delivered in December 1934 and officially unveiled on the following Easter Sunday. The Proclamation of the Republic with the names of its signatories was engraved on a bronze plaque. The sculpture is still in the Post Office, but it was moved, some years ago, to a window alcove in the front wall of the building so that passers-by could see it from O'Connell Street without the labor of entering the Post Office.

It has been argued, notably by Hugh Kenner, that by 1935 the Irish Literary Revival was already run down, having lapsed into a dispirited phase of itself, and that Beckett was the poet of that phase. Yeats, in his last years, did not permit himself to think so, but the stridency of his assertions may be taken as further evidence that the Revival had moved into its ironic days. In 1935, Beckett was at work on his novel, *Murphy*: he started work on it on August 20 and finished it, after much travail, by June 9 the following year. It was published, after several rejections, in 1938. In the fourth chapter of it, Neary is spotted by his associate Wylie in the Post Office:

In Dublin a week later, that would be September 19th, Neary minus his whiskers was recognized by a former pupil called Wylie, in the General Post Office, contemplating from behind the statue of Cuchulain. Neary had bared his head, as though the holy ground meant something to him. Suddenly he flung aside his hat, sprang forward, seized the dying hero by the thighs and began to dash his head against his buttocks, such as they are. The Civic Guard on duty in the building, roused from a tender reverie by the sound of the blows, took in the situation at his leisure, disentangled his baton and advanced with measured tread, thinking he had caught a vandal in the act. Happily Wylie, whose reactions at a street bookmaker's stand were as rapid as a zebra's, had already seized Neary round the waist, torn him back from the sacrifice and smuggled him halfway to the exit.

"Howlt on there, youze," said the CG.

Wylie turned back, tapped his forehead and said, as one sane man to another, "John o'God's. Hundred per cent harmless."

"Come back in here owwathat," said the CG.

Wylie, a tiny man, stood at a loss. Neary, almost as large as the CG though not of course so nobly proportioned, rocked blissfully on the right arm of his rescuer. It was not in the CG's nature to bandy words, nor had it come into any branch of his training. He resumed his steady advance.

"Stillorgan," said Wylie. "Not Dundrum."

The CG laid his monstrous hand on Wylie's left arm and exerted a strong pull along the line he had mapped out in his mind. They all moved off in the desired direction, Neary shod with orange-peel.

"John o' God's," said Wylie. "As quiet as a child."

They drew up behind the statue. A crowd gathered behind them. The CG leaned forward and scrutinized the pillar and draperies.

"Not a feather out of her," said Wylie. "No blood, no brains, nothing."
The CG straightened up and let go Wylie's arm.
"Move on," he said to the crowd, "before yer moved on."

… "Take my advice, mister –" He stopped. To devise words of advice was going to tax his ability to the utmost. When would he learn not to plunge into the labyrinths of an opinion when he had not the slightest idea of how he was to emerge? And before a hostile audience! His embarrassment was if possible increased by the expression of strained attention on Wylie's face, clamped there by the promise of advice.

"Yes, sergeant," said Wylie, and held his breath.
"Run him back to Stillorgan," said the CG.[2]

It speaks well for the CG, who is otherwise not spoken well of, that he knows the difference between Stillorgan and Dundrum; between a benign nursing home for the mentally distressed, called St. John o' God's, and a place of constraint for the criminally insane, an institution in Dundrum which housed mainly murderers and other men of violence. It speaks neither well nor ill for Wylie that he thinks Sheppard's statue depicts a woman, presumably on the evidence that there is no sign of trousers in the ensemble.

I take that episode in *Murphy* as an instance of the ironic note in the development of modern Ireland: it presupposes a mythic or Yeatsian phase, and plans to subvert it, profaning its holy ground. The fact that the two notes or modes are contemporaneous is not embarrassing. No

---

[2] Samuel Beckett, *Murphy* (London: Calder and Boyars, 1969 reprint of 1938 edition), pp. 28–29.

theory of intertextuality is required to indicate that one mood of a national life may be expressed beside a rival one. The mythic or heroic phase began – or was resumed, if you take a longer view – with Thomas Davis and the Young Ireland movement, Standish O'Grady, Douglas Hyde, Yeats, AE, and Lady Gregory: it did not end with the establishment of the Irish Free State or the clear evidence that the leaders of that institution were self-evidently unheroic. But, broadly speaking, the ironic phase became assertive if not dominant with the passage of the bill in 1925 outlawing divorce in Ireland, an act of oppression followed four years later by the passage of the Censorship of Publications Bill. The Constitution of 1937 brought this restrictive phase of government to its culmination. During the years of the Irish Literary Revival and afterwards, the masters of irony, directed against a state, a strange mixture of British government and Yeatsian mythology, included Joyce, the Synge of *The Playboy of the Western World* and *The Tinker's Wedding*, George Moore, Yeats in his satires on Dublin, Sean O'Casey, Beckett, Sean O'Faolain, Frank O'Connor, Brinsley MacNamara, Austin Clarke in his later poems, and Flann O'Brien. The inclusion of Yeats as mythographer and ironist is not a contradiction: since the unpleasantness at the first performance of *The Playboy of the Western World* in the Abbey Theatre on January 26, 1907, he had reason to know that his version of Ireland and its culture was locally resented.

The juxtaposition of Beckett's *Murphy* and Yeats's "The Statues" has its critical point in that context. Beckett recognized national values only to deride them. Yeats invoked such values on his own authority, and dared other people to spoil them. Beckett did not take much interest in the Protestant middle-class tradition from which he emerged, except that it enabled him to keep his distance from the Roman Catholic middle-class that was soon to take power in government and the professions. Yeats embarrassed his associates by the claim he made in the Senate for his origin – "no petty people" – and he responded by despising their embarrassment. He saw his early work as that of a cultural nationalist, preparing the ground for the emergence of a nation that could no longer be denied the right to exist. Beckett asserted that he had no interest in the Irish people any more than in the Finnish people or any other such entity. When his friend Thomas MacGreevy claimed, in a book on Jack Yeats, that Yeats's paintings were significant because of their relation to the Irish people and the noble cause of nationality, Beckett protested both in private and in public. He insisted that Jack

Yeats was a great painter for aesthetic reasons, not because his paintings could be put to the service of a national cause:

[Jack B. Yeats] is with the great of our time, Kandinsky and Klee, Ballmer and Bram van Velde, Rouault and Braque, because he brings light, as only the great dare to bring light, to the issueless predicament of existence.[3]

The distinctive quality of Jack Yeats's paintings was "strangeness so entire as even to withstand the stock assimilations to holy patrimony, national and other."[4] Beckett would have no dealings with the national cause; but then he came late upon the scene, as W. B. Yeats did not. Yeats was in at the beginning, or near it. He discovered or invented a race and laboured to turn it into a nation; at least that was his aim from the years culminating in the death of Parnell in 1891 till 1916 when Pearse and his military colleagues took the cause more spiritedly into their own hands.[5] By the time Beckett was sixteen, in 1922, the Free State was about to come into power. By the time he went to Paris, in November 1928, Ireland was resolutely on its way to becoming a nation among nations, even if it did not achieve full independence from the United Kingdom till 1948. Beckett was a latecomer, irony came easily to him.

But this did not inhibit him from admiring the selected work of his Irish elders and his contemporaries. Cioran met him one day in 1975 on the Avenue de l'Observatoire and they spoke of Swift. Beckett mentioned that he was rereading *Gulliver's Travels* and that he "had a predilection for the 'country of the Houyhnhnms' and particularly for the scene where Gulliver feels such terror and disgust at the approach of a female Yahoo."[6] I don't think Swift meant as much to Beckett as he did to Yeats and Joyce, but he was an irrefutable voice. Joyce could not be evaded, though I think Beckett regarded his tribute to him as sufficiently paid by his essay on *Work in Progress* and the obviously parasitic *Dream of Fair to Middling Women.* He was an assiduous playgoer at the Abbey, despite the fact that the theatre is dealt with harshly in *Murphy* when Murphy makes his will in the following terms:

With regard to the disposal of these my body, mind and soul, I desire that they be burnt and placed in a paper bag and brought to the Abbey Theatre,

---

[3] Samuel Beckett, *Disjecta: Miscellaneous Writings and a Dramatic Fragment,* ed. Ruby Cohn (New York: Grove Press, 1984), p. 97.

[4] Ibid., p. 149.

[5] Cf. David Lloyd, *Anomalous States: Irish Writing and the Post-Colonial Moment* (Dublin: Lilliput Press, 1993), pp. 59–87.

[6] Cioran, *Anathemas and Admirations,* p. 133.

Lr Abbey Street, Dublin, and without pause into what the great and good Lord Chesterfield calls the necessary house, where their happiest hours have been spent, on the right as one goes down into the pit, and I desire that the chain be there pulled upon them, if possible during the performance of a piece, the whole to be executed without ceremony or show of grief.[7]

Be that as it may, Beckett went on record to acknowledge the Yeats of *At the Hawk's Well* and, even more warmly, the Synge of *The Well of the Saints*, both of these plays in which something interminably waited for, like Godot, nearly arrives but doesn't. O'Casey he admired mainly, I think, because he was not Shaw. Beckett's most sustained tribute was given to the Yeats of "The Tower" in a short play for television, "but the clouds," written in 1976 and broadcast the following April. It is a ghost-play of lost love, an attempt to summon up a beloved woman who comes forth only to the extent of murmuring inaudibly the last lines of "The Tower":

> Till the wreck of body,
> Slow decay of blood,
> Testy delirium
> Or dull decrepitude,
> Or what worse evil come –
> The death of friends, or death
> Of every brilliant eye
> That made a catch in the breath –
> Seem but the clouds of the sky
> When the horizon fades,
> Or a bird's sleepy cry
> Among the deepening shades.[8]

It is fair to call Beckett an ironist in relation to the Yeatsian mythology of modern Ireland. But he was not compulsive in his irony: he was tender toward anything that concerned him. Toward his own early life, for instance. "I suppose all is reminiscence from womb to tomb," he told James Knowlson.[9] But he did not claim that reminiscence was a stable act of cognition. Anthony Cronin has drawn attention to a little episode in Beckett's early life that he cared enough about to allude to three times, in different terms and in contexts none of which is officially

---

[7] Beckett, *Murphy*, p. 151.

[8] W. B. Yeats, *The Variorum Edition of the Poems of W. B. Yeats*, ed. Peter Allt and Russell K. Alspach (New York: Macmillan, 1957), p. 416.

[9] Cf. James Knowlson, "Pipes and Tubes," in Morris Beja, S. E. Gontarski, and Pierre Astier (eds.), *Samuel Beckett: Humanistic Perspectives* (Columbus: Ohio State University Press, 1983), p. 16.

autobiographical.[10] In 1910 the Irish Aero Club gave a display over Leopardstown Racecourse in which several international aviators took part, looping the loop and doing other wondrous deeds. The Becketts lived nearby in Foxrock and they attended the show. The scene of Beckett's memory then shifts to Cornelscourt Hill Road, where as a young boy he walked home one day with his mother after going to the local grocery, Connolly's Stores, in Cornelscourt. In *Malone Dies* Beckett has this passage:

I was present at one of the first loopings of the loop, so help me God. I was not afraid. It was above a racecourse, my mother held me by the hand, She kept saying, It's a miracle, a miracle. Then I changed my mind. We were not often of the same mind. One day we were walking along the road, up a hill of extraordinary steepness, near home I imagine, my memory is full of steep hills, I get them confused. I said, The sky is further away than you think, is it not, mama? It was without malice, I was simply thinking of all the leagues that separated me from it. She replied, to me her son, It is precisely as far away as it appears to be. She was right. But at the time I was aghast. I can still see the spot, opposite Tyler's gate. A market-gardener, he had only one eye and wore sidewhiskers. That's the idea, rattle on.[11]

Beckett rattled on about this episode, more distractedly, in a story called "The End":

Now I was making my way through the garden. There was that strange light which follows a day of persistent rain, when the sun comes out and the sky clears too late to be of any use. The earth makes a sound as of sighs and the last drops fall from the emptied, cloudless sky. A small boy, stretching out his hands and looking up at the blue sky, asked his mother how such a thing was possible. Fuck off, she said. I suddenly remembered I had not thought of asking Mr Weir for a piece of bread.[12]

Many years later, in *Company*, Beckett returned to the scene:

A small boy you come out of Connolly's Stores holding your mother by the hand. You turn right and advance in silence southward along the highway. After some hundred paces you head inland and broach the long steep homeward. You make ground in silence hand in hand through the warm still summer air. It is late afternoon and after some hundred paces the sun appears above the crest of the rise. Looking up at the blue sky and then at your mother's face you break the

[10] Anthony Cronin, *Samuel Beckett: The Last Modernist* (London: Harper Collins, 1992), pp. 17 ff.
[11] Samuel Beckett, *Three Novels: Molloy, Malone Dies, The Unnamable* (New York: Grove Weidenfeld, 1991), p. 268.
[12] Samuel Beckett, *Stories & Texts for Nothing* (New York: Grove Press, 1967), p. 50.

silence asking her if it is not in reality much more distant than it appears. The sky that is. The blue sky. Receiving no answer you mentally reframe your question and some hundred paces later look up at her face again and ask her if it does not appear much less distant than in reality it is. For some reason you could never fathom this question must have angered her exceedingly. For she shook off your little hand and made you a cutting retort you have never forgotten.[13]

Mrs. Beckett, a high-toned Christian woman, would not have retorted in the idiom of the streets as given in "The End." It is impossible to say what the facts of the episode were, as distinct from the three versions we have of it: we have variations on a theme without the theme, so we are free to conflate them as we wish. I take the most revealing phrase to be "to me her son," wounded pride enforcing that precision of phrase. But on any account the episode rankled with Beckett and he recalled it, presumably in the hope of writing it out of his system. In his book on Proust, he ridiculed such gestures:

Voluntary memory (Proust repeats it ad nauseam) is of no value as an instrument of evocation, and provides an image as far removed from the real as the myth of our imagination or the caricature furnished by direct perception.[14]

Presumably the memory at work in the Cornelscourt episode is involuntary, and has to be respected. No irony is exerted in any of the three versions.

The same exemption from irony is evident wherever there is confluence between a sentiment that insists on being recalled and the place in which it occurred. Beckett hates time – "the poisonous ingenuity of Time in the science of affliction" –[15] but he is cordial enough toward place, or rather toward particular places, most of them in or around Dublin to begin with: Foxrock, Killiney Hill, the White Rock Strand, Leopardstown, watching the ducks in St. Stephen's Green (*Eh Joe*), Portobello Bridge, the Dublin city of the Bovril sign, Merrion Row, and McLoughlin's in *Dream of Fair to Middling Women*, the pier at Dun Laoghaire in *Krapp's Last Tape*, Leopardstown Railway Station in *All That Fall*, Barrington's Tower, the National Gallery, and the National Library in *That Time*, the Grand Canal in "First Love," the Forty-Foot swimming hole in *Company*, the Military Road near Glencree in *Mercier and Camier*, and the St. John o' God's of Stillorgan where Macmann lodged in *Malone Dies*. This list is

---

[13] Samuel Beckett, *Company* (London: John Calder, 1980), pp. 12–13.
[14] Samuel Beckett, *Proust* (London: John Calder, 1965), p. 14.   [15] Ibid., p. 15.

incomplete, as recourse to Eoin O'Brien's *The Beckett Country* will show. Even when Beckett's characters – to call them that rather loosely – turn aside from a recognizable place, the place is not humiliated, though the characters may be. There is a spot along the Military Road – I know it well – where a wayside cross keeps in mind the murder of an insurgent in the Troubles. When Camier and Mercier come upon it, their inability to remember its significance is repaired by the narrator, at no cost to the dead patriot:

What is that cross? said Camier.
There they go again.
Planted in the bog, not far from the road, but too far for the inscription to be
    visible, a plain cross stood.
I once knew, said Mercier, but no longer.
I too once knew, said Camier, I'm almost sure.
But he was not quite sure.

It was the grave of a nationalist, brought here in the night by the enemy and executed, or perhaps only the corpse brought here, to be dumped. He was buried long after, with a minimum of formality. His name was Masse, perhaps Massey. No great store was set by him now, in patriotic circles. It was true he had done little for the cause. But he still had this monument. All that, and no doubt much more, Mercier and perhaps Camier had once known, and all forgotten.

How aggravating, said Camier.
Would you like to go back and look? said Mercier.
And you? said Camier.
As you please, said Mercier.[16]

Places generally fare well in Beckett's fiction and plays, more so than the people found in them, as Austin Clarke discovered when he saw himself ridiculed as Austin Ticklepenny in *Murphy*. Even Terence MacSwiney, Lord Mayor of Cork, whom one would have thought exempt from irony by the manner of his death, is drawn into *Malone Dies* only as a test case for the human capacity of surviving for a while without solid nourishment, water permitted:

That reminds me, how long can one fast with impunity? The Lord Mayor of Cork lasted for ages, but he was young, and then he had political convictions, human ones too probably, just plain human convictions. And he allowed himself

---

[16] Samuel Beckett, *Mercier and Camier*, tr. Beckett (New York: Grove Press, 1974), p. 98.

a sip of water from time to time, sweetened probably. Water, for pity's sake! How is it I am not thirsty. There must be drinking going on inside me, my secretions.[17]

People are rarely allowed to engage the full attention of Beckett's figments. But his leaving Dublin for Paris coincided with his giving up the pleasure of malevolence.

Beckett's Ireland, then, is mostly places, but it is also the speech of those places, again treated with tenderness. Just as he recalled with something like pleasure his scenes of childhood with Foxrock as their center, so he remained open to the sounds and idioms of Irish English, Hiberno-English as it is called. One of the most memorable sequences in *All That Fall* occurs when Dan Rooney hears his wife speaking words and phrases inconsistent with her normal speech:

MR ROONEY: You have ceased to care. I speak – and you listen to the wind.
MRS ROONEY: No, no, I am agog, tell me all, then we shall press on and never pause, never pause, till we come safe to haven.
[Pause]
MR ROONEY: Never pause ... safe to haven .... Do you know, Maddy, sometimes one would think you were struggling with a dead language.
MRS ROONEY: Yes indeed, Dan, I know full well what you mean, I often have that feeling, it is unspeakably excruciating.
MR ROONEY: I confess I have it sometimes myself, when I happen to overhear what I am saying.
MRS ROONEY: Well, you know, it will be dead in time, just like our own poor dear Gaelic, there is that to be said.[18]

This is a generous allusion to the episode in the first chapter of *Ulysses* when the milk-woman says to Buck Mulligan, who has quoted Haines's opinion as an Englishman that "we ought to speak Irish in Ireland": "Sure we ought to ... and I'm ashamed I don't speak the language myself. I'm told it's a grand language by them that knows."[19] But *All That Fall* adds the nuance of Dan Rooney's "when I happen to overhear what I am saying." In Beckett, someone speaks – in a manner of speaking – and someone listens – at least intermittently – and often the two are one though not unambiguously the same.

The refined English that favors "never pause" and "safe to haven" is bound to appear a dead language to anyone who hears it from a distance,

[17] Beckett, *Three Novels*, p. 273.
[18] Samuel Beckett, *The Complete Dramatic Works* (London: Faber and Faber, 1986), p. 194.
[19] James Joyce, *Ulysses*, ed. Hans Walter Gabler with Wolfhard Steppe and Claus Melchior (New York: Random House, 1986), pp. 12–13.

like the Latin we have learnt and forgotten. To aspire to it from the unsafe haven of Hiberno-English is to yearn for a more comprehensive life than the one available to Maddy Rooney, ageing wife to a blind husband in Foxrock. It also entails her meaning beyond her means, an aspiration we have no reason to think she understands. It was in relation to *Endgame* that Stanley Cavell raised the question: must we mean what we say? "The discovery of *Endgame*," he maintained, "both in topic and technique, is not the failure of meaning (if that means the lack of meaning) but its total, even totalitarian, success – our inability *not* to mean what we are given to mean."[20] But Cavell discovers, without quite honoring the discovery, that you can defeat the oppressive authority of a language, or at worst hold it at bay, by various stratagems. One of them is to treat the forms of discourse as empty things, merely nominal. When Hamm and Clov try the alarm clock to see if it works, and listen to its ringing to the end, Clov says "The end is terrific" and Hamm says "I prefer the middle."[21] Another device is to treat as literal what is proposed as loosely figurative, reducing tropes to grammatical forms. That is what the skepticism of Deconstruction amounts to, as Paul de Man demonstrated by refusing to enter into the rhetorical spirit of the last stanza of Yeats's "Among School Children." He read it by pretending to have a tin ear and to be a mere grammarian.

There is another device that Cavell has not taken account of, mainly because (as a student of Austin and Wittgenstein) he assumes that a language is what it officially is and that we have no choice but to negotiate with it on its own terms. Gilles Deleuze and Felix Guattari designate as "a minor literature" the literature "a minority constructs within a major language."[22] They have Kafka in view, a Jew in Prague writing in German, but their designations have wider ambition: they might have referred to Yeats, writing in Hiberno-English while participating, willingly or not, in the larger ideological enterprise of writing in English. So far as I understand Deleuze and Guattari, the concept of a minor literature depends on a notion of territory. A territory is a place in which a majority writer writes in a majority language, as E. M. Forster writes *Howards End* or George Eliot *Middlemarch*. A territory raises two possibilities, de-territorial and re-territorial. In the de-territorial motive, an expression freed from its official form brings about a corresponding liberation of

---

[20] Stanley Cavell, *Must We Mean What We Say?* (Cambridge University Press, 1976), p. 117.
[21] Beckett, *The Complete Dramatic Works*, p. 115.
[22] Gilles Deleuze and Felix Guattari, *Kafka: Toward a Minor Literature*, trans. Dana Polan (Minneapolis: University of Minnesota Press, 1986), p. 16.

content and takes to itself a nomadic, irregular existence. It is the kind of existence a black writer has in America, or a Latino writer, or an immigrant trying to write in American English. Such a writer "finds his own point of underdevelopment, his own *patois*, his own third world, his own desert."[23] "A language of sense is traversed by a line of escape, in order to liberate a living and expressive material that speaks for itself and has no need of being put into a form."[24] According to the re-territorializing motive, a minority writer repairs the openness of his writing by joining it to official stabilities, the facts of a life, the hypothetical structure of a work, the self as an axiomatic entity only ostensibly broken, the image of a culture he or she would join, the conventions of making sense which one would adopt.

Deleuze and Guattari argue that there are only two ways open to "minor literature." One is to enrich the majority language artificially, to swell it up through all the resources of symbolism, of esoteric sense, having recourse – as in Gustav Meyrink, Max Brod, and other writers – to archetypes, Kabbala, and alchemy. Yeats's early poems attempt this device, though probably not in the service of the major literature. Kafka chooses the other way, according to Deleuze and Guattari:

He will opt for the German language of Prague as it is and in its very poverty. Go always farther in the direction of deterritorialization, to the point of sobriety. Since the language is arid, make it vibrate with a new intensity. Oppose a purely intensive usage of language to all symbolic or even significant or simply signifying usages of it. Arrive at a perfect and unformed expression, a materially intense expression.[25]

At this point, Deleuze and Guattari glance at a comparison of Joyce and Beckett. As Irish writers, both of them "live within the genial conditions of a minor literature." This is "the glory of this sort of minor literature – to be the revolutionary force for all literature": hence the utilization of English and of many other languages in *Finnegans Wake* and Beckett's recourse to French. The difference is that Joyce "never stops operating by exhilaration and overdetermination and brings about all sorts of worldwide reterritorializations." When Beckett writes in French, "he proceeds by dryness and sobriety, a willed poverty, pushing deterritorialization to such an extreme that nothing remains but intensities."[26] This second way may enable Beckett to escape from the fate of English, of having to mean what it says, by prescinding from those plenitudes, those enforced lucidities, totality,

---

[23] Ibid., p. 18.   [24] Ibid., p. 21.   [25] Ibid., p. 19.   [26] Ibid.

organic form, and all the other amenities. We do not interpret Beckett's writing by moving from the overt unknown to the known; from chaos and rigmarole to a known order elsewhere that would bring the writing to heel and make it behave itself. There is no myth, even as the last resort of interpretation, no literature or philosophy in which the writing may be safely lodged, no subjectivity in which the words on the page may find at least provisional stability. That is why the easy bits of Beckett's writing, the reminiscences of Dublin, are misleading: they allow us to pretend that in some way and at some level he may be read as any other writer. Beckett's relation to the society that gives rise to minor literature is equivocal, because the only pleasure he takes from that source is the beauty of its syllables. "Words have been my only loves, not many." He is not writing, as Yeats did, on behalf of a separatist mythology. He went to Paris and started writing mostly but not solely in French because he got tired of the echoes, the old allegiances, he got tired of listening to Dan Rooney and wanted to start over in a new language, with no debts incurred, no Ireland to care about.

Even in *Watt* (1953), a work of fiction he wrote first in English, he persisted in the ways of a minor literature, avoiding the official lordliness of making sense, contenting himself with slapstick pedantries and local intensities, going no further to seek a climax than by having one phrase speak pedantically to another. As here:

Watt's concern, while it lasted, was with the dog. But it did not last long, this concern of Watt's, not very long, as such concerns go. And yet it was a major concern, of that period, while it lasted. But once Watt had grasped, in its complexity, the mechanism of this arrangement, how the food came to be left, and the dog to be available, and the two to be united, then it interested him no more, and he enjoyed a comparative peace of mind, in this connexion. Not that for a moment Watt supposed that he had penetrated the forces at play, in this particular instance, or even perceived the forms that they upheaved, or obtained the least useful information concerning himself, or Mr Knott, for he did not. But he had turned, little by little, a disturbance into words, he had made a pillow of old words, for a head. Little by little, and not without labour. Kate eating from her dish, for example, with the dwarfs standing by, how he had laboured to know what that was, to know which the doer, and what the doer, and what the doing, and which the sufferer, and what the sufferer, and what the suffering, and what those shapes, that were not rooted to the ground, like the veronica, but melted away, into the dark, after a while.[27]

---

[27] Samuel Beckett, *Watt* (Paris: The Olympia Press, 1953), pp. 116–117.

Only a minor literature, operating in an irresponsible relation to a majority one – like an Irish actor playing in London – could enjoy these vain precisions, pursue the difference between "long" and "very long," measure the degree of heft in "upheaved." The words are nearly – nearly, not quite – leading a life of their own, scornful of such ulterior events as climaxes and resolutions. Whatever that life is deemed to be, it does not minister to any life we might think of ascribing to a speaker of these words. We have no such cause. The writing could be regarded as decadent, if one sign of decadence is a consideration of the word rather than the phrase, the phrase rather than the sentence, the sentence rather than the paragraph, the paragraph rather than the chapter or the book. This is Irish writing, in the sense in which we speak of an Irish solution to an Irish problem. The problem, for Beckett, is that there is no problem to be resolved, as Cavell evidently thinks there is; there is only the sensuous problem of composing one nomadic sentence and placing it beside another one, equally irregular, turning a few disturbances into words, making a pillow of old words, for a head. There is pleasure in it, too, at least some small pleasure, besides the labor it entails.

CHAPTER 12

William Trevor

William Trevor is an Irish writer by birth, and I take it he considers himself an Irish writer still. He left Ireland in 1954 and has settled in Devon. He was born in Mitchelstown, County Cork, on May 24, 1928 (but I have seen another birthday ascribed to him) to a family Protestant and middle-class. His father was a bank official with enough money to send him to school at Sandford Park, Dublin, and later to St. Columba's College, Rathfarnham, a school "with a reputation for aloofness, and skill on the hockey field."[1] At Trinity College, Dublin he read History but not with particular zeal. He left with an undistinguished degree and eventually found a reliable job in an advertising agency in London. In *Excursions in the Real World* (1994) he writes with equanimity of his early years:

I was born into a minority that all my life has seemed in danger of withering away. This was smalltime Protestant stock, far removed from the well-to-do Ascendancy of the recent past yet without much of a place in de Valera's new Catholic Ireland. The insult and repression that for centuries had been the response to Irish aspirations, the murders perpetrated by the Black and Tans, the heartbreak of the Civil War, were all to be expunged in de Valera's dream of a land "bright with cosy homesteads, whose fields and villages would be joyous with the sounds of industry, with the romping of sturdy children, the contests of athletic youths, the laughter of comely maidens; whose firesides would be forums for the wisdom of old age."[2]

Trevor has never objected to de Valera's dream of Ireland: he approves of it, apparently, and regrets only that it could not be fulfilled. He apparently had no objection to de Valera's determination to keep Ireland out of the Second World War. These sentiments may explain why his fiction exhibits none of the *ressentiment* of a diminished Anglo-Irish

* *The New York Review of Books*, February 22, 2001.
[1] William Trevor, *Excursions in the Real World* (New York: Knopf, 1994), p. 41.   [2] Ibid., p. xiii.

gentry or the lurid fantasy of Catholic power resorted to by other Protestant writers of similar background, such as Charles Maturin, Bram Stoker, and Sheridan LeFanu. The rise of Catholics to high place in Ireland does not seem to arouse in Trevor any special bitterness: he assumes that it was historically inevitable and therefore appropriate. Tender toward the Big House, he has seen the Protestant landed class in Ireland lapsing into a social existence mostly picturesque and decorative, but he has accepted this change with good grace and as patiently as other changes. In the novel *Fools of Fortune* (1983) he presents with appropriate dismay the burning of Kilneagh House, once a great house supposedly near Fermoy, County Cork, but he does not rail at the men who burned it, a squad of Black and Tans led by Sergeant Rudkin. A few of his stories, including "The Hotel of the Idle Moon," "The Distant Past," and "Mr. McNamara," could be read as allegories of the rise of Catholic Ireland and the fall of the Ascendancy, but no venom sours the narrative. Trevor has referred to "the melancholy nothingness that is the twentieth century's ugliest trade mark,"[3] but he has in mind mainly "the fashion in insurance-company architecture" in Dublin. You don't need to be of the withering Anglo-Irish Protestant class to hold that opinion.

The Hill Bachelors is a collection of twelve stories, seven of them set in Ireland or among Irish emigrants in England, four of them set among the English in England, and one in France. The best of them is the title story, a story of rural, remote Ireland, a family, and the constraints on a son who, out of a conviction of duty, stays on to look after his mother and gives up his chance of breaking away. The pervading genre of the stories is realism. Trevor has studied the arts of Dickens, Flaubert, Turgenev, Joyce, and other masters of the genre. His nearest companions in modern Irish fiction are Sean O'Faolain in urban stories and, in stories of Irish rural life, Mary Lavin and Frank O'Connor. Like these writers, Trevor seems to come to his stories by imagining a person or two or three people entangled in family or professional ties. The claims of plot and environment come later. His stories practice a distinction between "the real" and "the romantic" like the one proposed by Henry James in the Preface to *The American*:

The real represents to my perception the things we cannot possibly *not* know, sooner or later, in one way or another . . . . The romantic stands, on the other hand, for the things that, with all the facilities in the world, all the wealth and all

---

[3] Ibid., p. 78.

the courage and all the wit and all the adventure, we never *can* directly know; the things that can reach us only through the beautiful circuit and subterfuge of our thought and our desire.[4]

With few exceptions in his fiction, Trevor goes in for "the real." He sees or imagines a character, and asks himself what he – or more often she – would do with the problematic gift of life and the conditions at hand. As in "The Piano Tuner's Wives" from *After Rain*: suppose you were a blind piano tuner and you married Violet and some years later she died and after a decent interval you married Belle, a woman you had rejected in favor of Violet. How would you deal with Belle's conviction that the dead Violet was still deep in your life, leading you through houses and landscapes? How would Belle herself deal with that conviction? Pettie in *Death in Summer* (1998), Joseph Ambrose Hilditch in *Felicia's Journey* (1994), and Frau Messinger in *Nights at the Alexandra* (1987) seem to have begun as figures in Trevor's mind, waiting for whatever destiny he would give them, subject to the privilege of "the real" or verisimilitude.

Of the short stories in this genre, "Her Mother's Daughter" is outstanding. It is a story of a dreadful mother, living only to bring to publication the papers of her dead husband, a lexicographer, and meanwhile to punish her daughter Helena for the crime, it appears, of being alive. It is, in the end, a revenge play, and the daughter alone survives to tell the tale. Trevor has imagined the domestic scene so fully that every gesture gratifies our sense of "the real":

Before [her father's] death, conversations at mealtimes usually had to do with words. "Fluxion?" she remembered her father saying, and when she shrugged, her mother tightened her lips, her glance lingering on the shrug long after its motion had ceased.[5]

We cannot possibly *not* know those lips and that long glance. The precision of Trevor's irony in this story is masterful, especially when he enters Helena's mind and gives her, for the time being, the last word:

When she closed her eyes after lights-out, Helena saw her mother in the dark study, listing words and derivations, finding new words or words no longer used, all in loving memory.[6]

---

[4] Henry James, *The Art of the Novel: Critical Prefaces* (Boston: Northeastern University Press, 1984 reprint), pp. 31–32.
[5] William Trevor, *Collected Stories* (London: Penguin Books in association with The Bodley Head, 1993), p. 993.
[6] Ibid., p. 998.

The device by which Helena learns of her mother's death – a telephone call from the genially daft next-door-neighbor Mrs. Archingford to Helena who now works in the kitchens of a business firm – is characteristically telling. The funeral is persuasively low-key:

It was Mrs Archingford who had noticed the curtains not drawn back in the sitting-room of her mother's house, who had worried and had finally spoken to a policeman on the beat. Starvation was given as the cause of death on the death certificate: still struggling with the work in the study, Helena's mother had not bothered to eat. Not having visited her for more than three years, Helena had tried not to think about her while that time passed.

"You'll forgive me, dear, if I fail to attend the funeral," Mrs Archingford requested. "She didn't care for the look of me and no bones about it. Would be a trifle hypocritical, should we say?"

Helena was the only person who did attend the funeral. While a clergyman who had never known her mother spoke his conventional farewell she kept thinking of the busy kitchens of Veitch and Company – all that mound of food, while her mother had absentmindedly starved.[7]

In *The Hill Bachelors* Trevor is again preoccupied with character rather than with plot or incident. Nothing much happens in these stories, in any external sense. "A Friend in the Trade" is a good example. Start with Clione and James, a happy marriage. He deals in first editions and manuscripts, and together they run Asterisk Press, "publishing the verse of poets who are in fashion, novellas, short stories, from time to time a dozen or so pages of reminiscence by a writer whose standing guarantees the interest of collectors." Add a third party, a friend who deals in "nineteenth-century jottings," scraps of letters, abortive chapters of a novel by Dickens. Of course the third party is in love with Clione, but he has no designs on the marriage, he wants only to be in her vicinity. Trevor is more interested in these people as individuals and as he contemplates them than in any catastrophe that may befall them. There is no catastrophe: no vendetta, no murder, no suicide. Trevor is not in a hurry to see the lives of his people disturbed. Meanwhile he lavishes intelligence on the presentation of the third party, Michingthorpe:

But nothing that is outside himself, or part of other people, ever influences Michingthorpe. His surface runs deep, for greater knowledge of him offers nothing more than what initially it presents. Roaming the Internet is his hobby, he sometimes says.[8]

---

[7] Ibid., p. 1002.   [8] William Trevor, *The Hill Bachelors* (New York: Viking, 2000), pp. 96–97.

Readers of Trevor's fiction have remarked that he has mellowed in recent years. He seems willing to think that any crime or offence can be forgiven, provided there is some residue of love among the people involved. Sometimes he is content to look at someone and imagine what form her life will take before some necessity settles down on her. But I don't think he has disavowed the acerbity of his earlier stories. In *Excursions in the Real World* he describes going to a party given by the well-known Irish historian T. W. Moody and his wife at their home in Rathgar. A dispiriting occasion, apparently. The only praise Trevor can bring himself to utter is that "Dr. Moody and his wife meant well, and harmed no one."[9] But in a story, "The Time of Year," Trevor reverts to the same party, and uses the occasion to excoriate Moody (Professor Skully as he is called, but the man is unmistakable) and his wife, "as if they lived together in the dead wood of a relationship, together in this house because it was convenient." There is more detail in that vein:

Valerie continued to regard Mrs Skully's face and suddenly she found herself shivering. How could that mouth open and close, issuing invitations without knowing they were the subject of derision? How could this woman, in her late middle age, officiate at student parties in magenta and jade, or bake inedible cakes without knowing it? How could she daily permit herself to be taken for granted by a man who cared only for students with academic success behind them? How could she have married his pomposity in the first place? There was something wrong with Mrs Skully, there was something missing, as if some part of her had never come to life.

The Skullys "would go on ageing and he might never turn to his wife and say he was sorry."[10] Sorry for what? I barely knew Moody; I met him in Dublin two or three times, not often enough to form an opinion. A friend of mine who knew him better than I did tells me that he was pompous and boring, a man of managerial rather than creative talent. But I find Trevor's cruelty in this story shocking. What did Moody and his wife do to Trevor to incur such a drubbing?

Trevor's version of realism, like other versions in Russian, French, and English fiction, has a strong claim on our attention. We understand life mainly through the continuity of appearances and resemblances. Whatever happens has at least the privilege of having happened. Repetition is believing. Trevor takes pains to make us believe his stories. It is not enough that we suspend our disbelief while the story lasts. He is not a

[9] Trevor, *Excursions*, p. 69.   [10] Trevor, *Collected Stories*, p. 807.

historical novelist, but he gains credence for his stories by projecting them among historical events. "Of the Cloth," a story in *The Hill Bachelors*, has the Protestant minister Rev. Grattan Fitzmaurice sharing his love of Ireland with the Catholic priest Father Leahy:

For Grattan there was history's tale, regrets and sorrows and distress, the voices of unconquered men, the spirit of women as proud as empresses. For Grattan there were the rivers he knew, the mountains he had never climbed, wild fuchsia by a seashore and the swallows that came back, turf smoke on the air of little towns, the quiet in long glens. The sound, the look, the shape of Ireland, and Ireland's rain and Ireland's sunshine, and Ireland's living and Ireland's dead: all that.[11]

But this remarkably high style of sentiment is provoked by dismal circumstances: empty pews in Grattan's local churches, and a Catholic Church in Ireland shamed by scandal. When Father Leahy visits Grattan, a copy of *The Irish Times* on the table shows "the grinning countenance of Father Brendan Smyth being taken into custody by a grim-faced detective: *Paedophile Priest is Extradited*, the headline ran."[12]

Trevor sets other stories in a context that everybody is expected to know – films, advertising, brand names, popular songs:

They fell in love when *A Whiter Shade of Pale* played all summer. They married when Tony Orlando sang *Tie a Yellow Ribbon 'Round the Old Oak Tree*. These tunes are faded memories, hardly there at all, and they've forgotten Procol Harum and Suzi Quatro and the Brotherhood of Man, having long ago turned to Brahms.[13]

In "Lovers of Their Time" Norman Britt has "a David Niven moustache" and Hilda listens to "the Jimmy Young programme." These are economical devices to imply types, times, and social classes, but they show up the limitations of realism just as clearly as its values.

The first consideration is that if you ask readers to believe a story, you do well not to strain their credence. The narrator of "The Raising of Elvira Tremblett" says:

My father was bulky in his grey overalls, always with marks of grease or dirt on him, his fingernails rimmed with black, like fingers in mourning, I used to think .... Above the mantelpiece Christ on his cross had already given up the ghost.[14]

Interesting perceptions, but nothing in the story persuades me that the narrator is capable of them. He was never "mentally deficient," as his

---

[11] Ibid., p. 37. [12] Trevor, *The Hill Bachelors*, pp. 29–30.
[13] Ibid., p. 89. [14] Trevor, *Collected Stories*, pp. 647, 649.

parents feared he was. Living for the past thirty-four years in an insane asylum, he has always been able to report the events of his day. But the brilliance of apprehending the dirty fingernails as fingers in mourning is beyond his range. Trevor is doing his thinking for him.

Realism has several other problems. The camera in films and TV can do some realistic work better than narrative sentences can. I recall visual images and landscapes from the Pat O'Connor film *The Ballroom of Romance* more vividly than the descriptions and dialogue in Trevor's story. Realism also fosters the assumption that the actual and the real are one and the same. They are not. A fact becomes real only when it comes into a culturally significant relation. The tree near the wall at the end of Joyce's "The Dead" becomes real because it makes a place for Gretta's lover Michael Furey and for Gretta's seeing him getting his death in the rain. Like other realists, Trevor withholds himself in deference to the truth of the situation, but the conventions of realism urge him to proceed as if the truth were by definition social, worldly, and secular. Trevor's best fiction arises when he decides to question this notion and to give some expression to the beautiful circuit and subterfuge of our thought and our desire. Like the heroine of Trevor's *Reading Turgenev*, we are given a way out, even if it is a desperate subterfuge. Reality is more than the price of tomatoes, as Garcia Marquez has remarked.

But the most limiting disability of realism is that it lacks what W. B. Yeats called, somewhat mysteriously, "emotion of multitude." Yeats wondered why he found modern realistic plays unsatisfactory and he decided that it was because they lacked this emotion. Greek tragedy got it from the chorus, "which called up famous sorrows, even all the gods and all heroes, to witness, as it were, some well-ordered fable, some action separated but for this from all but itself." Shakespearean tragedy got it from the double plot, where a sub-plot copies the main plot "much as a shadow upon the wall copies one's body in the firelight." We think of *King Lear* "less as the history of one man and his sorrows than as the history of a whole evil time." Lear's shadow is in Gloucester, "who also has ungrateful children, and the mind goes on imagining other shadows, shadow beyond shadow, till it has pictured the world."[15] Yeats conceded that certain modern dramatists got the emotion of multitude by other means:

[15] W. B. Yeats, *Essays and Introductions* (London: Macmillan, 1961), p. 215.

Ibsen and Maeterlinck have created a new form, for they get multitude from the wild duck in the attic, or from the crown at the bottom of the fountain, vague symbols that set the mind wandering from idea to idea, emotion to emotion.[16]

There cannot be great art, Yeats claimed, "without the little limited life of the fable, which is always the better the simpler it is, and the rich, far-wandering, many-imaged life of the half-seen world beyond it."[17]

Most of Trevor's stories are content with the little limited life of the fable, closed in upon itself. They are stories of domestic malice, minor distress, discrepancies between husband and wife, the ending of a relation, dissatisfactions in an ostensibly Dutch interior, the tragicomedy of social life. Trevor is among the most skilful writers in maintaining the life of the fable. When he feels that the conflicts incurred in the story can be resolved, he lets the disputants resolve them without undue fuss. But often they can't be resolved and then, like Ibsen and Maeterlinck according to Yeats, Trevor looks to a half-seen world beyond them. He brings forward another perspective, as Joyce does systematically in the Homeric emphasis of *Ulysses* and more nonchalantly in *A Portrait of the Artist as a Young Man*. In the second chapter of the *Portrait* Joyce allows Stephen Dedalus to gain some relief from his feelings by finding them in Edmond Dantes, the "dark avenger" of *The Count of Monte Cristo*. When he passes a small whitewashed cottage outside Blackrock, Stephen imagines that a girl lives there, "another Mercedes," and that he rejects her "with a sadly proud gesture of refusal," saying: "Madam, I never eat muscatel grapes."[18]

Trevor is rarely as dashing as that, but he sometimes develops a story by opening it upon a half-seen world beyond the local conditions. His largest effort in this direction is *Reading Turgenev*. Mary Louise marries the local draper Elmer Quarry for security, not love. Gradually she realizes that she is in love with her cousin Robert, an invalid, and that he loves her. Robert reads to her from Turgenev's *Fathers and Sons*. When he dies, Mary Louise maintains their love by identifying herself with Yelena Nikolayevna in *On the Eve* and by projecting her life with Robert as a Russian idyll:

On the day after Elmer first invited her to the Electric Cinema, Robert arrived at the farmhouse. "No," she said when Elmer asked her to accompany him again, and went instead in search of the heron with her cousin. When they

---

[16] Ibid., p. 216.   [17] Ibid.
[18] James Joyce, *A Portrait of the Artist as a Young Man* (New York: Vintage Books, 1993), p. 58.

married they traveled in Italy and France. They sat outside a café by the sea, watching the people strolling by, Robert in a pale suit and a hat that matched it. He leaned across the table to kiss her, as he had the first time in the graveyard. Light as a butterfly, his kisses danced up and down her arm, from the tips of her fingers to her shoulders. The café orchestra began. They drank white wine.[19]

The story ends: "For thirty-one years she passed as mad and was at peace."[20]

In the title story of *After Rain* (1996) Trevor gains emotion of multitude by another device. Harriet, at the end of an affair, goes on vacation to the Pensione Cesarina, a small hotel near Ponte Nicolo that she used to go to with her parents, who are now separated. One afternoon she wanders into the local church of Santa Fabiola and sees an Annunciation by an unknown artist, "perhaps of the school of Filippo Lippi":

The angel kneels, grey wings protruding, his lily half hidden by a pillar. The floor is marble, white and green and ochre. The Virgin looks alarmed, right hand arresting her visitor's advance. Beyond – background to the encounter – there are gracious arches, a balustrade and then the sky and hills. There is a soundlessness about the picture, the silence of a mystery: no words are spoken in this captured moment, what's said between the two has been said already.[21]

Harriet leaves the church and walks back to the Pensione. It has been raining. She is thinking about the painting:

While she stands alone among the dripping vines she cannot make a connection that she knows is there. There is a blankness in her thoughts, a density that feels like muddle also, until she realizes: the Annunciation was painted after rain. Its distant landscape, glimpsed through arches, has the temporary look that she is seeing now. It was after rain that the angel came: those first cool moments were a chosen time.[22]

The story ends with an act of divination:

She hears the swish of the cleaner's mop in the church of Santa Fabiola, she hears the tourists' whisper. The fingers of the praying woman flutter on her beads, the candles flare. The story of Santa Fabiola is lost in the shadows that were once the people of her life, the family tomb reeks odourlessly of death. Rain has sweetened the breathless air, the angel comes mysteriously also.[23]

[19] William Trevor, *Two Lives: Reading Turgenev and My House in Umbria* (New York: Viking, 1991), p. 141.
[20] Ibid., p. 221.   [21] William Trevor, *After Rain* (London: Penguin Books, 1997), p. 91.
[22] Ibid., p. 94.   [23] Ibid., p. 96.

Here emotion of multitude is elicited from a larger perspective than Harriet's common understanding. It is a perspective that the "Annunciation" helps her to achieve. What it entails is an intuition on her part of mythic and natural forces at large. The Annunciation and rain are recognized as suffusing personal life without humiliating it. Harriet's sorrow is not removed, but it is distanced, it has become part of a more comprehensive sense of life. The episode is a minor instance of a motif to be found in Dickens's *Little Dorrit*, George Eliot's *Middlemarch*, and Henry James's *The Portrait of a Lady*. In each of these the heroine takes her sadness with her as she wanders among the ruins of ancient Rome. James writes of Isabel Archer:

She had long before this taken old Rome into her confidence, for in a world of ruins the ruin of her happiness seemed a less unnatural catastrophe. She rested her weariness upon things that had crumbled for centuries and yet still were upright; she dropped her secret sadness into the silence of lonely places .... [24]

In Dickens, George Eliot, and James, the larger perspective is gained by an extended sense of history and culture. Trevor sometimes gains it by appealing to certain Italian Renaissance paintings, but just as often by pastoral recognitions, intimations of continuity and recurrence in the natural world, the rhythms of winter and spring. In *My House in Umbria* Emily Delahunty muses to herself at the end:

Perhaps I'll become old, perhaps not. Perhaps something else will happen in my life, but I doubt it. When the season's over I'll walk among the shrubs myself, making the most of the colours while they last and the fountain while it flows. [25]

There is no reason to think that the colors will not recur or that the fountain will run dry.

The title story of *The Hill Bachelors* keeps these intimations alive, though the pastoral allegory is grim. The little limited life of the fable could not be simpler. After the death of his father, Paulie has to stay at home to take care of his mother. Home is a small farm among remote hills in Ireland. No girl of the present generation would even consider marrying into such loneliness, as Paulie finds when he talks of marriage to Patsy Finucane. After a while his mother offers to go and live with her married daughter Mena, but Paulie won't hear of it. "You're good, Paulie," his mother says:

---

[24] Henry James, *The Portrait of a Lady*, ed. Robert D. Bamberg (New York: W. W. Norton reprint, 1975), p. 430.
[25] Trevor, *Two Lives*, p. 375.

Guilt was misplaced, goodness hardly came into it. Her widowing and the mood of a capricious time were not of consequence, no more than a flicker in a scheme of things that had always been there. Enduring, unchanging, the hills had waited for him, claiming one of their own.[26]

These are not offered as Paulie's thoughts; he would not be able to understand them or to articulate them. It is Trevor, not Paulie, who comprehends this possessive relation between nature and man, between the hills and Paulie. We feel the emotion of multitude, as of subterranean forces come from afar; Paulie does not feel these forces, but he is led by them. He feels the necessity under which he lives. But perhaps on some primitive level of apprehension he realizes it and accepts its claim upon him.

---

[26] Trevor, *The Hill Bachelors*, p. 245.

CHAPTER 13

John McGahern

All Will Be Well is John McGahern's account of his life, from a grim childhood to the start of his career as a novelist with the publication of *The Barracks* (1963) and *The Dark* (1965), books that established him as one of Ireland's most impressive writers. He was born on November 12, 1934 in Dublin, the eldest child of a family that eventually came to seven children. He spent his early years in Ballinamore, County Leitrim. His mother was a teacher, employed when her health permitted in Aughawillian and other small, remote schools in Leitrim. She was an ardent believer in the Catholic faith that surrounded her. As McGahern recalls in *All Will Be Well*:

> Prayers were said each morning. Work and talk stopped in fields and houses and school and shop and the busy street at the first sound of the Angelus bell each day at noon. Every day was closed with the Rosary at night. The worlds to come, hell and heaven and purgatory and limbo, were closer and far more real than America or Australia and talked about almost daily as our future reality.[1]

His mother's most intense hope for her son was that he would become a priest and that she would live to attend his first Mass. She died of cancer in 1945. McGahern's father, like my own, was a police sergeant. McGahern's was one of the first generation of policemen (the *Garda Síochána*) established by the Irish Free State in 1922. Like my father, though for different reasons, Garda Frank McGahern had a commonplace career. He resented the fact that his service as an insurgent in the cause of Irish freedom during the War of Independence was meagerly recognized in the new state. He hated his job, couldn't wait to leave it, and took his duties as a policeman as lightly as he could get away with. He served in village stations, mostly in Cootehall, County Roscommon, without any prospect of promotion.

---

* *The New York Review of Books*, March 23, 2006, revised 2009.
[1] John McGahern, *All Will Be Well: A Memoir* (New York: Alfred A. Knopf, 2006), p. 13.

McGahern's memory of life in the barracks chimes with my own. I recall the hissing noise of the old carbide lamp attached to my father's bicycle as he got ready to go on "meet patrol," where he conferred, late at night, with other sergeants from local stations. And the annual warning that sergeants were required to deliver to local farmers that they must extirpate the ragwort in their fields or face a charge in the District Court. My father carried out these minor tasks more equably than McGahern's did: he didn't rage at necessities.

After McGahern's mother died, the children moved into "married quarters" in the barracks. John's mother, by all accounts, was a saint. There are no unlovely mothers in McGahern's fiction. His father was a brute: cold, violent, vindictive, charming to daughters and other women when he chose to be, but punitive and abusive to his son:

Up to now our mother had always been with us at home and in school. Now that she was gone we were at the mercy of our father – the scoldings, his sudden rages, the beatings he administered. While, in fits, he could charm and seduce us, when we did go towards him he found us tiresome and could not sustain what he had brought about. The protection our mother gave had not always been without danger to herself . . . . She had to be extraordinarily careful. Though my father was often coldly calculating, his general moods were so changeable that, apart from a passion for contrariness, he never knew his mind from one minute to the next.[2]

The local schools that McGahern attended were harsh; corporal punishment was the standard response to idleness, to any show of surliness, and to other misdemeanors. It has taken McGahern many years and four novels, *The Barracks, The Dark, The Leavetaking* (1974), and *Amongst Women* (1990), to write his anger to some degree out of his system. In *The Leavetaking* he repeats stories on this topic that he'd already told in *The Barracks*: good riddance is slow work.

McGahern, like myself, was given access as a boy to a local house that had choice sets of books in glass cases. Like myself, too, he picked out memorable passages that opened his mind, such as this speech in Book XI of the *Odyssey*, where the ghost of Achilles addresses Odysseus from the underground: "Speak not soothingly to me of death, O glorious Odysseus. I would choose, so that I might live on earth, to be the servant of a penniless man than to be lord over all the dead." With such informal teaching and the rudimentary lessons of schooling, McGahern went on to the Presentation Brothers' School, a good school in Carrick-on-Shannon, won a scholarship to St. Patrick's Training College in Drumcondra, Dublin, took a BA degree at University College, Dublin, and became a primary school teacher.

The Dark was an even more vengeful book than *The Barracks* on the same theme of father and son. When it was published, McGahern got more attention from the public than he could have wanted. The book was banned in Ireland on grounds of being "indecent or obscene." Worse still for his career, he married a woman in a registry office rather than a church, thereby rendering himself unfit for continued employment as a teacher in the Catholic *Scoil Eoin Bhaiste* (St. John the Baptist School) in Clontarf. It surprises me that he ever thought he could hold on to his job. "It must needs be that scandals come; but woe to him by whom the scandals come" (Matthew XVIII). McGahern has never forgiven the Catholic Church for his dismissal, though he acknowledges that if he is no longer in the Church, the Church continues to be much in him.[3]

In a country parish in Leitrim, social life, during the years to which McGahern has paid attention, was largely arranged in keeping with Catholic ceremonies and sacraments: not only the Angelus and the Family Rosary, said every night at home by those who said it at all, but Sunday Mass, New Year's Day, the Epiphany, St. Patrick's Day, Lent and its observances, Holy Thursday, Good Friday, Holy Saturday, Easter Sunday, the Corpus Christi Procession, the Feast of the Assumption, Christmas, Midnight Mass, and the recurrent Catholic births, weddings, and funerals. McGahern has denounced the Church in Ireland for its allegedly restrictive, sectarian practices, but this is hard to square with the books in which he presents the Church as having no influence whatever, apparently, on the personal and especially sexual lives of its flock. If you believed McGahern on the evidence of his novels and stories (and I don't, in this particular), you would conclude that any able-bodied lad in Ireland who went to a dancehall emerged from it a couple of hours later with a girl – often a nurse – who took him to her bed for a night of unprotected sex. In *The Pornographer*, the young man has sex with practically any woman he meets and, in London, makes one of them pregnant. He talks of an abortion, but she insists on having the child. At this point he abandons mother and child, goes back to Dublin, meets a girl, Nurse Brady, who

---

[3] Cf. "Catholicism and National Identity in the Works of John McGahern," interview between Eamon Maher and John McGahern: www.studiesirishreview.com/articles/2001/010304i.htm, p. 1.

is not at all dismayed by his behavior and is casual about her own. In the end, vaguely uneasy about his sexual activities in London, he plans to marry Nurse Brady and settle down with her in Leitrim. This is to count as a happy ending.

In the story "Bank Holiday" it takes a senior civil servant, Patrick McDonough, all of a weekend to meet a girl from New York, lunch with her, bring her walking along Dollymount Strand, share a raucous conversation with the poet Patrick Kavanagh in a Dublin pub, make love to the girl in his flat, and gain her agreement to marry "in everything but name." Maybe Yeats was right, if he was referring to Ireland in the first stanza of "Sailing to Byzantium" –

> That is no country for old men. The young
> In one another's arms, birds in the trees
> – Those dying generations – at their song,
> The salmon-falls, the mackerel-crowded seas,
> Fish, flesh, or fowl, commend all summer long
> Whatever is begotten, born, and dies.
> Caught in that sensual music, all neglect
> Monuments of unageing intellect ....[4]

– though little of that sensual music caught my attention in Ireland as it apparently caught Yeats's and McGahern's.

McGahern's fiction is predicated on the places he knows intuitively, especially Leitrim, where he has lived for many years. *The Leavetaking* and *The Pornographer* (1979) are both set in Dublin and London, but the settings are less suited to his gifts. McGahern's imaginative country is Leitrim and its environs. He has taken full possession of it, though one might remark that it is not a strenuously contested part of the world. His method is total submission to the conditions at large. It is a mark of his talent, as he says of a character called the Shah in *That They May Face the Rising Sun* (2002), "Where he blossomed was in the familiar and habitual, which he never left willingly."[5] If someone sits down to breakfast in a novel by McGahern, we are given the full menu:

He ate in silence from a large white plate: sausage, rasher, grilled halves of tomato, mushrooms, onion, black pudding, a thin slice of liver, a grilled lamb chop. From another plate he drew and buttered slices of freshly baked soda bread .... With an audible cry of satisfaction he reached for the slice of apple

[4] W. B. Yeats, *The Variorum Edition of the Poems*, ed. Peter Allt and Russell K. Alspach (New York: Macmillan, 1957), p. 407.
[5] John McGahern, *That They May Face the Rising Sun* (London: Faber and Faber, 2002), p. 38.

tart, the crust sprinkled with fine sugar. He poured cream from a small white jug. He drank from the mug of steaming tea.[6]

If there is work to be done in Leitrim, McGahern makes sure he himself can do it or at least knows how it is done: carpentry, cutting turf, making hay, keeping bees, fishing on the lake, dipping sheep, preparing a corpse for wake and burial. He knows things about Irish rural life that are new to me – that it's customary to stop all clocks in the house of the dead, for instance. No writer I know of since Walt Whitman has derived such pleasure from making lists:

The traders had already set out their stalls. Chain saws were displayed on a long trestle table beneath a canvas tent that bulged and flapped. From the open back of a van a man was selling animal medicines, sprays and drenches and large cans of disinfectant, sticks of caustic for removing horns, bone-handled knives with curved blades for dressing hooves. One whole side of a covered lorry was open. They had grease guns, tins of oil, top links for tractors, chains, pulleys, blue bales of rope. Close by was a van selling Wellingtons, work boots, rainwear, overalls. Elsewhere, shovels, spades, forks, hedge knives, axes, picks were displayed leaning against the side of a van. All kinds of tool handles stood in barrels.[7]

With such specification, "elsewhere" seems a moment's inattention.

In these novels, emotional relations between characters always spell trouble, as with Moran and his wife Rose in *Amongst Women*, but then there is the release of landscape, where McGahern's characters find peace and his prose achieves remarkable beauty, quiet and accepting:

They walked the fields. They looked at the stacked bales in the shaved meadows, already a rich yellow in the sun, and at the cattle and the sheep. They stood on the high hill over the inner lake and watched a heron cross from the wooded island to Gloria Bog. The day was so still that not even a breath of wind ruffled the sedge that was pale as wheat in the sun. The birch trees stood like green flowers until the pale sea merged with the far blue of the mountain.[8]

Or there is the gratification of work to be done – making hay, welding a broken sprocket, attending to bees, conducting an auction – or new images to be looked at, like the sea at Strandhill. To gain release from some domestic exacerbation or raised voices, McGahern's characters have only to look out a kitchen window, walk the fields, or let distant sounds become the music of what happens. As in *The Barracks*:

"Put coats on yourselves," Reegan at last took it into his head to play the part of father, "and no splashin' about of water. It's no time of the year yet for a wettin'."

---

[6] Ibid., p. 91.   [7] Ibid., p. 231.   [8] Ibid., p. 125.

A lovely blue dusk was on the water, a vapour of moon that'd climb to yellow light as the night came was already high. The sun had gone down to the rim of the hills they could not see beyond the woods, the spaces between the tree-tops burning with red light.

The sawmill came to a stop, then the stonecrusher in the quarries. Men called to each other and their voices came with haunting clarity across the frozen countryside. A bucket rattled where a woman was feeding calves in some yard.[9]

In *Amongst Women* the daughters appease their distress over Moran's treatment of them and his wife by taking it to the fields:

They passed the delicate white blossoms of wild cherry, Sheila striding along in angry resentment, Mona following in her shadow. The light of water showed through the tree trunks as they drew close to the narrow wood along the lake but only on the fringe of the trees they lost all resentment at the sight of the thick floor of bluebells beneath the trees. To advance further into the wood was to trample on the colour blue.
"There must be thousands."
"There's millions!"[10]

In the end, they survive by acting together:

They were already conspirators, they were mastered, and yet they were controlling together what they were mastered by.

Some readers in Ireland have complained that McGahern has stuck to his Leitrim with obstinacy, and has confined his attention to a few uneventful years there after the Second World War. They note that although the agricultural West of Ireland has been transformed by the European Union's Common Agricultural Policy, McGahern has shown little or no interest in farmers' access to wealth. Admittedly, Leitrim is one of the poorest counties in Ireland. Another source of complaint, in the eyes of some readers, is that McGahern has been indifferent to the "Troubles" in the North of Ireland since the Civil Rights marches of 1968, the rise of the Provisional Irish Republican Army, the various Loyalist paramilitary groups, internment without trial, Bloody Sunday, and the events leading to the Good Friday Agreement of April 10, 1998. These Troubles have provoked many Irish writers to respond to them in poems, novels, plays, and films – Seamus Heaney, Thomas Kinsella, John Montague, and Neil Jordan among them. But McGahern hasn't been stirred or provoked. The Northern situation "seems strange and foreign to me: it doesn't engage me

[9] John McGahern, *The Barracks* (London: Faber and Faber, 1963), p. 70.
[10] John McGahern, *Amongst Women* (London: Faber and Faber, 1991), p. 75.

personally."[11] He has settled, apparently, for the bizarre conclusion that the Northern situation is simply a quarrel between two sectarian states, the South in the service of Catholics, the North in the service of Protestants. There is no merit in protesting that the story of the North is more complex than McGahern's sense of it; he is free to ignore whatever he chooses to ignore. He is not obliged to concern himself with the current Ireland of greed followed by unemployment and distress, the Dublin of computers and the Irish Financial Center, the capitalism that has made Dublin one of the most expensive cities in the world. Why should he give his bounty to such images?

When *All Will Be Well* was first published in England, it was called simply *Memoir*. The change must have some point. The new title has as its immediate source the passage in "Little Gidding" in which T. S. Eliot writes:

> And all shall be well and
> All manner of thing shall be well
> By the purification of the motive
> In the ground of our beseeching.[12]

The ultimate source of this is the fourteenth-century mystic Dame Julian of Norwich in whose fourteenth "shewing" – or mystical vision – we read of her being told by the Lord that "all shall be well" through prayer and the grace of the Holy Spirit.[13] In McGahern's later fiction, prayer and grace have been translated into natural or secular terms. Community has displaced Church, the rhythm of the seasons has ousted theology.

This "conversion" took place after *Amongst Women*, but it was anticipated in a dramatic moment in that novel when Michael Moran is on his deathbed, attended by his daughters:

> "Why aren't you praying?" he demanded as if he knew he
>   was slipping away.
> They immediately dropped to their knees around the bed.
> "Thou, O Lord, wilt open my lips," Rose began.
> Tears slipped down their faces as they repeated the "Our Fathers" and
>   "Hail Marys." Maggie had begun her Mystery when it grew clear that
>   Moran was trying to speak. She stopped and the room was still.
>   The low whisper was unmistakeable: "*Shut up!*"[14]

---

[11] Ibid., p. 5.
[12] T. S. Eliot, *Collected Poems 1909–1962* (New York: Harcourt Brace and Company, 1963), pp. 206–207.
[13] Julian of Norwich, *Revelations of Divine Love* (London: Methuen, thirteenth edition, 1952), p. 85.
[14] McGahern, *Amongst Women*, p. 180.

In *That They May Face the Rising Sun* the conversion becomes a way of life, "turning each day into the same day, making every Sunday into all the other Sundays."[15]

That They May Face the Rising Sun is hardly a novel at all. There is no story, no plot, but a series of vignettes. There is a lake. There are a few characters with small farms on its shores. Joe and Kate Ruttledge, originally from the neighborhood, have come back from London to settle beside the lake. A few old friends drop in to see them, sometimes two or three times a day. The hospitality consists of tea for the women, whiskey for the men, ham sandwiches for everyone. Nothing happens except talk, bits of news, gossip, reminiscence. A cat catches a hare. Lambs are brought to the local factory. The seasons change, life goes on. Sometimes the narrative tone of voice is darkened, as it was often darkened in the early novels and stories: "In the end what does it matter?"[16] But the continuity of works and days is accepted as mattering, at least sufficiently to keep the talk going. This little community seems to utter itself in a voice of its own. In some passages it is not clear who is speaking or thinking; it is as if the weather spoke for everyone. Most of these characters still go to Mass on Sunday, but the altar they face is the rising sun.

It is in this sense that, as McGahern appears to say, all will be well. Individual acts of will are dissolved in custom. People are still seen as idiosyncratic, but there is no need to judge them, it is enough that they add color to the other lives around them. Inner experiences, if McGahern's characters have such stirrings, are rarely shown. In "The Wine Breath" – one of his best stories – a priest is delivered into the compulsion of memory and association by a hint of snow, the smell of crushed mint in his garden, the light he sees on bits of white beech. His life "had been like any other, except to himself, and then only in odd visions of it, as a lost life." When it had been "agreeable and equitable he had no vision of it at all."[17] He recalls his mother, who had been a seamstress, tearing up every dress, every piece of clothing she had ever made, before sinking into senility and death, but he does not try to divine the inner life that took such a violent turn. Generally in McGahern's stories, characters are alive in what they have to do or the local collisions of temper when they meet. Introspection counts for little of their vitality.

---

[15] McGahern, *That They May Face the Rising Sun*, p. 43.   [16] Ibid., p. 67.
[17] John McGahern, *The Collected Stories* (London: Faber and Faber, 1992), p. 183.

These considerations may help to explain McGahern's strange sense of his major precursors in Irish literature. He does not claim any strong relation to Swift, Yeats, Joyce, or Beckett. Some readers think of him in some relation to Beckett, but that seems extreme. Not being a poet, he is free of Yeats. He can circumvent Joyce by staying out of Dublin. The books he evidently admires are those in which the theme is life-as-such and the fact that particular lives are imagined, observed, and described matters in the beginning but not in the end. McGahern has not written in Irish, but he has remarked upon "the presence of the older language in the English we speak and use in Ireland, in many speech constructions, in its rhythms and its silences, and in those words withheld deliberately or left unspoken."[18]

In *That They May Face the Rising Sun* pieces of dialogue remember the Irish language they come from. "Patrick had no value on Edmund" comes into English from the Irish of "Ní raibh meas ag Phádraig ar Eamon," meaning that Patrick didn't respect Edmund.[19] McGahern has written warmly of one of the great enabling books of modern Irish writing, Tomás O Criomhthain's *An tOileánach* (translated by Robin Flower as *The Islandman*) and noted that O Criomhthain's "view of reality is at no time a personal view and is never at variance with the values of his society as a whole."[20] The place of McGahern's imagination is indeed Leitrim, its time the 1950s, but he does not write punctually to any occasion, or make a large point of it. The realism he practices does not subserve an event but the large rhythm of such events, a distinction also applicable to another book he admires, J. M. Synge's *The Aran Islands*. A typical paragraph in *All Will Be Well* reads:

In another week Mother came home. She was well and happy and went straight back to school. With her each morning we went up the cinder footpath to the little iron gate, past Brady's house and pool and the house where the old Mahon brothers lived, past the deep, dark quarry and across the railway bridge and up the hill by Mahon's shop to the school, and returned the same way in the evening. I am sure it is from those days that I take the belief that the best of life is life lived quietly, where nothing happens but our calm journey through the day, where change is imperceptible and the precious life is everything.[21]

The risk of ennui in the quiet life is clear, but it is a risk McGahern has very impressively negotiated.

---

[18] John McGahern, "What Is My Language?" *Irish University Review*, Vol. 35, No. 1 (Spring/Summer 2005), p. 2.
[19] McGahern, *That They May Face the Rising Sun*, p. 98.
[20] Ibid., p. 3.   [21] McGahern, *All Will Be Well*, p. 86.

CHAPTER 14

The early Roddy Doyle

Paddy Clarke Ha Ha Ha won the Booker Prize in 1993. Set on the north side of Dublin in 1966, it is the story of a ten-year-old boy, Paddy Clarke, told entirely in his voice. The events he speaks of are external. He doesn't keep a diary or express feelings as they occur to him. Everything in the book has happened in school or at home, on the streets of "Barrytown" or in the fields near the Clarkes' house. Paddy tells of these episodes shortly after they have happened, with a few references to earlier ones. Mainly he reports his daily life, ordinary things. We soon come to know him through his care for father and mother, his cruelty toward his young brother Francis ("Sinbad"), bouts of mischief-making for the thrill of it, petty thefts from local shops, spurts of vandalism, soccer on the street, games, fights. We also come to sense his resilience, the freshness of his small life, the unabashed timbre of his voice. Mostly his story amounts to loss. He wants to stop his father from fighting with his mother. He tries to anticipate his father's bad moods and to divert them by telling him a story or a joke. But it is no good. In the end, his father leaves home. The schoolboys jeer at Paddy:

> – Paddy Clarke –
> – Paddy Clarke –
> Has no da.
> Ha Ha Ha![1]

For no reason, Paddy rejects his best friend Kevin and beats him so savagely that the other lads at school boycott him. In the course of a year of losses, Sinbad becomes independent or indifferent and Paddy is left with the need of him. Barrytown is another loss: once it was mostly fields,

---

* *New York Review of Books*, February 3, 1994.
[1] Roddy Doyle, *Paddy Clarke Ha Ha Ha* (London: Martin Secker and Warburg, 1993, reprinted New York: Penguin Books, 1995), p. 281.

building sites, and open sewerage pipes, good for games and devilment, but much of this space is gone, the Corporation has built houses on it:

There were fields past the Corporation houses but they were too far away now. Past the Corporation houses. Somewhere else . . . . There were no farms left. Our pitch was gone, first sliced in half for pipes, then made into eight houses. The field behind the shops was still ours and we went there more often. Over at the Corporation houses, that end, wasn't ours any more. There was another tribe there now, tougher than us, though none of us said it. Our territory was being taken from us but we were fighting back. We played Indians and Cowboys now, not Cowboys and Indians.
   – Ger-on-IMO! (147)

The book tells of the time in which everything went wrong for Paddy. Mainly what went wrong was his father, a warmhearted man to begin with, thirty-three years old, with a wife, four children, and a job of some kind in Dublin. The Clarkes are not poor, they have secure meals and a car. But there is something wrong. Paddy's father becomes sullen, takes to the routines of drink, discontent, and violence. What does not go wrong is Paddy's mother, not only lovable but endlessly loving. In one of the most heartbreaking scenes the father, to give the car an outing, brings wife and children for a picnic to Dollymount Strand; it is a wet, gloomy day darkened further by his dour silence toward his wife.

   Roddy Doyle (Ruaidhri Ó Dúill) was born in Dublin in 1958. In 1980 he became a teacher and got a job teaching English and Geography at Greendale Community School, Kilbarrack, one of the northern suburbs of Dublin. *Paddy Clarke Ha Ha Ha* is his fourth novel, preceded by *The Commitments* (1987), *The Snapper* (1990), and *The Van* (1992). Doyle has also written two plays, *Brownbread* (1987), and *War* (1989).[2] Two of the novels have become deservedly popular films, *The Commitments* directed by Alan Parker in 1991, and *The Snapper*, which is still better, directed by Stephen Frears in 1993. *Paddy Clarke Ha Ha Ha* is not autobiographical. For one thing, Doyle's parents are still cordially married. Besides, his origin is not working class but middle class. He knows the place he writes about mainly by teaching there. He has since become a full-time writer. In Dublin in 2009 he established a creative writing centre, Fighting Words.

   Contemporary Irish writers have a particular problem of style: how to prevent Yeats, Joyce, or Beckett from taking over their minds and drowning out their voices. Writers older than Doyle – Seamus Heaney,

---

[2] Roddy Doyle, *Brownbread and War* (London: Secker and Warburg, 1992).

Derek Mahon, Thomas Kinsella, John Montague, John Banville, Eavan
Boland, William Trevor, Nuala ni Dhomhnaill – have tried to circumvent
these masters by turning toward less peremptory writers: Hopkins, Hardy,
Auden, Louis MacNeice, Patrick Kavanagh, Ivy Compton-Burnett. Or by
reading foreign writers in translation: Dante, Zbigniew Herbert, Sorley
MacLean, Calvino, Akhmatova. Or by going to foreign films. Or by
writing in Irish. Doyle's method has been to listen to his pupils in
Greendale and to their fathers in the local public houses. He has a
remarkable ear. On the strength of it, he imagines what an even more
thoroughgoing demotic English would sound like. Starting from Greendale and Kilbarrack he has invented Barrytown, a place impervious to the
idioms of Yeats, Joyce, and Beckett.

The fashionable side of Dublin is the south, taking the high roads from
Foxrock to Dalkey and Killiney. North Dublin has two upper-class
addresses; on the east coast, the Hill of Howth, Sutton to Malahide; on
the west side, the newly rich Castleknock. Taking the coast road to
Howth, if you turn left before Sutton, you come to one of the seedier
parts of Dublin, the working-class housing estates of Kilbarrack, Greendale, Darndale, and beyond these if you insist, Coolock, Artane, Raheny,
and Baldoyle. Parts of that area are rough, increasingly drug-ridden, but
not yet especially dangerous. This is Doyle's place, real to begin with and
then further imagined. Not a place I'd like to live in. Forty years ago, as a
young married couple with little or no money, my wife and I had to
choose between a dreary little house in Kilbarrack and a small bungalow
in Merville Estate, Stillorgan on the south side. We made the right choice,
Stillorgan, a more salubrious district with better schools and a higher
tone. But Stillorgan hasn't inspired any writers. There are allusions to
the south side in Beckett and Flann O'Brien. The railway station in
Beckett's *All That Fall* is Foxrock, but not as recognizably as Barrytown
is Kilbarrack.

The social lineaments of Barrytown are clear. It is a place of families:
normally, each of them has several children, an out-of-work father and a
put-upon mother. There are few jobs. In *The Van* Jimmy Rabbitte Sr., an
unemployed plasterer, goes into brief partnership with his friend Bimbo
to run a fish-and-chips van. They set up shop mostly outside a favorite
public house in Barrytown. The year is 1990, during the soccer World
Cup in which Ireland drew with England before being beaten by Italy.
Closing time brings out the customers, excited, hungry and drunk. Before
and after the fish-and-chips venture, Jimmy does his poor best to support
his family on the dole. In *The Snapper* his daughter Sharon gets pregnant

after a boozy party and refuses to name the man in the case. She does not consider having an abortion:

> – There's no way I'd have an abortion, said Sharon.
> – Good. You're right.
> – Abortion's murder.
> – It is o' course.[3]

In an average year, three or four thousand Irish women go to England to have an abortion. Most of these, I gather, are middle-class town women or else country women from any class. The Dublin working class doesn't seem to resort to abortions. Besides, the Single Mother's Allowance is just as good as the wage the girl would earn in a boring, poorly paid job at the check-out in a local supermarket. The out-of-wedlock child is simply added to the family; there is one more mouth to feed, but otherwise the addition doesn't make much difference.

Families may break up, as in *Paddy Clarke Ha Ha Ha*, but no other social institution in Barrytown has replaced the family. Not even the pub, the likeliest contender. Young people and their fathers go to the pub, drink, talk, laugh, and quarrel till closing time and in the intervals keep an eye on the TV set high in the corner. Making a night of it, the young ones go to the disco. Parents who stay at home watch TV, but if there's nothing good on, they read books. In *The Van* the mother, Veronica, is taking night classes and studying for the Leaving Certificate. Jimmy borrows from the local library *The Man in the Iron Mask* and swaps it with Veronica for *Lord of the Flies*. In *Paddy Clarke Ha Ha Ha* Paddy's father reads *The Naked and the Dead*, brings Paddy to the lending library at Baldoyle, and quotes in appreciation of his son a passage from Goldsmith's "The Deserted Village": "And still they gazed and still the wonder grew that one small head could carry all he knew" (27). But mainly the people of Barrytown get their sense of reality from TV and the lore of rock bands. *War* is based on the custom of having quiz competitions in the pub, most of the questions having to do with soccer and rock, both purveyed by TV. Who won the Football Association Cup in 1958? Bolton. "Wha' soccer team did the world famous singer from Spain, Julio Iglesias, play goalie for?" I don't know. For about a year, Doyle himself took part in such quizzes on Monday nights in the Foxhound Inn in Kilbarrack and the Cedar Lounge in Raheny.

---

[3] Roddy Doyle, *The Snapper* (London: Martin Secker and Warburg, 1990 reprinted Penguin Books, 1992), p. 6.

In the novels, mothers often stay at home to keep up with their favorite TV programs, *The Fugitive, Eastenders,* or *Thirty Something.* Fathers prefer reruns of *Hawaii 5–0* or *The Man from U.N.C.L.E.* Grandmothers insist on liking *The Virginian.* Parents watch the News not because they want to know what's happening outside Barrytown but because they like to ridicule newscasters and other experts. Languages get made that way. In *The Van* a sausage is called a dunphy because it looks like a prick and Eamon Dunphy, a soccer wiseacre on TV, is also a prick. In *The Commitments* Jimmy Rabbitte Jr. has the band study James Brown's body language on video and learn from Brown what is entailed in bringing soul to Dublin:

– Where are yis from? (He answered the question himself.) – Dublin. (He asked another one.) – Wha' part o' Dublin? Barrytown. Wha' class are yis? Workin' class. Are yis proud of it? Yeah, yis are. (Then a practical question.) – Who buys the most records? The workin' class. Are yis with me? (Not really.) – Your music should be abou' where you're from an' the sort o' people yeh come from. – Say it once, say it loud, I'm black an' I'm proud.

They looked at him . . . .

– The Irish are the niggers of Europe, lads . . . – An' Dubliners are the niggers of Ireland . . . . An' the northside Dubliners are the niggers o' Dublin. – Say it loud, I'm black an' I'm proud.[4]

The most striking features of Barrytown in the years denoted by *The Commitments, The Snapper,* and *The Van* are these: decline in the influence of the Catholic Church on working-class families; general indifference to modern Ireland and to the history of dissent and revolt from which the country slowly emerged; and incessant use of what my mother called bad language. In *Paddy Clarke Ha Ha Ha* the Clarkes still went to Mass and received Holy Communion. When a boy, Keith Simpson, was drowned in a pond, his funeral was a traditional Catholic event:

Da hugged Ma when he came home. He went up and shook hands with Keith Simpson's ma and da at the funeral. I saw him. I was with the school; everyone in the school was there, in our good clothes. Henno made each of us say the first half of the Hail Mary and the rest joined in for the second half, and that took up the time before we were brought to the church. Ma stayed in her seat. There was a huge queue for shaking hands, down the side and around the back of the church, along the stations of the cross. The coffin was white. Some of the mass cards fell off during the Offertory. They slapped the floor. The sound was huge. The only other sounds were someone at the front sobbing and the priest's stiff clothes, then the altar boy's bell. And there was more sobbing. (195)

---

[4] Roddy Doyle, *The Commitments* (New York: Vintage Books, 1989), pp. 8–9.

Such a tragedy would still be marked by a Catholic funeral on the same scale, but in Doyle's novels set in recent years, priests do not appear. Few parishioners go to Mass. The founder of Christianity is frequently invoked, but only as a residual expletive, Jaysis. Paddy Clarke thinks the best story he ever heard was the one about Father Damian and the lepers on Molokai, and he makes Sinbad play a leper, but even in 1966 it was only a game. According to *The Commitments, The Snapper,* and *The Van,* there is no sense of sin in Barrytown. No one feels guilt or shame. Or even misgiving. Reality is never presented as a private experience, something to be mulled over or worried about, it is always a social situation to be negotiated at the top of one's voice. Matters of concern to the rest of Ireland – the IRA, the UVF, murders in the North, Ireland's dealings with the European Community, financial scandals in high places – are of little interest to Barrytown. The world beyond J. Rabbitte's house at 118 Chestnut Avenue, Dublin 21, has mainly televisual presence: life exists to end up on TV. There is no reason to leave Barrytown, unless you ardently want a job, since all human life comes there in a shining box. In *The Van* Jimmy Sr. and Bimbo break this paradigm for one night. They blow their winnings on an expedition to Dublin City, visiting the smart lounges in Leeson Street, but all they discover is that the drink there is expensive and the women hard to get. They return, drunk, sad, and wise, to the Barrytown they should not have left.

Modern Ireland, its history and political life, is also a matter of indifference in Barrytown. In *The Commitments* Jimmy tries to raise the consciousness of his pals by telling them that Rock an' Roll is about real sex and real politics:

– Rock an' roll is all abou' ridin'. That's wha' rock an' roll means. Did yis know tha'? (They didn't.) – Yeah, that's wha' the blackies in America used to call it. So the time has come to put the ridin' back into rock an' roll. Tongues, gooters, boxes, the works. The market's huge.

– Wha' abou' this politics?
– Yeah, politics. – Not songs abou' Fianna fuckin' Fail or annythin' like tha'. Real politics.[5]

One of the quiz-questions in *War* is: "Who said 'Romantic Ireland's dead and gone. It's with O'Leary in the grave'?" Nobody gets it right. One contestant thinks that maybe Jack Charlton or George Hamilton said it to Jimmy Magee.

---

[5] Ibid., p. 8.

But there is a charmingly archaic scene in *Paddy Clarke Ha Ha Ha* in which a teacher, Miss Watkins, brings into class a tea-towel with the Proclamation of the Irish Republic on it "because it was fifty years after 1916":

It had the writing part in the middle and the seven men who'd signed it around the sides. She stuck it up over the blackboard and let us up to see it one by one. (20)

When Paddy sees that one of the signatories was Thomas J. Clarke, he says to James O'Keefe, "Thomas Clarke is my granda. Pass it on." Meanwhile Miss Watkins reads from the Proclamation:

Irishmen and Irishwomen: In the name of God and of the dead generations from which she receives her old tradition of nationhood, Ireland, through us, summons her children to her flag and strikes for her freedom. (21)

That's the last we hear of the dead generations. In Barrytown, no quarrel about Charles Stuart Parnell thwarts the Christmas cheer, such as it is. In *War* Bertie complains to the barman Leo that "the smell in the jacks is Paraic Pearse. It's mucho fuckin' terrible."

As for communication in Barrytown: in the novels, as in *Brownbread* and *War*, Doyle's instrument is speech, he rarely mentions anything that isn't already verbal, he doesn't deal in landscapes, cityscapes, backgrounds or settings. His sole context is whatever is enforced by dialogue and a short communal memory. The present tense is the only one, and it is fulfilled by speech. A disinterested observer would insist that the truth of Barrytown is economic and political, but Doyle's novels present that truth only when it has become hearsay, lore, and babble. People take the words of reality out of one another's mouths. Sex is never shown, but it gets talked about. Silence is rare. Reality is expressed as the babble of living room, pub, and the streets connecting them. From Doyle's version of these matters you would conclude that Barrytowners have learnt English only to the extent of words beginning with "f." Gaelic literature is often ribald, and the standard expletives turn up in *Ulysses*, mostly in the loud mouth of the British soldier Private Carr, but there is no precedent in modern Irish literature for the vernacular of Barrytown. Every third phrase is "fuckin' eejit," and of the remaining two, one of them is likely to be "ye bollix." These expletives are not necessarily mouthed in anger: often they are as routinely used as "very" or "quite" in polite societies.

Doyle's first three novels read like extended scripts for late-night TV. He had finished *The Commitments* before he thought of writing a play, but the novel sounds as if he made it up after having watched many showings of *Top of the Pops* and *MTV* and wondered how a soul band might come together for a while in Barrytown and then fall apart. In November 1985 a friend of Doyle's, Paul Mercier, invited him to attend a rehearsal of his new play, *Wasters*. Later, Doyle saw another of Mercier's plays, *Studs*, about a Sunday morning soccer team. These were put on in the SFX Centre, formerly the Saint Francis Xavier Hall, in north Dublin, a venue for heavy-metal bands, bingo, talent shows, auctions, and civil service examinations. The theatre company was Passion Machine, assembled by Mercier, John Sutton, and John Dunne. In September 1987 Doyle wrote *Brownbread* for Passion Machine; it's about three fellows who kidnap an American-born bishop. A farce, and not a very good one. *War* is a much better play, but it is technically difficult, complex in its movements, and needs expert acting and direction.

In the novels, and only less often in the plays, there are problems of local reference. In *Paddy Clarke Ha Ha Ha* mickey means penis, gick is excrement, spa meaning spastic is an insult, a dead leg is a numbing kick to one's calf, eccer means school homework, and the F.C.A. means Forsa Cosanta Aituil or the local defence force in time of war. Bits of Irish in the book are translated, but readers will be puzzled if they don't guess that Jervis Street refers to a hospital and that Charles Mitchell was a newscaster. When Paddy threatens to have Sinbad arrested and put into the Artane Boys Band, readers need to know that the Band is a famous attribute of the Artane Industrial School, a school for juvenile offenders. In a pub scene in *The Snapper* Jimmy Sr. urges Paddy, one of his cronies, to "do your Michael O'Hehir": "– Ah, for fuck sake, said Paddy. – Not again. All o'them horses are fuckin' dead."

This will be clear only to readers who know that Micheál – not Michael – O'Hehir was a famous racing commentator on Radio Eireann and the BBC. When Veronica says to Jimmy Sr. "Do you think I stick St. Bernard tags and washing instructions on the jumpers when I've finished knitting them?", readers have to divine that St. Bernard is a trade mark used by Dunne's Stores. In *War* you have to know that Jack Charlton played for Leeds United from 1953 to 1973 and later became the occasionally triumphant manager of the Republic of Ireland team. Such obscurities don't matter much in films. Those who go to see *The Commitments* are unlikely to pick up every syllable of the dialogue, but gestures and the context make the gist of it clear enough. Opacity on the page is harder to cope with.

In literary terms it is hard to say where Doyle's novels and plays come from. Not from Yeats or Beckett or even from Joyce. The first few pages of *Paddy Clarke Ha Ha Ha* show that Doyle has learnt from Joyce's *A Portrait of the Artist as a Young Man* how a boy's will appropriates reality by placing one deadpan sentence beside another:

Liam and Aidan turned down their cul-de-sac. We said nothing: they said nothing. Liam and Aidan had a dead mother. Missis O'Connell was her name.
– It'd be brilliant, wouldn't it? I said.
– Yeah, said Kevin. – Cool.
We were talking about having a dead ma. (1)

But Joyce's example doesn't otherwise bear upon Doyle's writing. Sean O'Casey's plays have a little more to do with them: the irreverence toward patriotism in *The Plough and the Stars*, for instance. But the correlation is slight. Brendan Behan's plays are likelier precedents. *The Hostage* is a possible precursor of Doyle's work; not his version in Irish, *An Giall*, but the music-hall knockabout show it became when Joan Littlewood put on an expletive-added version of it as *The Hostage* in Wyndham's Theatre, London in 1959. More recently we have had other adepts of rough verbal magic: Christy Brown's *My Left Foot*, Patrick McCabe's *The Butcher Boy*, Dermot Bolger's *The Journey Home*, Aidan Carl Matthews's *Lipstick on the Host*. Now everybody's doing it.

Paddy Clarke Ha Ha Ha is Doyle's best novel, the one most completely a novel rather than an extended script for a play. It is also, for adults, the most readable. And the most touching. Tenderness keeps breaking in upon scenes otherwise grim. Paddy's father is a slob but he is decent to the boy and when the boy comes second in his class, his father calls it "nearly first." Mrs. Clarke tells the boy to say " television," not "the telly," but that admonition, too, comes with love. Clarke tries to teach Paddy a Hank Williams song:

I WENT DOWN TO THE RIVER
TO WATCH THE FISH SWIM BY-YY-
BUT I GOT TO THE RIVER –
SO LONESOME I WANTED TO DIE-EE-IE – OH LORD – (87)

He also gives Paddy a present of George Best's *A Pictorial History of Soccer* with pictures of the greatest hits. For a while, Paddy thinks Best signed the book and that his father was in the great man's company. In one picture Manchester United are in the European Cup Final. Pat Crerand, Frank McLintock, and Best go up for a ball. Paddy decides, on internal evidence, that it was Best who flicked the ball into the back of the net. Paddy is growing up, learning more words, especially the bad ones. In one game

Kevin plays Zentoga, high priest of the great god Ciunas, meaning
Silence, and he wallops his mates with a poker till each of them produces
a satisfactorily bad word: shite, tits, diddies, and at last the big one:

> Fuck was the best word. The most dangerous word. You couldn't
>   whisper it.
> – Gee!

Fuck was always too loud, too late to stop it, it burst in the air above you and fell
slowly right over your head. There was total silence, nothing but Fuck floating
down. For a few seconds you were dead, waiting for Henno to look up and
see Fuck landing on top of you. They were thrilling seconds – when he didn't
look up. It was the word you couldn't say anywhere. It wouldn't come out unless you
pushed it. It made you feel caught and grabbed the minute you said it. When it
escaped it was like an electric laugh, a soundless gasp followed by the kind of laughing
that only forbidden things could make, an inside tickle that became a brilliant pain,
bashing at your mouth to be let out. It was agony. We didn't waste it. (132)

Would a boy of ten think that, precisely? Would he think "soundless," as
elsewhere would he say "hillock"? Hardly: for once or twice, Doyle is
putting words in Paddy's mind. But nearly always the words are convincingly Paddy's. Near the end, the fuck-words come out of him unless he
pushes them back, and there is no reason to think he will push them back
for long. There are fuckin' eejits around the next corner. We are well on
the way toward contemporary Ireland, or at least toward the Barrytown
version of it.

Select bibliography

Adams, Gerry, "We Have No Exit Strategy," *Ireland on Sunday*, March 8, 1998.

Agamben, Giorgio, *The End of the Poem: Studies in Poetics*, trans. Daniel Heller-Roazen (Stanford University Press, 1999).

Anderson, Perry, *A Zone of Engagement* (London: Verso, 1992).

Arnold, Matthew, *English Literature and Irish Politics*, ed. R. H. Super (Ann Arbor: University of Michigan Press, 1973).

"From Easter to August," *The Nineteenth Century*, Vol. 22 (September 1887).

"On the Study of Celtic Literature," in *Lectures and Essays in Criticism*, ed. R. H. Super (Ann Arbor: University of Michigan Press, 1962).

Bakhtin, M. M., *The Dialogic Imagination: Four Essays*, trans. Caryl Emerson and Michael Holquist (Austin: University of Texas Press, 1981).

Beckett, Samuel, *Company* (London: John Calder, 1980).

The Complete Dramatic Works (London: Faber and Faber, 1986).

Disjecta: Miscellaneous Writings and a Dramatic Fragment, ed. Ruby Cohn (New York: Grove Press, 1984).

Mercier and Camier (New York: Grove Press, 1974).

Murphy (London: Calder and Boyars, 1969 reprint of 1938 edition).

Proust (London: John Calder, 1965).

Stories & Texts for Nothing (New York: Grove Press, 1967).

Three Novels: Molloy, Malone Dies, The Unnamable (New York: Grove Weidenfeld, 1991).

Watt (Paris: Olympia Press, 1953).

Berger, Peter L. and Thomas Luckmann, *The Social Construction of Reality: A Treatise in the Sociology of Knowledge* (New York: Doubleday, 1966).

Blackmur, R. P., *Anni Mirabiles 1921–1925* (Washington: Library of Congress, 1956).

Outsider at the Heart of Things, ed. James T. Jones (Urbana and Chicago: University of Illinois Press, 1989).

Bloom, Harold, *Shakespeare: The Invention of the Human* (London: Fourth Estate, 1999).

Bowman, John, *De Valera and the Ulster Question 1917–1973* (Oxford: Clarendon Press, 1982).

Cassirer, Ernst, *The Philosophy of Symbolic Forms*, trans. Ralph Manheim (4 vols., New Haven: Yale University Press, 1953).

Cavell, Stanley, *Must We Mean What We Say?* (Cambridge University Press, 1976).

Cavell, Stanley, letter to Vicki Hearne, quoted in Hearne, "Tracking Dogs, Sensitive Horses, and the Traces of Speech," *Raritan*, Vol. 6, No. 4 (Spring 1986).

Cioran, E. M., *Anathemas and Admirations*, trans. Richard Howard (London: Quartet Encounters, 1992).

Clark, T. J., *Farewell to an Idea: Episodes from a History of Modernism* (New Haven: Yale University Press, 1999).

Coleridge, Samuel Taylor, *Biographia Literaria*, ed. James Engell and W. Jackson Bate, Bollingen Series 75 (2 vols., Princeton University Press, 1983).

Cowen, Walker (ed.), *Melville's Marginalia* (2 vols., New York: Garland, 1988).

Crane, R. S., *The Idea of the Humanities* (University of Chicago Press, 1967).

Cronin, Anthony, *Samuel Beckett: The Last Modernist* (London: Harper Collins, 1992).

Davis, Thomas, *Essays*, ed. D. J. O'Donoghue (New York: Lemma Publishing Company, 1974 reprint of 1914 edition).

Poems (Dublin: Duffy, 1853).

De Paor, Liam, *On the Easter Proclamation and Other Declarations* (Dublin: Four Courts Press, 1997).

Deleuze, Gilles and Felix Guattari, *Kafka: Toward a Minor Literature*, trans. Dana Polan (Minneapolis: University of Minnesota Press, 1986).

Derrida, Jacques, *Politics of Friendship*, trans. George Collins (London: Verso, 1997).

Writing and Difference, trans. Alan Bass (University of Chicago Press, 1978).

D'Etienne, Marcel, *Dionysus Slain*, trans. L. and M. Muellner (Baltimore: Johns Hopkins University Press, 1979).

Dowden, Edward, *Fragments from Old Letters E.D. to E.D.W: 1869–1892* (London: Dent, 1914).

Letters of Edward Dowden and His Correspondents (London: Dent, 1914).

Shakspere – A Critical Study of His Mind and Art (New York: Harper, 1875, third edition, 1918).

Doyle, Roddy, *Brownbread and War* (London: Secker and Warburg, 1992).

The Commitments (New York: Vintage Books, 1989).

Paddy Clarke Ha Ha Ha (London: Martin Secker and Warburg, 1993, reprinted New York: Penguin Books, 1995).

The Snapper (London: Martin Secker and Warburg, 1990, reprinted Penguin Books, 1992).

Eagleton, Terry, *Heathcliff and the Great Hunger: Studies in Irish Culture* (London: Verso, 1995).

Eliot, George, *The Writings of George Eliot: Essays and Leaves from a Note-Book* (Boston and New York: Houghton Mifflin, 1909).

Eliot, T. S., *After Strange Gods: A Primer of Modern Heresy* (New York: Harcourt, Brace, and Company, 1934).

Collected Poems 1909–1962 (New York: Harcourt, Brace, and Company, 1963).

On Poetry and Poets (New York: Farrar, Straus, and Cudahy, 1957).

Selected Essays: New Edition (New York: Harcourt, Brace, and World, 1964).

Selected Prose, ed. Frank Kermode (London: Faber and Faber, 1975).

The Use of Poetry and the Use of Criticism: Studies in the Relation of Criticism to Poetry in England (London: Faber and Faber, 1950 reprint).

"A Commentary," *The Criterion*, Vol. 14, No. 57 (July 1935).

"A Foreign Mind," *The Athenaeum*, No. 4653, July 4, 1919.

Ellmann, Richard, *Eminent Domain: Yeats among Wilde, Joyce, Pound, Eliot, and Auden* (New York: Oxford University Press, 1967).

The Identity of Yeats (New York: Oxford University Press, second edition, 1964).

Emerson, Ralph Waldo, *Representative Men* (Boston and New York: Houghton Mifflin, 1930 reprint).

Empson, William, *Some Versions of Pastoral* (London: Chatto and Windus, 1962).

The Structure of Complex Words (London: Chatto and Windus, 1971).

Foster, R. F., *W. B. Yeats: A Life, Vol. I: The Apprentice Mage 1865–1914* (Oxford University Press, 1997).

Frye, Northrop, *Anatomy of Criticism: Four Essays* (Princeton University Press, 1957).

"The Four Forms of Prose Fiction," *The Hudson Review*, Vol. 2, No. 4 (Winter 1950).

The Gonne-Yeats Letters 1893–1938: Always Your Friend, ed. Anna MacBride White and A. Norman Jeffares (London: Hutchinson, 1992).

Griffin, Dustin H., *Satires against Man: The Poems of Rochester* (Berkeley: University of California Press, 1973).

Grossman, Allen, *The Long Schoolroom: Lessons in the Bitter Logic of the Poetic Principle* (Ann Arbor: University of Michigan Press, 1997).

Poetic Knowledge in the Early Yeats: A Study of "The Wind among the Reeds" (Charlottesville: University Press of Virginia, 1969).

Hall, James and Martin Steinmann (eds.), *The Permanence of Yeats* (New York: Macmillan, 1950).

Harding, D. W., *Experience into Words* (New York: Horizon Press, 1964).

Harper, George Mills, *The Making of Yeats's "A Vision": A Study of the Automatic Script* (2 vols., London: Macmillan, 1987).

Hazlitt, William, *Works*, ed. P. P. Howe (21 vols., London: Dent, 1930–1934).

Hood, Connie K., "The Remaking of *A Vision*," in *Yeats: An Annual of Critical and Textual Studies*, ed. Richard J. Finneran (publishers vary, 1983–1999, Vol. 1, 1983).

Hopkins, Gerard Manley, *The Letters of Gerard Manley Hopkins to Robert Bridges*, ed. Claude Colleer Abbott (London: Oxford University Press, 1935).

Howe, Susan, "Melville's Marginalia," *The American Poetry Review*, Vol. 22, No. 1 (January–February, 1993).

Hume, David, *Inquiry Concerning Human Understanding*, ed. Charles W. Hendel (Indianapolis: Bobbs-Merrill, 1955).

A Treatise of Human Nature, ed. T. H. Green and T. H. Grose (London: Aalen, 1964 reprint).

Hutson, Lorna, "An Earlier Perspective," *The Times Literary Supplement*, May 30, 2003.

James, Henry, *The Art of the Novel: Critical Prefaces* (Boston: Northeastern University Press, 1984 reprint).

Letters, Vol. 1: 1843–1875, ed. Leon Edel (Cambridge, Mass.: Belknap Press of Harvard University Press, 1975).

The Portrait of a Lady, ed. Robert D. Bamberg (New York: W. W. Norton, 1975 reprint).

Jeffares, A. Norman, *A New Commentary on the Poems of W. B. Yeats* (London: Macmillan, 1984).

Yeats: A New Biography (London: Continuum, 2001).

Jeffares, A. Norman and K. G. W. Cross (eds.), *In Excited Reverie* (New York: Macmillan, 1965).

Jolas, Eugene, "The Revolution of Language and James Joyce," in *Our Exagmination Round His Factification for Incamination of Work in Progress* (London: Faber and Faber, second impression, 1961).

Joyce, James, *Finnegans Wake* (New York: Viking Press, 1939: London: Faber and Faber, 1939).

Occasional, Critical, and Political Writing, ed. Kevin Barry (Oxford University Press, 2000).

A Portrait of the Artist as a Young Man, ed. Hans Walter Gabler with Walter Hettche (New York: Garland, 1993).

Ulysses, ed. Hans Walter Gabler with Wolfhard Steppe and Claus Melchior (3 vols., New York: Garland, 1984).

Ulysses, ed. Hans Walter Gabler with Wolfhard Steppe and Claus Melchior (New York: Random House, 1986).

Julian of Norwich, *Revelations of Divine Love* (London: Methuen, thirteenth edition, 1952).

Kaiser, Walter, *Praisers of Folly: Erasmus, Rabelais, Shakespeare* (Cambridge, Mass: Harvard University Press, 1963).

Kelly, J. M., *The Irish Constitution*, ed. Gerard Hogan and Gerry Whyte (London: Butterworths, third edition, 1994).

Kenner, Hugh, *Joyce's Voices* (Berkeley: University of California Press, 1978).

The Poetry of Ezra Pound (Norfolk, Conn.: New Directions, reprinted 1974).

The Pound Era (Berkeley: University of California Press, 1971).

Samuel Beckett: A Critical Study (Berkeley: University of California Press, new edition, 1967).

"The Sacred Book of the Arts," in John Unterecker (ed.), *Yeats: A Collection of Critical Essays* (Englewood Cliffs, NJ: Prentice-Hall, 1963).

"Words in the Dark," in E. V. Rieu (ed.), *Essays by Divers Hands Being the Transactions of the Royal Society of Literature: New Series*, Vol. XXIX (London: Oxford University Press, 1958).

Kermode, Frank, *Shakespeare's Language* (New York: Farrar, Straus, Giroux, 2000).

Kierkegaard, Søren, *The Concept of Irony*, trans. Lee M. Capel (Bloomington: Indiana University Press, 1971).

Knowlson, James, "Pipes and Tubes," in Morris Beja, S. E. Gontarski, and Pierre Astier (eds.), *Samuel Beckett: Humanistic Perspectives* (Columbus: Ohio State University Press, 1983).

Kohn, Hans, *Nationalism: Its Meaning and History* (Princeton: Van Nostrands, revised edition, 1965).

Kristeva, Julia, *Nations without Nationalism*, trans. Leon S. Roudiez (New York: Columbia University Press, 1993).

Leavis, F. R., *The Common Pursuit* (London: Chatto and Windus, 1952).

"Joyce and the 'Revolution of the Word'," in *For Continuity* (Cambridge: The Minority Press, 1933).

"Milton's Verse," *Scrutiny*, Vol. 2, No. 2 (September 1933).

Lloyd, David, *Anomalous States: Irish Writing and the Post-Colonial Moment* (Dublin: Lilliput Press, 1993).

Nationalism and Minor Literature: James Clarence Mangan and the Emergence of Irish Cultural Nationalism (Berkeley: University of California Press, 1987).

Locke, John, *An Essay Concerning Human Understanding*, ed. Peter H. Nidditch (Oxford: Clarendon Press, 1975).

Lyons, F. S. L., *Charles Stewart Parnell* (New York: Oxford University Press, 1977).

MacCabe, Colin, *James Joyce and the Revolution of the Word* (London: Palgrave Macmillan, second edition, 2003).

McGahern, John, *All Will Be Well: A Memoir* (New York: Knopf, 2006).

Amongst Women (London: Faber and Faber, 1991).

The Barracks (London: Faber and Faber, 1963).

Collected Stories (London: Faber and Faber, 1992).

That They May Face the Rising Sun (London: Faber and Faber, 2002).

"What Is My Language?" *Irish University Review*, Vol. 35, No. 1 (Spring/ Summer 2005).

McGee, Thomas D'Arcy, *Poems* (Boston: Sadler, 1869).

Mangan, James Clarence, *Collected Prose: Prose 1840–1882 and Correspondence*, ed. Jacques Chuto et al. (Dublin: Irish Academic Press, 2002).

Selected Writings, ed. Sean Ryder (University College Dublin Press, 2004).

Marcus, Phillip L., *Yeats and Artistic Power* (New York University Press, 1992).

Moore, George, *Hail and Farewell* (2 vols., New York: Appleton, 1925 reprint).

Parnell and His Country (London: Swan Sonnenschein, Lowrey, 1887).

Murphy, William M., *Prodigal Father: The Life of John Butler Yeats 1839–1922* (Ithaca and London: Cornell University Press, 1978).

Nolan, Emer, *James Joyce and Nationalism* (London: Routledge, 1995).

O'Brien, Conor Cruise, "Passion and Cunning," in A. Norman Jeffares and K. G. W. Cross (eds.), *In Excited Reverie* (New York: Macmillan, 1965).

Pater, Walter, *Appreciations with an Essay on Style* (London: Macmillan, 1944 reprint).
    Imaginary Portraits (London: Macmillan, 1910, reprinted 1967).
    The Renaissance: Studies in Art and Poetry: The 1893 Text, ed. Donald L. Hill (Berkeley: University of California Press, 1980).
Peirce, C. S., *Selected Writings*, ed. Philip P. Wiener (Stanford University Press, 1958).
Pound, Ezra, *The Cantos* (New York: New Directions, 1975).
    Gaudier-Brzeska: A Memoir (New York: New Directions, fourth printing, 1970).
    "The Later Yeats," *Poetry*, Vol. 4, No. 11 (May, 1914).
    "The Return," *Poems and Translations* (New York: Library of America, 2003).
    "Status Rerum," *Poetry*, Vol. 1, No. 4 (January 1913).
Ransom, John Crowe, "The Future of Poetry," *The Fugitive*, February 1924, reprinted in Ransom, *Selected Essays*, ed. Thomas Daniel Young and John Hindle (Baton Rouge and London: Louisiana State University Press, 1984).
Richards, I. A., *Coleridge on Imagination* (London: Kegan Paul, Trench, Trubner, 1934).
Rosenthal, M. L., *Running to Paradise: Yeats's Poetic Art* (New York: Oxford University Press, 1993).
Salvadori, Corinna, *Yeats and Castiglione: Poet and Courtier* (Dublin: Allen Figgis, 1965).
Schmitt, Carl, *The Concept of the Political*, trans. George Schwab (New Brunswick: Rutgers University Press, 1976).
Senn, Fritz, *Joyce's Dislocutions: Essays on Reading as Translation*, ed. John Paul Riquelme (Baltimore: The Johns Hopkins University Press, 1984).
Sewell, Elizabeth, *Paul Valéry: The Mind in the Mirror* (Cambridge: Bowes and Bowes, 1952).
Shakespeare, William, *Complete Works*, ed. Hardin Craig and David Bevington (Glenview, Ill.: Scott, Foresman and Company, 1973).
Sidnell, Michael J., *Dances of Death: The Group Theatre of London in the Thirties* (London: Faber and Faber, 1984).
Sidney, Sir Philip, *The Countess of Pembroke's Arcadia*, ed. Albert Feuillerat (Cambridge University Press, 1926).
Stevens, Wallace, *Collected Poems* (New York: Vintage Books, 1990).
    Opus Posthumous, ed. Milton J. Bates (New York: Knopf, 1989).
Swift, Jonathan, *Correspondence*, ed. Harold Williams (5 vols., Oxford: Clarendon Press, 1963–1965).
    Gulliver's Travels, ed. Herbert Davis (Oxford: Basil Blackwell, 1959).
    Irish Tracts 1720–1723, ed. Herbert Davis (Oxford: Basil Blackwell, 1968).
    Prose Writings, ed. Herbert Davis et al. (16 vols., Oxford: Basil Blackwell, 1939–1974).
    "A Discourse concerning the Mechanical Operation of the Spirit," in *Prose Writings*, ed. Herbert Davis et al. (16 vols., Oxford: Basil Blackwell, 1939–1974), Vol. 1.

Symons, Arthur, *The Symbolist Movement in Literature* (New York: E. P. Dutton, revised and enlarged edition, 1919).

Taylor, Charles, *Sources of the Self: The Making of the Modern Identity* (Cambridge, Mass.: Harvard University Press, 1989).

Tennyson, Alfred, *Tennyson: A Selected Edition*, ed. Christopher Ricks (Berkeley: University of California Press, 1989).

Tertz, Abram, *A Voice from the Chorus*, trans. Kyril Fitzlyon and Max Hayward (New York: Farrar, Straus, and Giroux, 1976).

Torchiana, Donald T., "'Among School Children' and the Education of the Irish Spirit," in A. N. Jeffares and K. G. W. Cross (eds.), *In Excited Reverie* (New York: Macmillan, 1965).

Trevor, William, *After Rain* (London: Penguin Books, 1997).

Collected Stories (London: Penguin Books in association with The Bodley Head, 1993).

Excursions in the Real World (New York: Knopf, 1994).

The Hill Bachelors (New York: Viking, 2000).

Two Lives: Reading Turgenev and My House in Umbria (New York: Viking, 1991).

Trilling, Lionel, *Sincerity and Authenticity* (Cambridge, Mass.: Harvard University Press, 1972).

Trumpener, Katie, *Bardic Nationalism: The Romantic Novel and the British Empire* (Princeton University Press, 1997).

Tuve, Rosemond, *Elizabethan and Metaphysical Imagery: Renaissance Poetic and Twentieth-Century Critics* (University of Chicago Press, 1947, ninth impression, 1972).

Ure, Peter, *Yeats and Anglo-Irish Literature*, ed. C. J. Rawson (Liverpool University Press, 1974).

Valéry, Paul, *Analects*, trans. Stuart Gilbert, Bollingen Series 14 (Princeton University Press, 1970).

"Avant-Propos à la connaissance de la déesse," in *Oeuvres*, ed. Jean Hytier (Paris: Gallimard, 1957), Vol. 1.

Poésies (Paris: Gallimard, 1958 reprint).

Vendler, Helen, *Our Secret Discipline: Yeats and Lyric Form* (Cambridge, Mass.: Belknap Press of Harvard University Press, 2007).

Wade, Allan, *A Bibliography of the Writings of W. B. Yeats*, third edition revised by Russell K. Alspach (London: Rupert Hart-Davis, 1968).

Warren, Austin, *Rage for Order: Essays in Criticism* (University of Chicago Press, 1948).

Weinberger, Eliot (ed.), *American Poetry since 1950* (New York: Marsilio Publishers, 1993).

Welsford, Enid, *The Fool: His Social and Literary History* (New York: Farrar and Rinehart, 1935).

Wilson, Edmund, *Literary Essays and Reviews of the 1920s and 30s*, ed. Lewis M. Dabney (New York: Library of America, 2007).

Yeats, John Butler, *Letters to His Son W. B. Yeats and others, 1869–1922*, ed. Joseph Hone (London: Faber and Faber, 1944).

Yeats, W. B., *Autobiographies* (London: Macmillan, 1961).
  Autobiographies, ed. William H. O'Donnell and Douglas N. Archibald (New York: Scribner, 1999).
  The Collected Letters, Vol. Three: 1901–1904, ed. John Kelly and Ronald Schuchard (Oxford: Clarendon Press, 1994).
  Collected Plays (London: Macmillan, 1952).
  Collected Poems (London: Macmillan, 1952).
  The Cutting of an Agate (New York: Macmillan, 1912).
  Essays and Introductions (London: Macmillan, 1961).
  Explorations, selected by Mrs. W. B. Yeats (London: Macmillan, 1962).
  The Letters, ed. Allan Wade (London: Rupert Hart-Davis, 1954).
  Memoirs, transcribed and ed. Denis Donoghue (London: Macmillan, 1972).
  Mythologies (London: Macmillan, 1959).
  Mythologies, ed. Warwick Gould and Deirdre Toomey (New York: Palgrave Macmillan, 2005).
  Plays and Controversies (New York: Macmillan, 1924).
  The Poems, ed. Daniel Albright (London: Dent, 1994).
  Uncollected Prose, Vol. 1: First Reviews and Articles 1886–1896, ed. John P. Frayne (New York: Columbia University Press, 1970).
  The Variorum Edition of the Plays, ed. Russell K. Alspach (London: Macmillan, 1966).
  The Variorum Edition of the Poems, ed. Peter Allt and Russell K. Alspach (London: Macmillan, 1957).
  A Vision (London: Macmillan, second edition 1937, corrected 1962).
  A Vision: The Original 1925 Version, ed. Catherine E. Paul and Margaret Mills Harper (New York: Scribner, 2008).
  A Critical Edition of "A Vision" (1925), ed. George Mills Harper and Walter Kelly Hood (New York: Palgrave Macmillan, 1978).
  Words for Music Perhaps and Other Poems: Manuscript Materials, ed. David R. Clark (Ithaca and London: Cornell University Press, 1999).
  Yeats's "Vision" Papers, Vol. I: The Automatic Script: 5 November 1917–18 June 1918, ed. Steve L. Adams, Barbara J. Frieling, and Sandra L. Sprayberry (London: Macmillan, 1992).
  Yeats's "Vision" Papers, Vol. II: The Automatic Script: 25 June 1918–29 March 1920, ed. Steve L. Adams, Barbara J. Frieling, and Sandra L. Sprayberry (London: Macmillan, 1992).
  Yeats's "Vision" Papers, Vol. III: Sleep and Dream Notebooks, Vision Notebooks 1 and 2, Card File, ed. Robert Anthony Martinich and Margaret Mills Harper (London: Macmillan, 1992).
Yeats, W. B. (ed.), *The Oxford Book of Modern Verse 1892–1935* (New York: Oxford University Press, 1937).

Index